ALL ABOUT
HEDGE FUNDS

ALL ABOUT HEDGE FUNDS

Second Edition

Ezra Zask

New York Chicago San Francisco Lisbon London Madrid Mexico City
Milan New Delhi San Juan Seoul Singapore Sydney Toronto

The McGraw·Hill Companies

1 2 3 4 5 6 7 8 9 0   DOC/DOC   1 8 7 6 5 4 3

ISBN   978-0-07-176831-3
MHID   0-07-176831-9

e-ISBN   978-0-07-176832-0
e-MHID   0-07-176832-7

This publication is designed to provide accurate and authoritative information in regard to the subject matter covered. It is sold with the understanding that neither the author nor the publisher is engaged in rendering legal, accounting, securities, trading, or other professional service. If legal advice or other expert assistance is required, the services of a competent professional person should be sought.

—*From a Declaration of Principles Jointly Adopted by a Committee of the American Bar Association and a Committee of Publishers and Associations.*

Library of Congress Cataloging-in-Publication Data

Zask, Ezra.
   All about hedge funds / by Ezra Zask. — Fully Revised Second Edition.
      pages cm
   Includes bibliographical references.
   ISBN-13: 978-0-07-176832-0 (alk. paper)
   ISBN-10: 0-07-176832-7 (alk. paper)
   1. Hedge funds.   2. Investments—Management.   I. Title.
   HG4530.Z37 2013
   332.64'524—dc23

2012042805

McGraw-Hill books are available at special quantity discounts to use as premiums and sales promotions or for use in corporate training programs. To contact a representative, please e-mail us at bulksales@mcgraw-hill.com.

This book is printed on acid-free paper.

CONTENTS

Chapter 9

PART FOUR: HEDGE FUND PERFORMANCE: MOUNTING CRITICISM AND CHANGING BENCHMARKS

Chapter 10

Chapter 11

Chapter 12

Chapter 13

Chapter 14

PART FIVE: HEDGE FUND STRATEGIES

Chapter 15

Chapter 16

Chapter 17

Chapter 18

Chapter 19

Chapter 20

PART SIX: HEDGE FUNDS AND INVESMENT PORTFOLIOS

PART SEVEN: MANAGING HEDGE FUND PORTFOLIOS

I founded a hedge fund in 1991 and spent the subsequent 20 years in the hedge fund industry, participating in its amazing transformation. There were fewer than 1,000 hedge funds managing $58 billion in 1991 compared with over 10,000 funds managing $2 trillion today. The dominant hedge fund strategy in 1991 was "global macro," which entailed leveraged bets on the direction of global currency, interest rates, commodities, and stock markets, whereas today the strategies pursued by hedge funds are diversified and divided between equity, fixed income, global macro, and others. Finally, the investors in 1991 were predominantly wealthy individuals while today they are largely institutions, including pension funds, university endowments, and sovereign wealth funds (Figure 0.1).

It is fair to say that hedge funds have evolved from marginal investment vehicles for the rich into mainstream investments for the world's largest institutional investors, including CalPERS (the largest U.S. pension fund), the Yale Endowment, State of Massachusetts' $50 Billion Pension Reserves Investment Management Board, and the China Investment Corporation.

And yet, most people's knowledge of hedge funds comes from the news headlines, which tend to focus on the sensational aspects of the industry: the incredible wealth of some of its managers; the outsized gains (i.e., Paulson & Company, which made billions by correctly predicting the collapse of the U.S. housing market) and losses (i.e., Long-Term Capital Management, which lost billions in 1998 and caused a major crisis in the global financial system) of some of the larger funds; the frauds perpetrated by some managers (frequently including Bernard Madoff, who was *not* a hedge fund manager); its lack of transparency and escape from government regulation; the insider trading convictions of participants, notably Raj Rajaratnam and Raj Gupta; and the alleged role of hedge funds in the recent credit crisis.

The simple fact that the great majority of individuals are prohibited from investing in hedge funds amplifies the lack of widespread knowledge about hedge funds.

FIGURE 0-1

Growth of Hedge Funds: 1990–2011

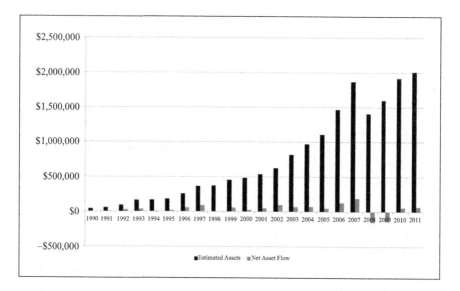

The purpose of the book is to provide an objective roadmap to the complex and rapidly changing world of hedge funds; to document the state of the industry today, describing the forces of change; and to provide some insight into its future direction.

The first edition, written by Robert Jaeger, has become a classic, widely renowned for its comprehensive description of the hedge fund industry and insightful analysis of hedge fund strategies. This is an opportune time to publish a second edition of this book. Hedge funds are inextricably linked to the larger financial and economic world and changes in the hedge fund industry are a mirror of global changes that include the credit crisis, the collapse of the investment banking industry, the global search for higher returns, the Madoff and insider trading scandals, the deleveraging of the global financial system, and the evolving regulation of the financial services industry: all have a profound impact upon—and are in turn affected by—hedge funds.

It is important to state what this book is not. First, it is not a "get rich quick" or even a "get rich slowly" book. Bookstores and e-books contain tons of information on how to make money with various investments, including hedge funds. There is a clear hunger for sure-fire solutions to the predicament faced by many investors—individual and institutional—of the combination of slowed economic growth, high debt levels, historically low interest rates, and a directionless stock market, all of which have made the investment decision increasingly frustrating. This book does not provide a path out of this bleak landscape.

This brings up a related point: this book is not a cheerleader or apologist for hedge funds. Over the years, the hedge fund industry has had an effective mantra that partially helps explain its extraordinary growth and helps justify its high fees, which goes something like this: hedge funds provide protection during market downturns; add diversity to an investment portfolio; produce favorable risk-adjusted returns compared with traditional stock and bond investments; and possess the ability to generate investment alpha. They are therefore an essential component of any investment portfolio.

These arguments are succinctly presented in a 2012 publication of the Alternative Investment Management Association, a hedge fund industry group, and KPMG, the consulting firm. The publication—"The Evolution of an Industry"—also contained a favorable endorsement by Richard H. Baker, President and Chief Executive Officer of the Managed Funds Association, the hedge fund industry's lobbying group.

However, hedge funds also have their critics.

Respected academics such as Burton Malkiel, author of *A Random Walk Down Wall Street*,[*] have long argued that hedge funds provide no benefit to investors. More recently, Simon Lack, a veteran of the industry, has argued that hedge funds are primarily a vehicle for siphoning investors' money into the pockets of hedge fund managers, leaving very little for investors.[†] Hedge funds are also criticized for causing or contributing to market turmoil, including during the recent credit crisis.

This book does not attempt to advocate, justify, or condemn; it seeks to document, analyze, and explain. Among the topics that will be treated in detail are the evolution and growth of hedge funds; the strategies and tools used by hedge funds; the performance and risk of hedge funds and their role in investment portfolios; the role of hedge funds in the larger financial markets and economic system; the industry's structure and evolution; hedge

---

[*] W.W. Norton & Company, New York, 2011.
[†] *The Hedge Fund Mirage: The Illusion of Big Money and Why It's Too Good to be True*; Wiley, New York, 2012.

fund losses and scandals and government regulation of hedge funds.

WHO SHOULD READ THIS BOOK

While this book will be of interest to most readers, it is organized to present topics that would primarily be of interest to one of four distinct audiences: the general reader, institutional investors, retail investors, and industry professionals.

The General Reader

Because of their increasingly important role in the financial and investment worlds, any informed citizen should know more about hedge funds than what can be gleaned from the media. The book is organized to systematically explain them in a nontechnical manner so that the general reader will be able to answer the questions I inevitably get from friends and neighbors: What is a hedge fund? How do they work? Can I invest in one? Should I invest in one? Are the headlines I read true?

Hedge funds are unique in their organization and they use complex and unfamiliar strategies and techniques. They regularly inhabit new and unusual markets. In addition, because hedge funds span global markets and interact with a wide range of actors—including banks, governments, and investors—they provide important insights on the key issues in the global financial system and efforts to deal with the ongoing financial crisis.

Finally, general readers will also find interest (and occasional titillation) in the descriptions of some of the outsized personalities and unique strategies that are part of the hedge fund world.

Institutional Investors

The hedge fund world is segmented into a "retail" sector dominated by wealthy investors and, increasingly, average ("retail") investors, and an "institutional" sector dominated by pension funds, sovereign wealth funds, and endowments. I have made an effort to address the differing interests of these segments when relevant, especially in the latter chapters of the book on the role of hedge funds in an overall investment portfolio.

Institutional investors manage "other people's money" and therefore are faced with fiduciary responsibility to their investors. They invest large amounts of money with a long-term time horizon under formal regulatory and institutional mandates. Institutions are concerned with how hedge funds fit into their overall investment portfolio that, for many institutions, is experiencing a shortfall that needs to be addressed in a difficult environment.

Institutions view hedge funds in the context of modern portfolio theory, asset allocation, and risk management. They use such concepts as "alpha," "alternative beta," "Sharpe ratio," and "value at risk," in evaluating hedge funds and their potential contributions to their overall investment needs.

Institutional investors are also using their size and sophistication to bring about the "institutionalization" of hedge funds; changing hedge funds' modus operandi by gaining increased transparency into their strategies, operations, and risks; pressing for a reduction of fees; and ensuring that there is more of an alignment of the interests of hedge fund managers and investors.

Individual High-Net-Worth and "Retail" Investors

As a general rule, this group of investors is interested in a practical and useful roadmap to a very complicated and, to most, unfamiliar investment world. The person who is thinking about investing in hedge funds needs solid information about the strategies and tools used by hedge funds, as well as the potential return and risks of different types of hedge fund strategies. Most importantly, they need information to allow them to cut through the hype and decide whether hedge funds are a suitable investment for their specific needs and objectives.

The book describes in some detail the alternatives available to investors, starting with the eligibility requirements they need to meet to invest in traditional hedge fund and hedge fund of fund limited partnerships. In the past several years, a number of vehicles have been developed for investors that wish to access hedge fund strategies; notably mutual funds and exchange-traded funds (ETFs) that adopt some of the strategies and tools of hedge funds such as leverage, short selling, and derivatives, as well as hedge fund "replicators" who strive to provide returns comparable to those of hedge funds in a mutual fund or ETF structure. Finally, SEC-registered funds of hedge funds in the United States and UCITS-registered funds in Europe have provided investors with another channel to invest in hedge funds and hedge fund–type programs.

Financial and Hedge Fund Industry Professionals, Regulators, and Academics

For industry insiders and fellow travelers, the book will analyze the changes in the hedge fund industry and provide some ideas for future development of strategies, products, and regulations.

The specific topics covered in this book that will be of special interest to this audience include:

- Changes in the regulation of hedge funds and the financial services industry and their effect on hedge funds
- Changes in the organization of the financial services industry—for example, the changing role of investment banks and brokers—and the impact on the role of hedge funds
- Developments in hedge fund strategies, such as statistical arbitrage and direct lending
- Changes in the investor mix, including sovereign wealth funds, retail investors, and, most recently, wealthy investors from China
- Changes in the organization and functioning of hedge funds as they adapt to the segmentation of their investor base and the very different needs of "retail" and "institutional" investors
- Changes in the finances, economics, and structure of the hedge fund industry itself, including the consolidation of the industry; pressure on hedge fund fees; the changing role of fund of hedge funds; and the increasing overlap and competition between hedge funds, mutual funds, and other asset managers

ACKNOWLEDGMENTS

I would like to thank Robert Jaeger, the author of the classic *All About Hedge Funds*, for providing the foundation upon which this book was built.

I would like to thank Philip L. S. Deely, CAIA, for his extensive and ongoing research and editorial support in the course of writing this book.

Major Themes and Organization of the Book

While the book covers a wide range of topics, it is also guided by a number of recurring themes. It is important to make these themes explicit at the start because they define the major issues confronting hedge funds, their investors, and their regulators.

HEDGE FUNDS ARE REMARKABLY DIVERSE

Unlike mutual funds, which are constrained by regulation and investor expectations to conform to rigid and well-defined categories, hedge funds cover a wide and varied territory. The very fact that hedge funds have the flexibility to evolve and change their strategy makes it impossible to develop a fixed typology of the industry.

There are hedge funds that closely resemble mutual funds; they pursue primarily long-only investment in equities using traditional financial analysis to identify overvalued and undervalued stocks. In fact, many of the practitioners of this type of hedge funds came from the "long-only" world. It seems only natural, therefore, that hedge funds have started long-only mutual funds and mutual funds have founded vehicles that adopt some of the hedge fund strategies and tools, notably the use of leverage and short selling.

In sharp contrast are hedge funds such as Steven Cohen's SAC Capital Advisors that have a fast-paced, opportunistic orientation to the market, often driven by trends and movements in the market themselves. "Black box" quantitative hedge funds, such as Jim Simons' Renaissance Technologies and David Shaw's D.E. Shaw Group, are another distinct hedge fund category, as are commodity trading advisers such as David Harding's Winton, many of whom utilize statistical models to drive their investment decisions.

At another extreme are hedge funds that pursue strategies based on the discretion of their managers; strategies that can vary widely and change quickly. Prominent here are the so-called global macro funds—exemplified by George Soros' Soros Fund Management, Bruce Kovner's Caxton Associates, Paul Tudor Jones's Tudor Investment Corporation, and Louis Bacon's Moore Capital Management—that scour the world for opportunities and adopt strategies and instruments to suit a variety of markets.

There are "niche" hedge funds that exploit relatively narrow markets and strategies such as mergers and acquisitions (M&A) arbitrage, convertible bonds, or specific sectors (i.e., financial, energy, or high tech) or specific countries or regions (i.e., Brazil, China, Russia, Europe, or Asia).

Finally, a combination of the changes in the financial industry and the "war chest" accumulated by some of the larger hedge funds has blurred the lines between hedge funds, investment banks, and private equity firms and caused hedge funds to provide loans for mergers and acquisitions and initial public offerings (IPO) and invest in companies with the goal of affecting the companies structure; a strategy known as "activist" investing practiced by hedge funds, including Warren Lichtenstein's Steel Partners and Daniel S. Loeb whose Third Point LLC's targets have included Yahoo and Procter & Gamble.

THE HEDGE FUND INDUSTRY IS CHANGING

The hedge fund industry is changing in fundamental ways. The increasing consolidation and concentration among hedge funds has a parallel in the mutual fund industry, which went through a similar change in the 1980s. If we project this trend into the future, hedge funds look likely to mimic mutual funds and asset management companies in becoming larger, more concentrated, and more hierarchical. Hedge funds are also increasingly competing with mutual funds and asset management companies for both institutional and retail customers, causing changes in their products and organization. It is noteworthy that these changes coincide with retirement of the first generation of hedge fund managers.

Another area of change is the increased crossover of functions between hedge funds and other financial firms, notably banks, investment banks, and private equity firms. The credit crisis (and subsequent regulatory initiatives such as Dodd–Frank and Basel III) have unmoored the functions of traditional banking and investment banking and provided a window for hedge funds to assume some of their functions, notably risk trading and financing of M&A transactions, as well as providing financing in "special situations" such as distressed company debt and trade financing. Activist hedge funds are also changing the landscape in the area of corporate finance and shareholder rights.

INSTITUTIONALIZATION OF HEDGE FUNDS

Today's hedge fund world is not the same as that of the 1990s. Hedge funds have evolved from small and nimble firms often driven by outsized personalities catering primarily to the wealthy. The industry is now dominated by increasingly large hedge funds catering to institutional investors who view hedge funds as an integral part of their portfolio.

Along with this change has come increased concentration and consolidation According to PerTrac, a hedge fund industry information company, single-manager hedge funds with over $1 billion under management account for only 3.9% of all hedge funds, but account for about 60% of all hedge fund assets.[‡]

In response to their changing investor base and to new government regulations, hedge funds have beefed up their organization in areas such as risk management, marketing, operations, and compliance. In a self-fulfilling cycle, the additional resources needed to service institutional investors and comply with government regulations have favored the larger hedge funds at the expense of the smaller ones, in turn further concentrating assets with the larger firms.

---

‡ PerTrac's Annual Database Survey, April 30, 2012.

FINANCIAL HEADWINDS: LOW INTEREST RATES, SLOW GROWTH, AND CREDIT CONTRACTION

In the two decades leading up to the credit crisis in 2007, hedge funds—along with the asset management industry—enjoyed a tailwind of falling interest rates, economic expansion, and increased tolerance for leverage and derivative structures. Falling interest rates and easier credit standards led to an increase in asset valuation in major markets, and also to markets—especially bond markets—that had pronounced trends. Hedge funds responded to these new opportunities to devise investment strategies based on leverage and rising markets.

The current financial landscape is one of low interest rates, a reduction in leverage and credit, and volatile and unpredictable markets. In this environment, the expected returns from hedge funds have declined dramatically from double digit at the start of the decade to the point where an 6% annual return is considered extremely attractive.

This trend dovetails with the "yield shock" of investors who, faced with interest rates in the low single digits and volatile equity markets, are desperately seeking additional return on investment. The need for return is compounded by the deterioration in the "assets side" of the balance sheet of individuals, institutions, and governments whereby the growth of debt and expenses are outpacing the return on their investments.

DEBATE OVER HEDGE FUND BENEFITS

For close to two decades, hedge funds—along with private equity, commodities, and "real assets—have been presented as "alternative investments"; a necessary component of a portfolio that also includes stocks and bonds (the so-called traditional investments). Hedge funds, consultants, and academics claimed that hedge funds produced risk-adjusted returns superior to traditional investments, while also offering protection from market crashes and reducing risk through portfolio diversification. An oft-stated mantra was that anywhere from 5% to 20% of a portfolio should be invested in hedge funds.

However, over the past several years, these assumptions have been increasingly tested, challenged, and denied on a number of fronts. First, the underlying data used to analyze the performance of hedge funds has come under repeated attack, to the point where some critics deny the validity of any aggregate analysis of hedge fund returns or performance. Second, a number of analyses of hedge fund performance have indicated that hedge funds do not provide the additional or "alpha" returns (i.e., returns that come from manager skill) above traditional investments, especially given the major drag on performance caused by the unique hedge fund fee structure. A particularly trenchant criticism of hedge fund performance, which will be described and analyzed in detail below, has been presented by Simon Lack, who argues that the overwhelming majority of hedge fund returns have actually gone to the hedge fund managers, with a meager sliver handed to investors.

Finally, the relatively poor performance of hedge funds both during the credit crisis, when hedge funds in aggregate lost 20%, as well as in subsequent years has undermined the claims that they offered superior absolute returns that were uncorrelated to the major stock and bond markets.

HEDGE FUNDS AND THE GLOBAL FINANCIAL SYSTEM

To understand hedge funds, you have to understand how they fit into the overall financial system. Two features are especially important. First, they are often seen as part of the so-called shadow banking system of interconnected actors that includes bank vehicles, sovereign wealth funds, hedge funds, and private equity firms and that is "greased" by leverage and collateral. As important consumers of this leverage, hedge funds have a symbiotic relationship with banks and brokers and play a key role in this system.

Second, hedge funds are an important factor in most financial markets and major players in the derivatives world, and their importance will only increase as trading shifts from banks to hedge funds. This has made hedge funds a target for government regulation, to the extent that there is a distinct possibility that some time in the future larger hedge funds may be designated as "systematically important entities," which would lead to an additional layer of regulation and disclosure.

ORGANIZATION OF THIS BOOK

This book is divided into seven major parts, each composed of several chapters. It is also populated with separate "side boxes" that contain information related to the main body of the book but whose inclusion in the text would disrupt the narrative flow. These boxes will include case studies of hedge funds, hedge fund strategies, and hedge fund managers. They will also include some of the more technical and mathematical material that needs to be incorporated to gain a proper understanding of hedge funds, especially when we delve into some the hedge fund strategies and measures of performance and risk.

Part One: Introduction to Hedge Funds

The introduction provides a roadmap to the world of hedge funds, including the key characteristics of hedge funds and how they differ from other investment vehicles, notably mutual funds. Next are the regulations that govern eligibility for investing in hedge funds and the dos and don'ts that govern hedge fund behavior under existing and pending regulations, including the provisions of the Dodd–Frank Act. The following part describes the organization of a typical hedge fund and hedge fund management company, including the process of investing in hedge funds: the offering documents involved and fee structures of investment managers. The final chapter discusses the hedge fund service providers that are part and parcel of the hedge fund industry.

Part Two: Hedge Fund Toolkit

This part begins by providing readers with an overview of two of the main tools in the hedge fund toolkit: short selling, which allows managers to wager that stock prices are going to fall, and leverage, whereby hedge funds borrow monies to increase the return (and risk) potential of their investments. This part describes the mechanics by which hedge funds employ these tools, as well as the risks inherent in each, especially in the face of tail-risk type events, such as the Credit Crisis, and the failure of Long-Term Capital Management.

The final chapter in this part looks at derivatives, the oft-maligned instruments whose astronomical growth over the last two decades shows few signs of slowing. It addresses the growth of the derivatives market, the mechanics of futures, forwards, options and swaps, and the issues that have arisen as a result of constantly expanding derivatives market- trading both on exchanges and over-the-counter.

Part Three: History and Overview of the Hedge Fund Industry

This part discusses the origins of hedge funds, how hedge funds evolved as an industry and how they fit into the larger domestic and global financial system, especially in the post–credit crisis environment. This part will discuss issues including the changing client base and the consolidation of the industry, the valuation of hedge funds and fund of hedge funds in a mergers and acquisitions context, and tax issues and the concept of the "new power brokers."

This part also describes the controversy surrounding the "shadow banking" system, the purported systemic risk that hedge funds pose to the financial system and their potential benefits to the market. Lastly, this part provides an overview of the credit crisis, including the role of hedge funds, and dissects one of the largest hedge fund failures: Long-Term Capital Management.

Part Four: Hedge Fund Performance: Mounting Criticism and Changing Benchmarks

This part takes on the highly controversial issue of how hedge funds perform and the equally controversial issue of how to measure hedge fund performance. The part begins with the problems inherent in hedge fund data, including a number of biases that are unique to hedge fund data, which is voluntarily provided by hedge fund managers. Next is a description of various hedge fund indices that attempt to measure hedge fund performance in the aggregate and for specific strategies, and a discussion of the differences between investible and non-investible indices.

The next chapter discusses the debate over the popular theory that smaller hedge funds outperform their larger brethren. It also addresses an issue that rarely gets raised: even if (thousands of) small hedge funds in aggregate do statistically outperform thousands of larger hedge funds, can investors make use of this knowledge to their economic advantage?

The following chapter provides readers with an overview of the statistical measures commonly used in the industry to measure performance, and risk, including standard deviation, the Sharpe and Sortino ratios, and skewness and kurtosis. The discussion also looks at the tools that investors employ in the tricky task of separating alpha from beta in an effort to measure manger skill.

The part continues the investigation into hedge fund performance at the aggregate level, by applying the most commonly used measures of risk and performance to the overall hedge fund universe and to various strategy groups, and by delving deeper into the questions surrounding hedge fund alpha.

The final chapter describes the controversy over whether or not hedge funds provide value to their investors. Related issues are the persistence of returns, the division of the spoils of hedge fund returns between investors and hedge fund managers, and the extent to which the interests of hedge fund managers and investors converge or diverge.

Part Five: Hedge Fund Strategies

This part provides detailed information on the full range of hedge fund strategies, with special attention to the risk and return of various hedge fund strategy types. The part is organized to provide a framework that can be used to describe and evaluate the various strategies. This framework includes, for each strategy:

- The markets in which a hedge fund operates, by function (i.e., equities, fixed income, commodities), by sector (i.e., financial services, energy), and by geographic region (i.e., country, region, or global)
- The tools and techniques used by different strategies, notably the use of leverage and derivatives, and the extent to which a strategy is "systematic" (i.e., a result of a quantitative, rule-driven process) or involves discretion on the part of the managers
- The historical performance characteristics of different hedge fund strategies and their behavior in various types of markets

Part Six: Hedge Funds and Investment Portfolios

This part places hedge funds in the context of an investment portfolio that also includes stocks, bonds, and other assets. This will also place the discussion in the context of the controversy over modern portfolio theory and the extent to which markets are or are not efficient. This is especially important for institutional investors, whose decisions regarding the role of hedge funds are often driven by overall asset allocation. The part also describes some of the tools that derive from modern portfolio theory, notably portfolio optimization, and discusses the industry practices for creating optimal portfolios.

The following two chapters look at behavioral finance, and its challenges posed to the efficient markets hypothesis, and the growing trends towards institutionalization of hedge funds, including how institutions such as endowments and pensions invest.

This part concludes with a look at hybrid products and alternatives to traditional hedge funds, including mutual funds that contain hedge fund characteristics, actively managed ETFs, hedge fund "replication" strategies that attempt to replicate hedge fund performance using liquid futures and options markets, and SEC-registered fund of hedge funds.

Part Seven: Managing Hedge Fund Portfolios

The last chapters of the book address the crucial areas of risk management, portfolio construction, and due diligence, areas that have gained in prominence following large losses by many hedge funds during the credit crisis and the exposure of the Madoff Ponzi scheme, the Bayou fraud, as well as other instances of fraud. The discussion will cover issues of manager selection, various risks present in all hedge funds—such as market risk and operational risk—and the techniques that are commonly used for measuring and attempting to manage these risks. The discussion will include an examination of quantitative risk measurements—such as value at risk—and the limitation of their usefulness due to the "fat tails" distribution of returns and "black swan" events.

Finally, the discussion turns to notable hedge fund implosions, and the hedge fund due diligence issues they raise, a topic that has gained special importance following the failure of investors to uncover the Madoff fraud for over 20 years, as well as more recent insider trading scandals.

Appendices and Resources

Information on hedge funds is not as readily available as for other investment vehicles. Part six provides a number of resources that will be useful to the reader including:

- A glossary of hedge fund terms
- Hedge fund due diligence document
- Overview of major hedge fund replication products
- Internet resources for hedge fund news and research
- Index of regulatory agencies overseeing hedge funds worldwide
- Bibliography of hedge fund books and articles

PART ONE

Introduction to Hedge Funds

What Is a Hedge Fund?

There is no universally accepted definition of a hedge fund, either legal or industry-wide. The term is believed to have been coined by a journalist in the 1950s to describe a private investment fund managed by Alfred Winslow Jones, who used long and short equity positions to "hedge" the fund's overall exposure to stock market movements. Today, hedge funds are no longer confined to one market and very often do not "hedge" their portfolio against market movements. It is much more useful to describe hedge funds by a set of characteristics that most hedge funds have in common. While some of these characteristics are also shared by other investment firms and not every hedge fund has all the characteristics, taken together these features do represent a definable group of entities that most industry participants would recognize as hedge funds. These features include the following:

- Hedge funds pool assets from multiple investors in a limited partnership structure with a general partner and investment manager.

- They are offered to a restricted group of investors that meet regulatory criteria as qualified investors.

- Hedge funds may not market themselves and can offer shares only on the basis of a private placement memorandum.

- They are largely exempt from the Securities and Exchange Commission (SEC) regulation governing investment companies, although this has changed to some extent with the implementation of the new Dodd-Frank legislation.

- Investors face restrictions on the redemption of their units or shares that may be as short as three months or as long as several years.

- Hedge funds have high investment minimums.

SEC DEFINITION OF HEDGE FUNDS

The SEC, which has gained considerable supervisory authority over hedge funds as a result of the Dodd-Frank Act, defines hedge funds as follows:

What are hedge funds?
Like mutual funds, hedge funds pool investors' money and invest those funds in financial instruments in an effort to make a positive return. Many hedge funds seek to profit in all kinds of markets by pursuing leveraging and other speculative investment practices that may increase the risk of investment loss. Unlike mutual funds, however, hedge funds are not required to register with the SEC. Hedge funds typically issue securities in "private offerings" that are not registered with the SEC under the Securities Act of 1933. In addition, hedge funds are not required to make periodic reports under the Securities Exchange Act of 1934. But hedge funds are subject to the same prohibitions against fraud as are other market participants, and their managers have the same fiduciary duties as other investment advisers.

What are "funds of hedge funds"?

A fund of hedge funds is an investment company that invests in hedge funds—rather than investing in individual securities. Some funds of hedge funds register their securities with the SEC. These funds of hedge funds must provide investors with a prospectus and must file certain reports quarterly with the SEC.*

---

*"Investor Bulletin: Hedge Funds." www.sec.gov/investor/alerts/ib_hedgefunds.pdf (accessed 12/26/12)

- Hedge funds make extensive use of leverage, short selling, and derivatives.
- They are often active traders and speculators seeking to provide "absolute returns"— i.e., positive returns in up or down markets.

HEDGE FUNDS AND MUTUAL FUNDS

Mutual funds manage approximately $12 trillion in assets compared to around $2 trillion managed by hedge funds. Unlike hedge funds, mutual funds are open to all investors and have no minimum investment. As a result, they have a much wider investor base of both individuals and institutions. As I discuss in greater detail later in the book, mutual funds are adopting some of the strategies of hedge funds. However, even these are distinct because of the distinct features of mutual funds compared to hedge funds.

The SEC describes mutual funds as follows:

- A mutual fund is a company that pools money from many investors and invests the money in stocks, bonds, short-term money-market instruments and other securities or assets.

Some of the traditional, distinguishing characteristics of mutual funds include the following:

- Investors purchase mutual fund shares from the fund itself (or through a broker of the fund).
- The price that investors pay for mutual fund shares is the fund's per share net asset value (NAV) plus any shareholder fees.
- Mutual fund shares are "redeemable," meaning investors can sell their shares back to the fund (or to a broker acting for the fund).
- Mutual funds generally create and sell new shares to accommodate new investors. In other words, they sell their shares on a continuous basis.
- The investment portfolios of mutual funds typically are managed by separate entities known as "investment advisers" that are registered with the SEC.

Hedge Funds Compared with Mutual Funds		
	Hedge Funds	**Mutual Funds**
Regulation	Registration required under the Dodd-Frank Act for larger hedge funds	Extensive SEC regulation
Short selling	Only limited by availability of stocks or derivatives	Maximum 30% of profits
Public knowledge	Presently word of mouth; limited advertising coming	Advertisement and widespread sales and distribution
Investment tools	Any legal means	Limited leverage, derivative use shorting
Fees	Management fee (1–2% of assets) and performance fee (typically 20%)	Limited to percent of assets (no performance fees)
Minimum investment	Typically $1,000,000+	Small
Investors	99–499 "qualified purchasers" and "accredited investors"; some retail investors	Unlimited
Liquidity	Three months to five years	No lockup; immediate redemption
Structure	Partnership (onshore) and limited liability corporation (offshore)	Public vehicle
Benchmark	No fixed benchmark; absolute return or peer group	Return against market benchmark
Investor document	Private placement memorandum	Prospectus registered with SEC
Organization	Limited partnership (U.S.); corporation (abroad)	Corporation
Status of investors	Limited partners	Shareholders

In addition to the rigorous regulation of mutual funds, a key difference with hedge funds is that mutual fund managers are constrained by their limitation on short positions and their need to adhere to benchmarks. The limitation on short positions means that mutual funds will always have a greater correlation to the markets (stocks, bonds, etc.) than hedge funds. The adherence to benchmarks place limits on the extent to which mutual fund managers are able to actively manage their portfolios.

While some mutual funds are identified as "actively managed," the meaning is completely different than hedge funds. In broad terms, mutual funds can be "index" funds, which means that they seek to exactly track a benchmark index such as the S&P 500. When a mutual fund is described as "active" the manager seeks to outperform the benchmark index by a relatively small amount.

Take an example of a mutual fund that seeks to replicate the S&P 500 index and compare it to an "actively managed" mutual fund with the same index benchmark. Both funds' returns will closely mirror the returns of the S&P 500. If the S&P 500 index declines by 20%, the index fund will decline by the same amount and the index fund will decline by almost the same amount (say between 19% and 21%).

This is significantly different than a hedge fund which would seek to make money for investors even in the fact of a stock market decline of 20%. The extent to which they succeed is the topic of a later chapter.

HEDGE FUND ORGANIZATION

There is a widespread mistaken notion about the exact meaning of "hedge fund." A hedge fund is a passive investment pool—the vehicle into which the partners place their money. Hedge funds are established as limited partnerships (typically in Delaware) or corporation (offshore), which issue units or shares to limited partners. A hedge fund has no employees or physical presence. A limited partnership hedge fund vehicle is structured as follows:

- The *general partner* (*GP*) (a.k.a. *sponsor*) is typically the creator of the fund. The GP usually manages the fund and has broad powers along with fiduciary responsibilities to the other (limited) partners.

FIGURE 1–1

Illustration of a Typical Hedge Fund Structure

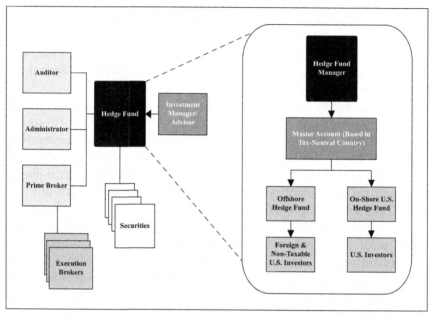

- The *limited partners* (*LP*) (a.k.a. *investors*) contribute capital and receive some form of ownership or partnership interest.

What is often mistakenly taken as the hedge fund is the investment manager (a.k.a. investment adviser) hired by the hedge fund (more specifically the GP of the hedge fund) to actively manage this pool of money on behalf of the investors. The portfolio managers and decision makers are employees of the investment manager. However, while the investment manager is hired by the hedge fund, in practice the GP is normally the investment manager and invests substantial amounts, often the great majority, of his or her total assets in the fund. The complex organization of a fund along with its service provider is diagrammed in Figure 1–1.

PRIVATELY OFFERED TO A RESTRICTED GROUP OF INVESTORS

Mutual funds are "sponsored" by an organization such as Fidelity or Vanguard. Shares in mutual funds are typically offered to the general public on the basis of a prospectus by brokers, investment advisers, financial planners, banks, or insurance companies. Mutual funds are supported by a significant amount of marketing and advertising. All this is in the context of compliance with the relevant investment laws and under the registration and supervision of the SEC.

Hedge funds can only be offered privately to investors who must meet certain legal requirements as "qualified investors" and "accredited investors" based on their wealth, income, and sophistication, and who can bear the possibility of large losses. These requirements have limited hedge fund investors to high-net-worth individuals and institutions. However, there are increasing opportunities for individuals who do not meet these criteria to invest in hedge fund products, or in investments that mimic some of the characteristics of hedge funds.

A private offering means that a hedge fund cannot advertise, although that will change to an unknown extent as a result of the JOBS Act. Investment in a hedge fund is offered via a document known as a *private placement memorandum* (or *offering documents*), which serves a similar function as the mutual funds' prospectus but which, as the name implies, is not registered with the SEC.

DODD-FRANK ACT AND HEDGE FUND REGULATION

Two overarching laws govern the investment management industry: the Securities Act of 1933 and the Investment Adviser Act of 1940, along with their many amendments. Hedge funds (along with other entities such as private equity firms) are exempt from many of the provisions of these laws. In exchange for these exemptions, the Congress limited the ability of hedge funds to market to small investors. In effect, the Congress said we will leave hedge funds largely unregulated, but they can only cater to wealthy individuals and institutions, and only reach out to them through private channels and word of mouth.

Under the provisions of the Dodd-Frank Act, hedge funds that have more than $150 million in assets under management—must register with the SEC and to file several documents and provide certain information. The Dodd-Frank Act does not change the fact that investments in hedge funds units (or shares) are not registered under the Securities Act of 1933, which governs most publicly issued investment securities.

However, it is important to point out that hedge funds have always been subject to laws that prevent fraudulent and other illegal activities, as witnessed by the recent spate of prominent arrests and conviction of hedge fund managers and employees for insider trading and for running Ponzi schemes.

RESTRICTED REDEMPTION RIGHTS

By law, mutual funds must honor investor redemption requests within seven days; although in practice, redemption is made within a day or two. Shareholders in a mutual fund return their shares to the fund and are paid their share of the funds' net asset value. Hedge fund shares or units, on the other hand, may only be redeemed on a periodic basis, typically either quarterly or annually, although they can be much longer. Most hedge funds also require notice before the redemption period. For example, hedge funds that have a three-month restriction on redemptions may require that investors notify the fund of their intent to redeem shares a month before the three-month period begins. In effect, this means that investors must wait four months to see their funds. As discussed at length below, there are investment considerations that underlay these restrictions having to do with the economic benefits of allowing hedge fund managers to invest with the knowledge that they will be able to deploy the funds for a minimum amount of time. The same considerations are behind the restrictions imposed by private equity firms, which limit customer access to their funds for five years or more.

In addition, the GP is normally allowed to suspend redemptions for a variety of reasons or to place some or even the entire fund in a segregated account called a "side pocket," where the portfolio is essentially locked up until the GP decides to allow redemptions.

MAY USE LEVERAGE, SHORT SELLING, DERIVATIVES

A number of financial techniques and instruments are widely associated with hedge funds. In fact, hedge funds (along with investment banks) are the primary users of some of these instruments, especially for speculative purposes. The industry has had close links to the derivatives world from its earliest days, when many hedge funds were closely associated with the futures and options exchanges. The expertise of hedge funds with derivatives and complex financial structures (futures, forwards, options, swaps, structured products) is now widespread within the industry. They are a regular feature of hedge funds involved in the fixed-income markets, which are extensive users of both futures and swaps, and the equity markets through stock index options and options on individual securities. In more recent times, this expertise has placed hedge funds front and center in the mortgage crisis as major users of mortgage-backed securities and credit default swaps.

A trademark of hedge funds is their ability to "short" markets either as short sellers of stocks or through the use of derivatives in fixed income, currency, and commodity markets. Hedge funds' active use of shorting has repeatedly brought them into conflict with governments who blame hedge funds shorting for declines in the value of stocks and currencies. Finally, many hedge fund strategies and fund of funds vehicles rely on credit from banks and investment banks to leverage or enhance their returns (and risks) using vehicles such as repurchase agreements, credit lines, total return swaps, and the leverage inherent in many derivatives.

ACTIVE MANAGERS SEEKING TO PRODUCE ABSOLUTE RETURNS

Hedge fund managers are often described as "active managers seeking absolute return." In the mutual fund industry, there are broadly two types of funds. Index funds attempt to replicate the returns of an index (e.g., the S&P 500). Active managers seek to provide returns higher than a relevant index. However, active managers typically seek small enhancements to the index and are tightly constrained in terms of how much they can deviate and the tools (i.e., leverage, short selling, and derivatives) they can use.

In the hedge fund arena, all managers are active in the sense that their objective is to deliver a positive return to investors under all economic and market conditions utilizing all the tools at their disposal. Hedge funds are not constrained to beat the S&P 500, which has had declines of 40% or more. As absolute return managers, with the tools to short a market, their objective is to make money whether the S&P 500 declines or rises. In reality, hedge funds are judged by some benchmarks and do not always achieve this absolute return.

SPECULATION, TRADING, INVESTMENT, AND GAMBLING

Hedge funds are often said to speculate, with the inference that they take greater risk with their clients' money than other investment managers. It would be useful to deal with this early in the text and clear up some misconceptions about the related concepts of speculation, trading, and investment and gambling.

First, *trading* is merely the selling or buying of any security, and is therefore a part of any form of any investment strategy, including those of mutual funds.

Next, there are differences between speculation and gambling: speculation is taking a calculated risk, where the outcome can be rationally (if imperfectly and incorrectly) analyzed. On the other hand, the outcome of gambling is entirely dependent on pure chance and totally random outcome for results. While hedge funds certainly gamble, they at least attempt to speculate and put much time and effort into analyzing the potential outcome of their trading decisions.

It is more difficult to differentiate between investment and speculation. It would be tempting to neatly distinguish between hedge funds (speculators) on the one hand and "responsible" investors on the other. However, even Ben Graham, the noted financial adviser and author of the classic investment book *The Intelligent Investor*, finds it difficult to separate the two. He describes the prototypical investor as "one interested chiefly in safety plus freedom from bother." He admits, however, that "some speculation is necessary and unavoidable, for in many common-stock situations, there are substantial possibilities of both profit and loss, and the risks therein must be assumed by someone."

Finally, economic theory ascribes a significant economic and social benefit to what is commonly thought of as speculation. By buying and selling instruments, it often provides liquidity in markets that in turn helps establish realistic prices, narrow spreads between purchase and sales, and assume risks that enable hedgers to gain certainty in their businesses. The classic example here is of a farmer who is able to plant a field with greater certainty because a "speculator" has taken the other side of a futures contract on the price of wheat.

CHAPTER 2

Regulation of Hedge Funds

Four main laws govern the investment industry: the Securities Act of 1933, the Securities and Exchange Act of 1934, the Investment Company Act of 1940, and the Investment Advisers Act of 1940. As the names imply, the Securities Act of 1933 governs the issuance and trading of securities while the two 1940s acts govern investment firms and investment advisers. The most recent law, the Dodd-Frank Act, has changed some fundamental aspects of these laws but kept many provisions intact.

These laws exempt certain firms—including hedge funds and private equity firms—from certain provisions, notably those relating to registration and supervision by the U.S. Securities and Exchange Commission (SEC). However, hedge funds that qualify for these exemptions must also accept certain restrictions, especially in the type of investor that can invest in the fund as well as limitations to their activities in marketing and approaching clients.

In summary, the exemptions provided to hedge funds are as follows:

- Hedge funds are not subject to the Securities Act of 1933 because they do not engage in public offerings.

- Hedge funds do not fall under the purview of the Securities and Exchange Act of 1934 because they are not publicly traded companies.

- Hedge funds are not subject to the Investment Company Act of 1940 because (1) hedge funds are not mutual funds that solicit funds from the public and (2) they offer investment advice only to private clients.

HEDGE FUND EXEMPTIONS FROM SECURITIES REGULATIONS

Figure 2–1 provides an overview of hedge fund exceptions by the SEC.

Securities Act of 1933

Interest in a hedge fund are "securities"

The Securities Act of 1933 requires that securities be registered with the SEC. According to the law, an interest in a hedge fund *is* a security. However, Section 4(2), which provides the most important provision for hedge funds exemption, states that "[t]he provisions of section 5 shall not apply to transactions by an issuer not involving any public offering," which includes hedge funds.

FIGURE 2–1

Overview of Hedge Fund SEC Exemptions

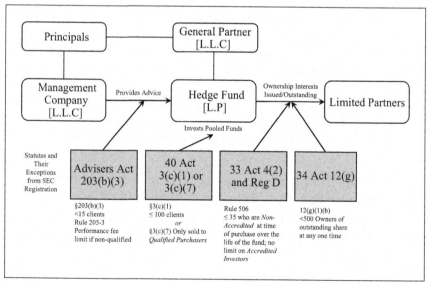

Regulation D "safe harbor"

Regulation D is a "safe harbor" allowing hedge funds to satisfy the Section 4(2) exemption noted above (i.e., that they do not make public offerings) provided that they do not "use general solicitation or advertising to market the securities," and that all but 35 investors in the fund are "accredited investors," as defined by Rule 506.

Rule 506: accredited investors

Rule 506 defines an *accredited investor* as a natural person that has:

1. $1 million net worth
2. $200,000 in income in last 2 years; $300,000 when combined with spouse

Institutions that are accredited investors must have a minimum of $5,000,000 in *invested* assets (not net worth) to qualify as accredited investors.

No general advertising

Prohibition on advertising by hedge funds includes no newspaper ads or radio or television shows.

Securities and Exchange Act of 1934

Funds with 500 investors and $10 million in equity must register with the SEC

The Securities Exchange Act of 1934 requires a company to register with the SEC if it has more than $10 million in assets *and* more than 500 investors. Registration subjects funds to annual and other periodic reporting requirements. Hedge funds with more than $10 million in equity can opt out of this reporting requirement if they have no more than 499 investors.

Investment Company Act of 1940

Hedge funds exempted under Sections 3(c)(1) and 3(c)(7)

The Investment Company Act of 1940 requires that an *investment company* must disclose its financial condition and investment policies to investors on a regular basis. However, hedge funds qualify for exclusion from the definition of investment company under the act's 3(c)(1) and 3(c)(7) provisions.

1. Section 3(c)(1) excludes any issuer whose outstanding securities are beneficially owned by not more than 100 investors and is not making public offerings of its securities.
2. Section 3(c)(7) excludes any issuer whose outstanding securities are owned by "qualified purchasers" and is not making public offerings of its securities.

Investment Advisers Act of 1940

Requires investment advisers to register with the SEC

The Advisers Act defines an *investment adviser* as "any person who, for compensation, engages in the business of advising others, either directly or through publications or writings, as to the value of securities or as to the advisability of investing in, purchasing, or selling securities, or who, for compensation and as part of a regular business, issues or promulgates analyses or reports concerning securities."

Exemption under Section 203(b)(3) for advisers who have less than 15 clients over a 12-month period

Hedge funds that have had fewer than 15 clients during the preceding 12-month period are not required to register as investment advisers under Section 203(b)(3).

Commodities Exchange Act CPO and CTA Registration

The Commodity Exchange Act (CEA) may subject hedge funds that trade financial and commodity futures to register as a commodity pool operator (CPO) or a commodity trading adviser (CTA), which requires disclosure, record keeping, and periodic reporting in compliance with the Commodity Futures Trading Commission rules. Hedge funds can claim exemption from registration as a CPO or CTA. Rule 4.13(a)(3) of the CEA exempt asset pools from registering as CPOs if they privately place ownership interests to accredited investors (as defined in Rule 501 of Regulation D). The CEA also contains Rule 4.13(a)(4), which exempts pools from registering as CPOs if they place ownership interests to certain highly sophisticated persons, including qualified purchasers (as defined in Section 2(a)(51) of the Investment Company Act). Hedge fund advisers can also be exempt from CTA registration under Section 4m(1) of the CEA, which provides exemption for CTAs with 15 or fewer clients.

"Blue Sky" Laws

The above security laws are enforced by the SEC and other exchanges or agencies at the federal level. There are also "blue sky" laws, which are the securities laws of the individual states and enforced by the state's securities administrator. Generally, a state requires that hedge funds make a "blue sky filing" if an investor resides there. In addition, small hedge funds (generally those with less than $25 million in assets) are exempt from registration under the Investment Advisor Act (under Section 203(b)(3)) but may still need to register under state regulation, which varies from state to state.

RECENT CHANGES UNDER THE DODD-FRANK ACT

The Dodd-Frank Wall Street Reform and Consumer Protection Act (Dodd-Frank Act), passed largely in response to the credit crisis, represents the most comprehensive securities legislation since the New Deal laws, and includes provisions for the regulation of hedge funds. Title IV of the Act "Regulation of Advisers to Hedge Funds and Others" mandates that hedge funds with between $25 million and $150 million in assets under management (AUM) will be required to register with the state in which they operate, while hedge funds that operate in over 15 states or have over $150 million in AUM will be required to register with the SEC.

The SEC attempted to require the registration of hedge funds by administrative edict in 2004. However, the courts overturned this attempt in 2006 in the case of Goldstein, et al. v. Securities Exchange Commission. The Dodd-Frank Act makes registration a legal requirement.

Title IV: Regulation of Advisers to Hedge Funds and Others

Section (1) of the title requires hedge funds and private equity advisors to register with the SEC as investment advisers and provide information about their trades and portfolios. The information is primarily gathered to be shared with the Financial Stability Oversight Council (FSOC), a group comprising the major regulatory agencies with the mandate of determining the sources of systemic risk. The inclusion of hedge funds, private equity firms, and other members of the "shadow banking" system were deemed essential for the FSOC to be able to gauge the potential for systemic risk.

Hedge funds that register under Dodd-Frank are required to provide information on Form PF (Reporting Form for Investment Advisers to Private Funds and Certain Commodity Pool Operators and Commodity Trading Advisors). Form PF is formidable and calls for extensive information on the funds' AUM; leverage and sources of financing; use of derivatives; fund strategies and risks; their largest market positions; the types of investors in the fund; and their "gatekeepers"—auditors, prime brokers, and marketers that service the funds.

Registered funds will also be required to have a compliance officer and set up policies to avoid conflicts of interest.

Under the new rules, advisers with AUM between $150 million and $1.5 billion will have to report on an annual basis. Advisers with AUM of $1.5 billion or greater will be required to file quarterly. Large hedge fund advisers (those with $1.5 billion or more in AUM) will have to file within 60 days after their quarter end. Smaller advisers and large private equity fund advisers will have to file within 120 days after their fiscal year.

Section (3) of the title exempts from registration advisers to private funds with AUM of less than $150 million as well as advisers to "family offices." A number of large hedge funds, notably that of George Soros, have converted to family offices partly to avoid the registration and disclosure requirements of Dodd-Frank.

Another provision of Dodd-Frank greatly restricts the role of banks in their ability to invest and/or sponsor hedge funds and private equity funds. Banks may constitute no more than 3% of the NAV of a hedge fund, and may have no more than 3% of their Tier 1 capital invested in private funds.

JOBS Act and Hedge Fund Advertising

Congress passed the Jump start Our Business Startups (JOBS) Act in 2012. The Act will greatly increase the ability of hedge funds to market their services. As described above, hedge funds are allowed to solicit funds under the exemption provided by Rule 506, which allows for the offering of securities primarily to accredited investors so long as such offering is not accomplished through general solicitation or general advertising (e.g., publishing an advertisement in a newspaper or on TV, or announcing the new fundraiser on the sponsor's website or at a public seminar).

However, the JOBS Act lifts the Rule 506 restriction on general solicitation and general advertising so long as the sponsor has taken reasonable steps to verify that all purchasers are accredited investors. Once rules go into effect, hedge funds will be permitted to market new funds through print, broadcast, and Internet advertisements; notices posted on their websites; and media interviews. It also allows presentations at seminars and other forms of interaction with potential investors. However, the antifraud provisions contained in the Investment Advisers Act of 1940 and in the rules promulgated thereunder will continue to apply, which include (in the case of registered investment advisers) prohibitions on the use of testimonials and specific requirements when listing past performance information in connection with the offer and sale of private fund securities.

The effect of the JOBS act, however, may be limited in practice—at least in the immediate future—for a number of reasons: First, the larger and more established hedge funds do not need to advertise to solicit funds; in fact, many have turned away prospective investors. Second, the hedge fund industry has developed a network that connects investors with funds throughout the world. The network is built on personal relationships, events that bring together investors and funds, databases that allow investors to evaluate some aspects of hedge fund performance, and professional marketers that have extensive contacts among investors. This network does not depend on advertising. Third, hedge funds have an incentive to maintain a relatively low profile to avoid the adverse publicity they sometimes generate among regulators or the general public. Finally, hedge funds may be eager to maintain their "brand name" with wealthy investors and especially institutions that may view mass media advertising as a diminution of that brand.

EUROPEAN ALTERNATIVE INVESTMENT FUND MANAGERS DIRECTIVE

While the focus of hedge fund regulation has centered on the Dodd-Frank legislation, a regulation proposed for the European Union (EU)—the Alternative Investment Fund Managers Directive (AIFMD)—is likely to have far greater impact on hedge funds. The directive, which will become law in July 2013, addresses the following issues:

1. Domicile—Depending on how the legislation is implemented, there is a real possibility that hedge funds and hedge fund managers may have to establish domicile in Europe in order to market their products within the EU.

2. Reporting—Managers will have to register with their national regulator (essentially the Financial Services Authority in the United Kingdom since 80% of EU-based hedge funds are in London) and provide information on investment strategy and the instruments and leverage they will utilize. The added operational and software capability this reporting will require will favor larger hedge funds with deeper pockets.

3. Depository Requirements—All hedge funds will have to appoint a single independent depository (custodian or prime broker) to safeguard the funds. Non-EU funds may have a depository either within the EU or in their "home country" (main location) or country of domiciliation. However, the non-EU depository must be subject to the same level of EU regulation in the "home" jurisdiction as they would be in the EU, which may present a problem for some hedge funds.

4. Leverage—The directive adopts restrictions on leverage as well as a revised measurement of hedge funds whose overall effect will be to reduce hedge fund leverage to the degree that it may change the model of traditional hedge funds.

5. Valuation Policy—The AIFMD mandates that all assets of a fund will be independently valued either by an independent entity (i.e., an administrator) or by the hedge fund—as long as it is not valued by the portfolio management function or the area that sets remuneration policy for the fund. The overall effect may be to make it less attractive for hedge funds to invest in potentially illiquid investments.

EUROPEAN REGULATORS MAY LIMIT HEDGE FUND
COMPENSATION

The European Securities and Markets Authority (ESMA) has stated
that it expects national EU regulators to extend to hedge funds bonus
restrictions that are already imposed on banks. ESMA's guidance suggests that hedge funds would have to defer between 40% and 60%
of bonuses over several years, and that at least half of the bonuses
would have to be paid in equity-linked instruments related to the fund
rather than outright cash bonuses. Part of the proposed regulation
would include a "clawback" provision that would allow a hedge fund to
cancel a bonus or an equity-linked instrument if the recipient lost money
for the fund in subsequent years. The motivation for the regulation is
to align the interests of hedge fund managers and their investors at
least insofar as it should deter hedge funds from pursuing short-term
strategies that may provide them with an immediate bonus payout but
come back and harm investors in the longer term. A classic example
would be a short option or an option-like strategy that paid the hedge
fund an immediate premium but may incur large losses in the future.

WHO ARE HEDGE FUND INVESTORS?

Because hedge funds are exempt from a wide variety of securities
and investment adviser regulations, hedge funds historically have
been available only to accredited investors and large institutions,
and have limited their investors through high investment minimums. The specific regulatory limitations on hedge fund investors
vary according to the legal organization of each hedge fund.

Subscription documents that investors sign to purchase hedge
fund units generally ask investors to provide the information
needed to assure they meet the investor requirements for the fund.
However, in general, hedge fund investors must fall into one of two
categories, each with its own investor limitations.

Section 3(c)(1) and Regulation D Rule 506
Exempt Funds

Hedge funds established as Section 3(c)(1) funds under the Investment
Adviser Act of 1940 are limited to 99 investors. Furthermore, each investor must be an *accredited investor*, which is defined as an individual

(or individual and spouse) with a net worth of at least $1 million and an income of more than $200,000 (or $300,000 with spouse) in each of the preceding two years. (A Rule 506 fund may have an unlimited number of accredited investors and up to 35 nonaccredited investors.)

Section 3(c)(7) Exemption Funds

These funds are limited to 499 investors (recently changed to 1,999), all of whom are *qualified purchasers*, defined as a natural person who (with their spouse) "owns not less than $5,000,000 in investments." Also allowed are certain trusts, foundations, and family offices, as well as advisers that manage more than $25,000,000 in investments on behalf of qualified purchasers.

FIDUCIARY AND LEGAL DUTIES OF HEDGE FUND MANAGERS

The standard description one finds of *hedge funds* inevitably claims that hedge funds are "unregulated" or "largely unregulated." This presents an impression of an out-of-control industry able to operate without restrictions or prohibitions, accountable to no one but their investors (if even those), to the extent their investors know what they are doing and are in a position to redeem their funds or influence the managers.

This is not the case. In fact, even before the passage of the Dodd-Frank Act, the SEC stated that:

> Like mutual funds, hedge funds pool investors' money and invest those funds in financial instruments in an effort to make a positive return. Many hedge funds seek to profit in all kinds of markets by pursuing leveraging and other speculative investment practices that may increase the risk of investment loss.

> Unlike mutual funds, however, hedge funds are not required to register with the SEC. Hedge funds typically issue securities in "private offerings" that are not registered with the SEC under the Securities Act of 1933. In addition, hedge funds are not required to make periodic reports under the Securities Exchange Act of 1934. But hedge funds are subject to the same prohibitions against fraud as are

other market participants, and their managers have the same fiduciary duties as other investment advisers.

In addition, hedge fund managers that are general partners owe the fund and the fund's limited partners a fiduciary responsibility of placing the fund's and limited partner's interest ahead of their own. Fiduciary duties are not the same as laws; however, they do place duties and restrictions on hedge fund managers' behavior and, while not enforceable in the same way as laws, may lead to lawsuits on the part of investors if these duties are violated.

While there is no fixed definition of fiduciary responsibility, there is a broad consensus in the investment industry that investment managers owe their investors a set of duties that include at least the following:

- To manage the hedge fund in the best interest of the fund and its investors

- To place the interest of the limited partners before those of the general partner

- To disclose all conflicts of interest.

Hedge Funds under the Investment Advisers Act of 1940

The new regulations will be become more meaningful by the regulators' access to hedge fund activities gained through the registration requirement of the new legislation, which places registered hedge funds under the regulation of the Investment Advisers Act of 1940. Again, the SEC has stated that:

> The Securities and Exchange Commission is adopting a new rule that prohibits advisers to pooled investment vehicles from making false or misleading statements to, or otherwise defrauding, investors or prospective investors in those pooled vehicles. This rule is designed to clarify, in light of a recent court opinion, the Commission's ability to bring enforcement actions under the Investment Advisers Act of 1940 against investment advisers who defraud investors or prospective investors in a hedge fund or other pooled investment vehicle.

CHAPTER 3

Hedge Fund Organization

This chapter covers certain organizational issues of hedge funds, including the types of documents associated with hedge funds, issues of redemptions and fees, and the important issue of the alignment (or misalignment) of interest between hedge fund managers and investors.

OFFERING DOCUMENTS

Before investing in a hedge fund, investors are presented with a variety of documents, each with a specific purpose. Investors need to keep in mind that these documents are written by attorneys to protect the interests of the general partner and/or the investment company. As such, a primary purpose of these documents is to ensure that their legal liability has been reduced as much as possible through the use of disclaimers. This is not to say, however, that they do not include valuable information about the fund, its strategy, and its risks.

Hedge funds normally also provide potential investors with several types of marketing materials, including PowerPoint presentations, newsletters, and other documents, as well as making representations at meetings and in phone conversations.

It is important that all these documents and discussions are viewed as a whole since each document addresses different points and has a different purpose. Many investors, especially institutional investors, retain attorneys to review the documents and may be able to negotiate concessions in some of the agreements.

Private Placement Memorandum

Section 3(c)(1) of the U.S. Investment Company Act of 1940, which established the terms under which hedge funds are exempt from SEC registration, states that funds must issue a private placement memorandum (PPM) as a prospectus to potential investors when raising capital, either initially when launching the fund or on an ongoing basis to new investors or investors looking to purchase new units.

The PPM is also referred to as an offering circular, offering memorandum, or private offering memorandum for the interest of shares of a hedge fund. The PPM is required to disclose all material terms of the interests of shares being offered to investors, the details of the general partner or the members of an offshore hedge fund's board of directors, information about the investment adviser and the management agreement, material risks factors for an investment in the hedge fund, regulatory matters, tax aspects, and information about the administrator and the fees it charges.

A hedge fund may only seek investment from potential investors with whom it has a preexisting relationship. To legally solicit an individual investor, the hedge fund must establish this relationship before sending the PPM on for consideration. Another avenue is for a hedge fund to work with a third-party marketer or broker-dealer, who must be registered with the SEC, and are allowed to solicit their own established relationships on behalf of the hedge fund.

In broad terms, these documents are similar to a mutual fund prospectus and provide detailed discussions of the following topics:

- The investment program, including any limitations to the investment manager's discretion in terms of instruments or position limits
- The structural terms such as the relationship of the fund to the general partner, investment manager, and, importantly,

the key service providers, including broker, administrator, custodian, auditor, and attorneys

- Information on the management company and the managers
- Information on how the market and economic situation affected past performance
- The fees and expenses that investors would have to pay out of financial results
- The alert to investors that they may lose all or part of their investments
- The alert to investors that past performance does not guarantee future success of the fund

A private placement often provides detailed information on the hedge fund's proposed strategy, including the types of investments it will make and instruments it will use, and the fund's allowable leverage capacity or level. PPMs also address potential conflicts of interest between the general and limited partners. The PPM also describes in detail how fees are calculated and charged. In order to arrive at fees, it also describes the method for calculating the fund's net asset value (NAV).

PPM Table of Contents

A typical Table of Contents for a PPM indicates the topics that are treated:

- Investment objective and policies
- Risk factors
- Fees and expenses
- Management of the fund
- The manager
- The investment adviser
- The prime broker and custodian
- The subadministrator
- Brokerage

- Net asset value
- Tax considerations
- Subscription and redemption of shares
- Distribution and selling restrictions
- Dividends and distributions
- Shareholder reports
- Legal counsel and auditors
- Anti–money laundering regulations

Limited Partnership Agreement

To invest in a limited partnership, investors need to sign a Limited Partnership Agreement (LPA), also known as the governing legal document. The LPA covers the relationship between the general partner and the limited partners, delineating their respective powers and responsibilities. The LPA is used by partners in a business to establish the rights and liabilities of the general partner(s) who actively manages affairs of the business and the limited partner(s) who are passive investors and have no role in management. In practice, the role of limited partners is severely restricted; they have no role in the operation of the partnership. However, the general partner's authority is restricted by the fact that he or she owes a fiduciary duty to the limited partners to place the interest of the fund and of the limited partners ahead of his own. The LPA also describes issues such as the formation of the partnership, name and place of business, terms of partnership, and contributions of capital.

Subscription Documents

The actual purchase of units in a hedge fund is done by submitting a signed limited partner "subscription agreement" along with sending the investment funds to the administrator. A subscription agreement details the amount of capital the applicant will contribute to the partnership as well as his or her responsibilities and authority in the company. The agreement establishes the partnership's expectations of the new member and defines his role within the existing management structure. All limited partners must be approved by the general partner.

This document describes the amount of money the investor is investing in the hedge fund and the number of "units" that this amount purchases. The subscription agreement also details the terms under which an investor can purchase additional units as well as the procedure for the redemption of shares. The subscription agreement typically includes questions about an investor's financial background, especially their qualification and suitability for exemption under the SEC securities regulations as "qualified purchasers" or as an "accredited investor."

Side Letters

Side letters between a hedge fund and certain investors are relatively common in the industry. They typically provide for preferential treatment to the investor in the form of lowered fees, lesser redemption restrictions, and increased transparency into the fund's operation. They are typically given to early investors or particularly large investors in a fund.

HEDGE FUND REDEMPTIONS AND REDEMPTION GATES

Investors in a typical hedge fund can only redeem funds on a quarterly, semiannual, annual, or longer basis. The period during which an investor is unable to redeem their shares is known as the "lockup" period. In practice, there are many variations of redemption rights. For example, some funds allow for an early redemption upon the payment of a penalty fee, typically around 3–5% of the amount being redeemed.

Hedge fund general partners typically give themselves wide discretion in their ability to suspend or restrict redemption. These restrictions are generally written in broad terms in the offering documents in order to give the general partner wide latitude as to when and how they impose these restrictions. During the credit crisis, scores of hedge funds made liberal use of this power. This became so prevalent that *BusinessWeek* was driven to declare "Hedge Funds Frozen Shut" (March 4, 2008). During the crisis, the hedge funds that suspended redemption to one degree or another included such leading names as Tudor, Fortress, Highbridge Capital Management, Permal Group, Centaurus Capital, Goldman Sachs, D.E. Shaw, Farallon Capital Management, Deephaven, GLG, and many others.[*]

A typical clause in the PPM addressing the issue of redemptions reads as follows:

> "The General Partner, <u>in its sole and absolute discretion</u>, has the right to suspend withdrawals by Limited Partners under certain circumstances specified in the Partnership Agreement including, without limitation, when, as a result of political, economic, military or monetary events, the existence of a natural disaster, force majeure, act of war or terrorist attack or other circumstances outside the responsibility of the General Partner, disposal of the assets of the Partnership is not reasonably or normally practicable, without being seriously detrimental, <u>in the judgment of the General Partner</u>, to the interests of the Partners." (*Hedge Fund Law Report*, July 29, 2009)

There are several types of redemption restrictions (in addition to the initial "lockup") that many hedge funds have, including:

- *Redemption restrictions* are the most common form of limit on the partners. They are outright limitations on redemptions and may be partial (i.e., investors can redeem a portion of their assets) or total (i.e., allowing for no redemptions).

- *Redemption gates* allow the manager to suspend redemptions once they have reached a predetermined percentage of the fund's overall assets, typically between 10% and 25% of the fund's assets. The gate may be discretionary on the part of the manager, or automatically imposed once the percentage trigger has been reached.

- *Establishing side pockets* is another common form of restriction on redemptions, especially for funds that have assets that have become highly illiquid, such as owning bonds of bankrupt

---

[*] It is important to check if there are any "side letters" between the fund and an investor that modifies the terms of the fund for that investor, including lockup and redemption terms.

companies or countries or when exchange regulations prevent remitting the assets, as happened during the Russian debt crisis in 1998. In recent years, side pockets were extensively used to segregate mortgage-backed securities that the manager felt could only be sold at "fire sale" prices, well below their "fair value" because of temporary market conditions, but that will increase in value once these conditions are gone. In practice, side pockets are established when a fund is split into liquid and illiquid share class with investors holding a stake in both share classes. Redemptions can continue on the liquid part (as well as new money through subscriptions), while redemptions are suspended on the illiquid shares.

- *Liquidation* refers to unwinding a fund and returning remaining assets to the investors. This is normally only done when redemption requests are too high to continue the fund or the manager decides to wind up the fund. This was a regular occurrence during the credit crisis, as in the case of Peloton, a $2 billion hedge fund that suffered fatal losses in mortgage-backed securities.

Some Limitations on Redemption Restrictions

While most hedge funds provide their managers with broad authority to suspend redemptions, there are, in practice, limitations to this power. First, the manager, as general partner, owes the traditional fiduciary duties of loyalty and care to the limited partnership (i.e., the fund) and its limited partners/investors. In practice, this limits the actions of the general partner to those that do not breach these duties and provide a boundary to the manager's behavior. This has sometimes been expanded to the manager's duty to act "in the best interest of the fund." Second, redemption restrictions are normally implemented so that no class of investors is unfairly affected compared with other investors.

Justification for Restrictions on Redemptions

While the presumptive power of general partners to suspend redemptions may seem onerous, there is actually an economic rationale for at least some discretionary authority as a benefit to all the partners in a fund. Redemption restrictions are sometimes justified with the argument that they allow the fund to "live to fight another day" by preventing forced liquidation. They are also justified as a mechanism to prevent investors from self-inflicted damage. This argument was presented by Professor Marcus K. Brunnermeier in an influential paper written in 2005 called "Predatory Trading," which Professor Brunnermeier explains as follows:

> Predatory trading is "trading that induces and/or exploits the need of other investors to reduce their positions . . . If one trader needs to sell, others also sell . . . This leads to price overshooting and a reduced liquidation value for the distressed trader. Hence, the market is illiquid when liquidity is most needed. Further, a trader profits from triggering another trader's crisis, and the crisis can spill over across traders and across markets.

The point here is that every investor has an incentive to flee the fund first to avoid being stuck in the crowd as all investors attempt to flee at once through a narrow door. Another often-used analogy is that of someone yelling "fire!" in a crowded theater and the need for an orderly exit strategy to prevent harm. Redemption restrictions are a way of controlling predatory trading by allowing the general partner to act in the interest of the investors despite their instinct to flee.

As described above, a related rationale for redemption gates is often used in the case of a hedge fund that holds illiquid securities in its portfolio, that is, those that can only be sold at a steep discount to their "real" value or whose sale would have a negative impact on the price of the security. In extreme cases, there may be no market for a security.

In addition, redemption limits are sometimes justified as a matter of fairness to all the investors in a fund. The logic here is as follows: If a large group of investors redeem their shares or units in a portfolio that includes illiquid securities or in a volatile environment, the manager would be forced to liquidate the more liquid securities first, leaving the remaining investors "holding the bag" with a portfolio of the more illiquid securities. Here, a redemption limit could be said to be fair to all the investors.

Finally, redemption restrictions are justified as a matter of aligning the strategy of a fund with its funding source. If a fund's strategy is dependent on making investments that may take a certain amount of time to reach fruition, it seems reasonable that the funding for the strategy (i.e., the investors) be matched to the needed time. In fact, there is a correlation between the limits on redemptions and the liquidity of the underlying hedge fund investments. For example, hedge funds that invest in highly liquid instruments (i.e., high cap stocks, U.S. Treasury or high-grade corporate bonds, liquid futures contracts) typically offer relatively short redemption periods (as short as two or three months), while hedge funds that invest in distressed company debt may have redemption restrictions of one year or more.

HEDGE FUND MANAGEMENT AND INCENTIVE (PERFORMANCE) FEES

While the hedge fund industry has come under pressure to reduce their traditional fee structure, especially from institutional investors, the standard in the industry is still a management fee of between 1% and 2% of the assets under management (AUM), and an additional 20% of the returns earned by the fund on the AUM (Figure 3–1). (In fact, a study by Bank of America Merrill Lynch shows that management fees have actually crept up over the years, with average fees of 1.8% for funds launched in 2011.) This fee

FIGURE 3–1

Average Management Fee by Launch Date

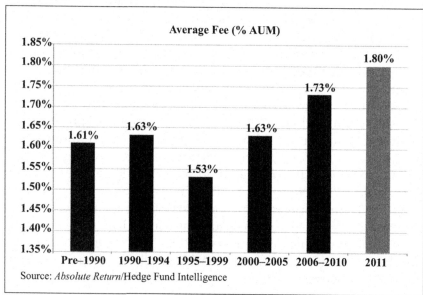

Source: *Absolute Return*/Hedge Fund Intelligence

structure is often referred to as 1 and 20 or 2 and 20. (In addition, expenses related to the operation of a hedge fund, including administrative, brokerage, legal, etc., are deducted from the asset pool.)

Typically, the management fee of 1–2% of AUM is taken out of the fund's assets by the administrator at the beginning of each month on the basis of the administrator's calculation of AUM. Thus, a fund with $100 million in AUM would charge investors an annual management fee of between $1 and $2 million. Except for exceptional situations, management fees are paid regardless of the fund's performance.

Incentive fees are typically 20% of returns earned by the fund (after deducting the management fee and other fund expenses) and normally paid by investors to the general partner (or more accurately taken by the manager from the fund) on a quarterly basis. The amount of incentive fee is often (but not always) contingent on two factors.

Hurdle Rates

Many hedge funds only start to accumulate an incentive fee once the funds' earning or profits have passed a hurdle rate, typically a short-term Treasury bill rate. The logic here is that the investor has the alternative to place their assets in a risk-free investment rather than a hedge fund, and the hedge fund should be able to return at least this risk-free rate. For example, a hedge fund with a hurdle rate of 2% will only start to pay incentive fees to the manager once the returns of the fund have gone above 2%.

High-Water Mark

If a hedge fund losses money in its management of client assets, it must first make up this loss before it can earn any new incentive fees. The level the fund must reach before it can start to earn incentive fees is known as the "high-water mark." In practice, many funds ceased earning incentive fees after severe losses in 2008 and 2009. Many of these hedge funds are still below their high-water mark today. Figure 3.2 shows that a whopping 62% of hedge funds were below their high-water mark in 2011.

As an example, a hedge fund managing $100 million that earns a return of 10% during a year (i.e., $10 million)—an excellent return in this environment—would pay the fund manager $2 million in

FIGURE 3-2

U.S.-Based Funds Above/Below Their HWMs by Year

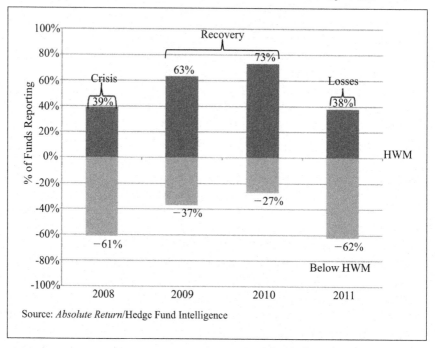

Source: *Absolute Return*/Hedge Fund Intelligence

incentive fee. If there is a hurdle rate of 3%, the amount eligible for incentive fee would be $7 million (i.e., 7%) and the manager's incentive compensation would be $1.4 million.

Assume that the manager had lost 10% ($10 million) in a given year on an investment pool of $100 million. The manager would then only be eligible for incentive compensation after he recouped the $10 million. To see the hardship imposed by the high-water mark calculation, note that in order to earn $10 million on the remaining $90 in assets, the manager must now make 11.11% on the remaining assets under management.

It should be noted that some highly successful and desirable hedge funds charge a management fee of up to 5% and an incentive fee of up to 50%. This is not really a concern for most investors since these funds tend to be either closed to new investors or allow new investors to enter on rare occasions.

The impact of hedge fund fees and hurdle rates on the experience of an investor are shown in Table 3–1.

TABLE 3-1

Fee Calculations

Year	Gross Return	Hurdle Rate	Management Fee(%)	Incentive Fee (% of Profits)	Incentive Fee (% of Assets)	Total Fee	Net Return	Beginning NAV	Ending NAV	Ending HWM
Year 1	5%	0%	2%	20%	0.60	2.60%	2.40%	$100.00	$102.40	$102.40
Year 2	5%	0%	2%	20%	0.60	2.60%	2.40%	$102.40	$104.90	$104.90
Year 3	20%	0%	2%	20%	3.60	5.60%	14.40%	$104.90	$120.00	$120.00
Year 4	–10%	0%	2%	20%	0.00	2.00%	–12.00%	$120.00	$105.60	$120.00
Year 5	16%	0%	2%	20%	0.00	2.00%	13.60%	$105.60	$119.90	$120.00
Year 6	8%	0%	2%	20%	1.14	3.14%	4.86%	$119.90	$125.70	$125.70

Year	Gross Return	Hurdle Rate	Management Fee(%)	Incentive Fee (% of Profits)	Incentive Fee (% of Assets)	Total Fee	Net Return	Beginning NAV	Ending NAV	Ending HWM
Year 1	5%	3%	2%	20%	0.00	2.00%	3.00%	$100.00	$103.00	$103.00
Year 2	5%	3%	2%	20%	0.00	2.00%	3.00%	$103.00	$106.10	$106.10
Year 3	20%	3%	2%	20%	3.00	5.00%	15.00%	$106.10	$122.00	$122.00
Year 4	–10%	3%	2%	20%	0.00	2.00%	–12.00%	$122.00	$107.40	$122.00
Year 5	16%	3%	2%	20%	0.00	2.00%	13.60%	$107.40	$122.00	$122.00
Year 6	8%	3%	2%	20%	0.00	2.60%	5.40%	$122.00	$120.60	$128.60

Source: Adapted from: CAIA Association, Mark J. P. Anson, PhD, CFA, Donald R. Chambers, Keith H. Black, Hossein Kazemi. *CAIA Level 1: An Introduction to Core Topics in Alternative Investments*, 2nd ed. Hoboken, NJ: John Wiley & Sons, Inc. 2012. Reprinted by permission.

THE ALIGNMENT (AND MISALIGNMENT) OF HEDGE FUND MANAGER AND INVESTOR INTEREST

One of the ongoing debates in the hedge fund world is the extent to which the interests of the hedge fund manager are the same as those of investors. (This is actually a problem, known as the "agency problem," whenever the management of a company differs from its owners, as for example in the case of corporations). The issue of hedge fund fees is one of the battlegrounds for this debate. The argument runs as follows: when a hedge fund is relatively small, the management fee would normally only be sufficient to cover the expenses of running the fund, which means that the manager must earn an incentive fee to make a "reasonable" income. However, when a hedge fund becomes large, the management fee can be large enough so that a manager can make a comfortable living without taking much risk. The economics favor the manager in this scenario because hedge funds have economies of scale, which means that expenses do not grow nearly as quickly as AUM. In other words, if the AUM doubles (along with the management fee), the fund may only need to increase its expenses (i.e., personnel, space, technology, etc.) by 20%. In this situation, the interests of the hedge fund manager (i.e., to grow the assets of the fund) may diverge from those of the investors, who are interested in a return on investment.

It may occur to the reader that managers whose returns have become mediocre as they become more interested in collecting management fee than incentive fees face the risk that investors would pull out their money. However, in case of large, formerly successful, hedge funds, there is an inertia among investors that keeps assets stable, or even increasing, so that many managers are willing to take that chance. They can take comfort from the many mutual funds that have underperformed their indices for years or decades but still retain their investors.

CHAPTER 4

Hedge Fund Service Providers

Hedge funds survive because of a network of service providers —prime brokers, administrators, custodians, auditors, and attorneys—that cater to their complex needs and requirements. In turn, hedge funds have been instrumental in shaping the service providers. In fact, some features of the modern financial world— notably shorting, repurchase agreements, and prime brokerage— have grown to the extent they have as a direct result of the need to service hedge funds.

ACCESS TO MARKETS AND CONSOLIDATION OF TRADING ACTIVITIES

In broad terms, the prime broker acts as a conduit between hedge funds and the financial marketplace by providing transaction execution, clearing and settlement services where hedge funds can access a wide range of markets and products, such as equities, fixed-income securities, commodities, and currencies, as well as derivative products, including options, futures, and swaps. Importantly, prime brokers also provide leverage to hedge funds.

The prime brokerage relationship allows a hedge fund to trade with multiple brokers, yet have their trades and settlements concentrated with the prime broker. This arrangement offers the advantage that hedge funds can trade with the brokers that offer the best service and pricing, but still have settlement, information, and funding reside in a master account with one broker.

Because the prime broker has access to the transactions of their hedge fund client from multiple brokers, they are in a position to provide consolidated reporting, margin financing, and efficient back-office processing. Prime brokers offer sophisticated transaction, information, and risk management systems to hedge funds, including what is known as "straight-through processing" of transactions, where a the prime broker processes and settles a transaction and the information is passed on to the hedge fund electronically and integrated with its back-office systems. In effect, the prime broker becomes a part of the back office of the hedge fund. The level and sophistication of these services have accelerated in recent years as competition among prime brokers for the lucrative hedge fund business has increased.

Prime brokers need to trade, process, and settle trades in a wide variety of instruments for hundreds of hedge funds—an undertaking that requires significant capital investment—and is one of the reasons that prime brokerage is dominated by a small number of large firms. (The migration of more and more trading to hedge funds will only work to reinforce this trend.) Avoiding this expense also explains why most hedge funds are willing to "outsource" much of the work to the prime broker while retaining the essential control, accounting, and risk management functions in-house (Figure 1–1).

Ten Largest Prime Brokers 2012

Prime Broker	Prime Brokerage Assets under Management (in millions)
Goldman Sachs	13.7%
Credit Suisse	12.3%
JP Morgan	11.5%
Morgan Stanley	10%
UBS	7.4%
Deutsche Bank	7.1%
Citibank	3.6%
Barclays Capital	3.5%
Bank of America/Merrill Lynch	3.5%
Newedge	3%

Source: HedgeFundIntelligence

Prime brokerage is a highly profitable business for banks and brokers, although the reduction of leverage has impacted the profit. Once a hedge fund chooses a prime broker, it tends to use that broker for multiple services, generating multiple sources of revenue. Furthermore, it is difficult for a hedge fund to change prime brokers after it has integrated into the broker's financing, information, and transaction processing system.

Until the Lehman Brothers and Bear Stearns failures, the norm was for a hedge fund to have one prime broker and many executing brokers. After Long-Term Capital Management nearly bankrupted the major Wall Street firms, brokers/dealers were intent on avoiding a similar experience. As a result, they increased their diligence of hedge fund's financial condition and insisted that hedge funds consolidate their activities with one bank so they had a handle on the fund's overall leverage and market exposure.

OTHER PRIME BROKERAGE SERVICES

As we discussed above, hedge funds rely on their prime brokers for leverage, whether in the form of loans, lines of credit, margin financing, repurchase agreements, and derivatives. While hedge funds can gain leverage from several brokers and banks, prime brokers have a distinct advantage because they have direct access to a hedge fund's accounts and assets, which are the collateral used by prime brokers when they extend credit by repurchase agreements, collateral financing, and other forms of credit. They also rely on prime brokers (as well as other brokers) for customized derivatives such as total return swaps, exotic options, swaptions, and credit derivatives.

Brokers also lend stock shares to hedge funds for use in shorting stocks. Brokers have access to many shares through an arrangement known as "securities lending," where they lend shares that large institutions such as mutual funds, pension funds, and insurance companies leave with them for custody safekeeping. The broker receives a fee from the hedge fund for this service, which it shares with the ultimate shareowner.

Finally, prime brokers provide fund raising assistance to hedge fund through a service known as "capital introduction," where brokers introduce their hedge fund customers to potential investors, including high-net-worth individuals, fund of funds, and institutional investors. An indication of the profitability of prime brokerage is that this service is offered to hedge fund customers without charge.

ADMINISTRATORS AND CUSTODIANS

Hedge fund administration and custody has assumed increased importance as a result of the Madoff Ponzi scheme (more specifically, the fact that it went on undetected for two decades), the difficulty of valuing mortgage- and credit-related products during the credit crisis of 2007–2009, and the proliferation of hedge fund side pockets and liquidations spawned by the crisis. The Madoff crisis led to a greater emphasis on the verification of assets, a function of both administrators and custodians, while the credit crisis emphasized the importance of valuation of illiquid securities, one proximate cause of the credit crisis.

There is a pronounced trend toward independent administrators (as opposed to a hedge fund performing the administrative function) as well as toward independent custodians (as opposed to prime brokers automatically gaining custody of assets they clear or trade on behalf of a hedge fund). More and more, investors are demanding independent proof and documentation of basic fund facts—that is, that assets exist, positions are true, valuation is arm's length, and cash reported is real.

In fact, an increasing number of investors consider a review of the administrator and his role in a hedge fund as part of the due diligence process before investing with that fund. The increased importance of independent administrators has led some prime brokers and accounting firms to launch administration services.

Functions of an Administrator

Hedge fund administration performs a set of functions that the majority of hedge funds outsource to external, independent specialist companies. Administration means, in effect, the management of a hedge fund (in the sense of the pooled investment vehicle) in virtually all aspects of the day to day operations, except the actual investment of the assets, which is the responsibility of the investment manager. Among the duties of the administrator are the following:

- Calculation of the net asset value (NAV) per share or unit or partnership, including the calculation of the fund's income and expenses, normally on a monthly basis.
- Pricing of securities and verifying the assets held in the fund's portfolio.
- Preparation of semiannual and annual accounts for audit by fund's accounting firm.
- Maintenance of the fund's financial books and records.
- Reconciliation of daily and monthly broker statement.
- Supervision of the orderly liquidation and dissolution of the fund (if required).
- Liaising with the investment manager or adviser, the custodian, the brokers, and other service providers.
- Calculating, confirming, and arranging payment of all subscriptions, redemptions, fees, and expenses.
- Liaising with prospective investors and sending out the offering documentation.
- Most administrators are cosignatories with the investment manager or the sole signatory on the bank accounts. This is to prevent managers from running off with the fund's money.
- Carrying out anti–money laundering due diligence on investors.
- Administrator may also be responsible for ensuring that the fund complies with the terms of its offering memorandum, including investment restrictions.

As with other service providers, there has been a pronounced trend toward consolidation among administrators and the entry of large banks into the area.

Pricing of securities
The credit crisis brought to the fore the issue of valuation of hedge fund assets, especially for illiquid securities, including private se-

curities, structured notes, complex over-the-counter derivatives, credit derivatives, distressed credit, and mortgage-backed securities. The practices assumed by the administrator for pricing securities are often spelled out in the legal offering documents. They often call for coordination with the investment manager and/or general partner and the custodian.

For most hedge fund portfolios, the independent verification of the prices of their assets and liabilities, which are also used to calculate the fund's NAV, is relatively straightforward because most assets are actively traded on exchanges or over-the-counter markets. The problems come with hard-to-value and illiquid securities. Since the credit crisis, many hedge funds have their assets frozen in side pockets or behind redemption gates. In addition, administrators are frequently responsible for the valuation of securities when a fund is liquidated.

It is preferable that administrators get prices from independent third-party brokers using a method that involves multiple brokers. However, the offering documents or administration agreement with the hedge fund may provide that the administrator obtain prices directly from the hedge fund. The latter would be a logical source since they trade in these securities and would likely have their own valuation methods. However, there is clearly a potential for conflict of interest since a hedge fund's valuation of securities would also affect their reported NAV or performance, which are used to attract or keep customers as well as to calculate the manager's management and incentive fees.

Complex derivatives such as exotic options or structured debt products may be so customized or illiquid that valuation is only possible using a pricing model that was developed or modified by the hedge fund, again increasing their reliance on the hedge fund. Also, as the mortgage-backed security market showed, models may not be very good at realistic pricing, especially during a turbulent market.

Some checks that are part of "good practice" for administrators include the following: First, the offering documents and administration agreement often lays out a procedure for valuation of hedge fund assets, including illiquid ones. Second, pricing decisions are made in coordination with the administrator, board or general partner, and the investment manager. Finally, when possible, a recognized independent pricing vendor is used to verify the "marks" used by the administrator.

Administrators also provide service to fund of hedge funds that do not typically trade individual securities; rather, their assets are units or shares in other hedge funds. Because the number of administrators is relatively small and fund of hedge funds may invest in a large number of hedge funds, it is likely that an administrator will service both a fund of hedge funds and the underlying hedge funds. In that case, the fund of hedge funds is typically serviced through a separate legal entity from the one servicing the hedge funds.

Verification of existence of assets

One of the functions of an administrator is to reconcile the information it possesses regarding a hedge fund's portfolio with custodial and brokerage statements, thereby adding another level of protection that assets are as claimed. The verification of the existence of assets in a fund is usually quite simple if the fund's assets are exchange traded and held by a prime broker or independent custodian. However, after Madoff, where custody of assets was central to the Ponzi scheme, administrators sometimes go one step further in verifying the assets.

Increased transparency

The growing power of institutional investors, many with fiduciary responsibility, has led to the call for increased transparency of hedge fund positions, pricing, and assets. Because administrators carry this information on their books, they have become a logical source of these services. Some administrators have gone so far as to provide daily NAV for funds they administer, especially in the case of managed accounts. The call for transparency has also led to increased contact between the administrators and the hedge fund investors, and administrators have been developing products and programs specifically for institutional clients.

Changing Custody Practices

Traditionally, a hedge fund's prime broker also acted as the fund's custodian. There is a strong economic rationale for this since brokers provide leverage and equity financing, where the assets maintained

FAIR VALUE PRICING

There is general recognition in the financial world that the market value of a security may deviate from its "fair value." The Financial Accounting Standards Board (FASB) issued "Statement of Financial Accounting Standards No. 157: Fair Value Measurements" (FAS 157) in September 2006 to set out a method for valuing assets in different market settings. While FAS 157 is meant to apply to accounting reporting, it has become more widely used as a benchmark for the valuation of securities. According to FAS 157, fair value is the amount at which an asset could be bought or sold in a current transaction between willing parties, or transferred to an equivalent party, other than in a liquidation sale. There are three types of fair value method depending on the market for a given security.

Level 1 valuation is based on "quoted prices in active markets for identical assets or liabilities," with the caveat that the reporting entity must have access to that market. An example would be a stock trade on the New York Stock Exchange.

If Level 1 prices are not available, the fair value is based on the method of Level 2 or Level 3 estimates.

Level 2 valuation is based on information available in the market other than the direct price of the asset being valued. The board provided for a second level of inputs that can be applied for fair valuation in three situations: the first involves less-active markets for identical assets and liabilities; the second arises when the assets being valued are similar to, but not the same as, those traded in a market; a third situation exists when no active or less-active markets exist for similar assets and liabilities, but some observable market data is sufficiently applicable to the reported items to allow the fair values to be estimated. The Black–Scholes valuation method, which is based on observable market inputs, is an example of Level 2.

Level 3 valuations are based on "unobservable inputs," which are not based on independent sources but on "the reporting entity's own assumptions about the assumptions market participants would use." Further, the entity may only rely on internal information if the cost and effort to obtain external information is too high. Clearly, these are valuations that require the most oversight and checking.

in custody with the prime broker serve as collateral. Furthermore, prime brokers have developed technology around portfolio accounting systems and web-based reporting that are based on their having direct access to the securities in their custody accounts. Hedge funds have come to depend on these for their daily reporting and position maintenance.

After the Lehman bankruptcy, many hedge funds have become more concerned with the counterparty risk and the wisdom of placing all the fund's assets with the prime broker for settlement and safekeeping. The past years have seen a trend whereby assets that are not required as collateral are being moved to a traditional global custodian, including those managed by administrators and custody banks.

For hedge funds that maintain custody accounts with their prime brokers, there is an emphasis on the provision of segregated custody accounts to safeguard their fund's holdings and tighter control over rehypothecation, the practice of lending out securities kept in custody, to prevent a replay of the Lehman Brothers' bankruptcy when hedge funds and others found that their assets had been rehypothecated to offshore entities, causing them difficulties in reclaiming their assets.

The move toward independent custodians presents a challenge for prime brokers to provide operational support and leverage financing without direct access to the hedge funds' assets or a full view of the fund's portfolio.

LAWYERS AND ACCOUNTANTS

Finally, hedge funds are heavily reliant on lawyers and accountants. Attorneys are needed to help establish the various hedge fund entities and in the preparation of private placement memorandum and other offering and subscription documents. They are also needed to help hedge funds meet their compliance with various regulations and regulatory filings, especially in light of the many changes in the present environment.

Accountants are also a necessary part of the hedge fund world for the key reason of providing investors with audited financial statements. Many investors, especially institutional investors, will not invest with a hedge fund if it does not produce regular audited results. It is important to note that, while administrators produce NAV calculations and help accountants in their audits, only accounting statements are recognized as definitive in documenting a hedge fund's financial situation.

PART TWO

Hedge Fund Toolkit

Short Selling and Leverage

To achieve their objectives, hedge fund managers use a "toolkit" that contains the following tools:

- Short selling
- Leverage (borrowing)
- Derivatives

It should be made clear that many hedge funds do not use any of the tools while others only make use of one or two of these tools, and even then to a limited extent. In addition, these tools are not unique to hedge funds and are extensively used by banks, investment banks, and, to a limited extent, by mutual funds. However, these tools are closely associated with hedge funds that tend to use them more regularly than other firms. Also, the tools are more central to the strategies and business models pursued by hedge funds than, say, mutual funds, where they are mostly peripheral to their strategy.

The association of these tools with hedge funds has placed hedge funds in the center of a number of controversies. Short selling has repeatedly been blamed for causing periodic declines of stocks, bonds, commodities, or currencies, and has been the target of government restriction and regulation in the United States and abroad. Similarly, leverage has been identified as a leading contributor to the severity of the credit crisis. Finally, derivatives, notably credit default swaps and mortgage-backed securities, have been called "financial weapons of mass destruction" by Warren Buffett in describing their ability to create havoc in financial markets.

The characterization of hedge funds as addicted to high leverage, aggressive short selling, and large-scale use of derivatives is a stereotype that does not apply to the great majority of hedge funds. As we discuss later in the book, a hedge fund's strategy largely determines the tools it will use. For example, a global macro fund is much more likely to use derivatives and leverage than a typical long/short equity fund. Similarly, leverage is more closely linked to hedge funds pursuing fixed income than to equity hedge funds, which also explains why hedge fund implosions are much more common among fixed-income and global macro funds.

While "derivatives" and "leverage" may conjure images of excessive speculation and losses, when used in moderation they may actually reduce risk and provide hedge funds with the ability to pursue strategies not available to other investment firms. In fact, the "hedge" component of hedge funds would be impossible without the ability to sell short or use derivatives. In this chapter, we will explore short selling and leverage, then look at derivatives in the following chapter.

SHORT SELLING

Short selling is the sine qua non of hedge funds, as implied by the "hedge" component of hedge funds. To "go short" or "sell short" or "take a short position" or "shorting the market" means to establish a position on a market or individual security such that the position will benefit if the price of the market or security declines. In the simplest example, a short position on IBM stock will make money if the price of IBM declines. Conversely, a short seller will lose money if the price of IBM goes up.

There are several ways of "going short" depending on the specific market and instrument. To give just a few examples:

- Shorting an individual stock, the classic type of short selling.

- Shorting the Japanese yen, other currencies or commodities using a future, forward, swap, or option.

- Shorting the S&P 500 index or other stock market indices, both domestic and international, using stock index futures or options.
- In a more complex and more recent type of transaction, a hedge fund can short the credit of a mortgage-backed security or a corporate bond by selling a credit default swap.

Short Stock Sales

The short sale of an individual stock is a strategy used in a number of hedge fund strategies. For example, long/short equity hedge funds short stocks on the basis of their view of the direction of the stock's price, or related pair of stocks. Other strategies, including convertible arbitrage, merger (risk) arbitrage, and capital structure arbitrage will short a stock as part of a strategy that involves multiple instruments. Short bias funds will short stocks that they expect will decline in price more than other stocks.

Mechanically, a short stock sale is achieved as follows:

1. The hedge fund initiates the position by borrowing a stock from a broker/dealer. The dealer will in turn normally borrow the stock from customers who maintain long positions in the stock with the broker in return for a small fee. This transaction is known as "securities lending." Many large institutional investors such as pension funds, insurance companies, and mutual funds allow securities in their portfolios to be loaned out as a way of earning incremental income.
2. The fund then sells the stock in the open market and deposits the proceeds in a margin account with the broker/dealer as collateral for the borrowed stock.
3. To close out the position, the fund will buy the stock in the open market and return the shares to the lending dealer.

Risks in Short Sales

Short selling is not simply the opposite of buying and holding a stock position. It requires specialized skill and introduces a level of complexity and risk not found in long stock positions. It is for this reason that managers whose background is entirely or predominantly on the long side, for example, working for a traditional mutual fund, sometimes find it difficult to adapt to the hedge fund world. There are a number of risks that are unique to shorting stocks:

1. *Unlimited loss potential:* In a traditional long position, the manager's losses are limited to the amount he spent to purchase the stock. However, in a short position, the loss is theoretically infinite since the price of the stock can rise without limit.

2. *Stock loan difficulties:* Short positions in stocks with high levels of *short interest* (i.e., high demand by hedge fund and others to short the stock) may be difficult to implement. For example, the stock may be impossible to borrow, or can only be borrowed at a high cost.

3. *Stock "call-in":* A stock loan may be "called-in" by the stock lender, causing the manager to buy the stock at the market price, which may mean forcing a loss.

4. *Margin call:* If the price of the stock rises and triggers a margin call from the broker, the hedge fund must come up with additional collateral or purchase the stock at the market price, typically at a loss since the margin call implies the stock's price has most likely risen.

5. *Short squeezes:* A short squeeze is a sharp increase in the price of a stock caused by short sellers attempting to cover their short positions at the same time. This is especially acute for stocks that are thinly traded or where supply is limited. A recent example is the sharp rise in the price of Porsche stock as hedge funds that had shorted the stock scampered to purchase the stock to cover their large short positions. However, there was a limited supply of Porsche shares, which caused a spike in their price and resulted in billions of dollars in losses for the hedge funds.

Shorting the Stock Markets or Stock Market Sectors

In contrast to the shorting of individual stocks discussed above, hedge fund managers can short stock market sectors (such as technology or energy) or large segments of the market in the United States (i.e., S&P 500 or Russell 2000) or abroad (i.e., Japan's Nikkei or U.K. FTSE). These short positions—which may be taken to hedge sector or market specific risks of a long stock portfolio or as speculative positions—are typically taken with equity index futures or options, or with exchange-traded funds. The mechanisms for this type of strategy are very different from stock sales and more closely resemble the short selling used in fixed-income or currency markets and are addressed below.

Controversy over Short Selling

There is a long-standing, global debate about the role of short selling in financial markets. This applies to short selling in all markets. The discussion here is limited to short selling of individual stocks. Short selling in other markets (i.e., currencies, fixed income, and commodities) are addressed below. Critics assert that short sales are a destabilizing force, artificially driving down stock prices below their "true" value. Defenders of short sales argue that they make financial markets more efficient by revealing negative information about companies with overvalued stock and by assisting the process of "price discovery" for these shares.

Regulators have by and large decided that short selling needs to be regulated, especially in times of market stress. As a result, there are some restrictions on short selling (in addition to the margin requirement). For example, exchange regulations dictate that selling a stock short can only be done on an uptick or a flat-tick, that is, when the most recent movement in the stock's price has increased or remained flat.

In the United States, short selling is regulated by the SEC's Regulation SHO, which places limits on "naked short sales"—short sales where the broker does not actually have the stock being shorted. Regulation SHO includes "locate requirement," which specifies that market participants seeking to lend a stock for a short sale must either arrange to borrow, or at least have reasonable grounds to believe that a security can be borrowed within the typical three-day delivery time for stock settlement.

During the credit crisis, government regulators in the United States and abroad imposed draconian limitations on short selling, banning the practice for shares of financial stocks, which were under attack as a result of their exposure to subprime mortgages. There is no consensus about whether these measures were successful, although it seems clear that governments will not be reticent about repeating their bans in the future if for no other reason than their popularity with the general public.

LEVERAGE (BORROWING)

Leverage is essentially borrowing money in order to increase the amount of capital that can be used to take market positions. The idea behind leverage is familiar: think about the purchase of a house with mortgage financing. If the home buyer puts 20% down on a $100,000 house and finances the remaining $80,000 with a mortgage, they have effectively leveraged their $20,000 in assets by a factor of 4. The home buyer has turned $20,000 in capital into a $100,000 purchase.

There are a number of ways to express this leveraging: as a ratio (in this case 4:1), as a percentage (400%), or as a percent increment between the amount of capital and the amount financed (300%).

Direct and Indirect Leverage

Hedge funds can leverage their capital either directly or indirectly.

Direct Leverage

- *Bank borrowings:* Hedge funds can take out margin loans (buying securities on margin) from banks and broker/dealers. For example, assuming a 20% margin on security ABC, a hedge fund could buy $10 worth of securities by paying only $2 upfront and having the bank supply the remaining $8 in the form of a loan. To protect its loan balance, the bank requires the hedge fund to deposit an agreed amount of securities as collateral. If the market value of the ABC securities drops, the bank can require additional collateral from the hedge fund (margin call) to further protect itself.
- *Repurchase agreements ("repos"):* Widely used by hedge funds to finance debt security purchases, a repo transaction

involves a bank or broker/dealer agreeing to sell a security to a hedge fund for a given price and then buying it back later at a higher price. In a repo transaction, the hedge fund purchases a security (stock or bond) and uses the security to borrow from a broker in order to purchase additional securities. The amount of leverage is limited by the "haircut," which is the margin that the hedge fund must post to protect the bank against adverse market movements.

Indirect Leverage

- *Short selling:* Short selling is the practice of selling securities borrowed from banks or other counterparties. Funds raised from the sale of these borrowed securities are used to buy other securities, effectively providing the hedge fund with leverage.

- *Derivatives and structured products:* Another way that hedge funds can gain leverage is through derivative instruments, which include futures, options, and swaps. Unlike stock short sale, where the leverage is restricted by a 50% margin requirement, leverage on derivatives is dictated by the exchanges or banks that act as counterparties to the hedge fund. For example, the purchase of a futures contract is typically done using a margin account where the buyer needs to post a collateral that is only a fraction of the nominal amount of the contract. Similarly, the purchase of a $1 million option on IBM stock requires a premium that may be as little as 3% of the contract amount, or $30,000. Certain instruments such as currencies, commodities, and fixed income are often highly leveraged, especially in the "over-the-counter" (i.e., nonexchange) market where leverage can be as high as 30:1.

LEVERAGE AND RISK

Because leverage allows a hedge fund to use their capital to take larger market positions, it increases the risk to the hedge fund. Of course, the hedge fund manager would only leverage their capital if they assume that the probability of profiting from a position

REPURCHASE AGREEMENT MARKET

Hedge funds obtain short-term funding for the purchase of securities via the repurchase agreement market. This market also allows hedge funds to obtain leverage.

Effectively, a repo is a securitized loan. Although sometimes structured as long-term agreements, typically the loans are short term, often overnight, and entail the purchase of a security or securities by a bank from a hedge fund (or any entity in need of cash), with the simultaneous pledge by the hedge fund to repurchase the security at a higher price. The difference in price is the borrowing cost that the hedge fund pays for the privilege of accessing the bank's cash between the sale and repurchase dates.

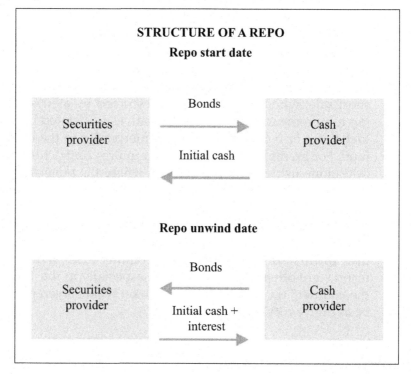

STRUCTURE OF A REPO

Repo start date

Bonds

Securities provider — Cash provider

Initial cash

Repo unwind date

Bonds

Securities provider — Cash provider

Initial cash + interest

While a repo is legally the sale and subsequent repurchase of a security, its economic effect is that of a secured loan. Economically, the party purchasing the security makes funds available to the seller and holds the security as collateral. If the repoed security pays a dividend, coupon, or partial redemptions during the repo, this is returned. The difference between the sale and repurchase prices paid for the security represents interest on the loan. Indeed, repos are quoted as interest rates.

Lenders will often "haircut" the collateral, and apply this haircut to the amount of cash they disperse through the agreement. Haircuts vary primarily on the basis of the volatility and liquidity of the securities being sold and then repurchased. Less liquid securities command a higher haircut. The size of the haircut determines the number of times a hedge fund can utilize a security in order to obtain leverage.

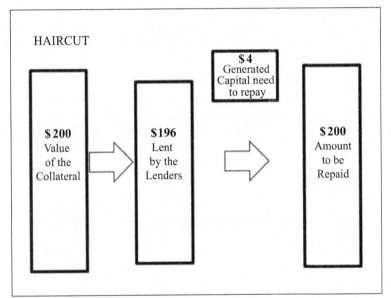

HAIRCUT

$4
Generated
Capital need
to repay

$200
Value
of the
Collateral

$196
Lent
by the
Lenders

$200
Amount
to be
Repaid

Repos often reference a Master Repurchase Agreement (MRA) or a Global Master Repo Agreement (GMRA), which serves as a starting point for negotiation.

(including the cost of borrowing funds for leverage) is greater than the risk. While hedge funds are sometimes portrayed as addicted to excessive leverage, this view needs to be modified by two observations: first, hedge funds are not nearly as highly leveraged as is sometimes assumed; second, there is a complicated relationship between leverage and risk.

Actual Hedge Fund Leverage Is Relatively Low and Concentrated in Certain Strategies

A common myth is that hedge funds are highly leveraged compared with other financial firms. In fact, research shows that a third of hedge funds do not utilize any leverage. Research also shows that bigger funds use more leverage than smaller funds; between two and five times their investment capital. According to data from Credit Suisse, the average hedge fund ended 2011 with a leverage of 1.5: in other words, for every $1 of client money a hedge fund had at the end of the year, a bank or broker lent out a further $0.6 to the average hedge fund.

In fact, it appears that hedge funds are less highly leveraged than banks. As shown in Figure 5–1, banks—who also leverage their assets by using derivative instruments or borrowing—have considerably higher leverage than hedge funds. In certain periods during the height of the credit boom that preceded the credit crisis, investment banks such as Lehman Brothers leveraged their capital by as much at 40 times.

Relationship Between Leverage and Risk

Applying leverage to an asset or portfolio is not inherently riskier than an unleveraged equivalent because the overall risk of a portfolio is a *combination* of the amount of leverage applied and all the risks of the assets that are being leveraged, including market, credit, and liquidity risks. Thus, applying leverage to an asset with little volatility (i.e., U.S. Treasury bond) may actually result in less risk than holding a volatile asset without leverage (i.e., a high yield bond). It is therefore important for investors to look past the leverage number (although this is clearly important) and evaluate the overall hedge fund risk. It is thus important to disaggregate the returns of a hedge fund manager to determine how much is a function of the underlying asset positions versus the leverage applied to these positions. Finally, it is important to keep

FIGURE 5-1

Hedge Fund and Bank Leverage

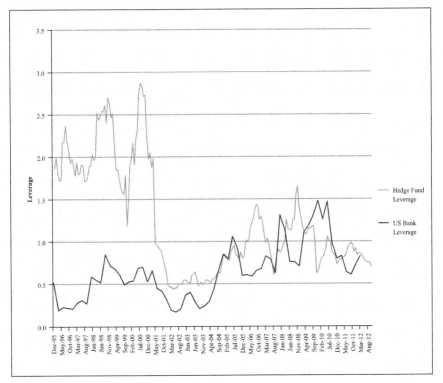

in mind that leverage obtained through derivatives may not show up in a hedge fund's leverage calculation.

The relationship between asset risk and leverage also varies by the type of strategy pursued by the hedge fund. Certain hedge fund strategies (e.g., merger arbitrage or convertible arbitrage, equity market neutral) have low market risk, and can therefore utilize a relatively high leverage, while other strategies (e.g., emerging market debt and global macro) have significant asset risk and may not be able to carry excessive leverage.

As Ray Dalio, the founder of Bridgewater, states, "If investors can get used to looking at leverage in a less prejudicial, black-and-white way—'no leverage is good and any leverage is bad'—I believe that they will understand that a moderately leveraged, highly diversified portfolio is considerably *less* risky than an unleveraged non-diversified one." ("Engineering Targeted Returns and Risks," by Ray Dalio, *Pension & Investments Magazine*, August 18, 2004.)

Long-Term Capital Management, Credit Crisis and the Great Deleveraging

The extent of hedge fund leverage has changed over the years for a number of reasons. As Figure 5–1 shows, hedge fund leverage has declined on two occasions: once after the Long-Term Capital Management (LTCM) crisis in 1998 (and the follow-up collapse of the tech bubble in 2001), when hedge funds leverage decline from a high as 8:1 in the mid-1992 to a low of under 1:1 in 2001; and again following the credit crisis in 2008. Hedge fund leverage increased between 2003 and 2007 as a result of low interest rates and an increase in available credit, which encouraged hedge funds to borrow. When the price of assets, especially mortgage-backed assets, declined and liquidity dried up, the leverage multiplied the losses incurred by hedge funds.

Hedge fund leverage is dependent on the amount that banks and investment banks are willing to lend. One of the reasons for the deleveraging following the LTCM crisis is that Wall Street firms realized the full extent of their outstanding loans to LTCM and the potential threat to their own existence that may have come from these loans. Similarly, the credit crisis resulted in a severe reduction of lending by Wall Street firms and international banks, thus forcing a reduction in hedge fund leverage. One of the lessons that emerged from these two events is that an effective way of controlling the amount of leverage assumed by hedge fund is by limiting the amount of lending that banks and broker/dealers can extend. This has been the focus of government efforts in the United States and abroad, who have been raising the amount of capital banks need to support their lending activities, in effect limiting banks' lending capabilities to hedge funds. It is therefore highly unlikely that hedge fund leverage will rebound to its previous levels in the foreseeable future.

CHAPTER 6

Derivatives: Financial Weapons of Mass Destruction

"**W**e view them as time bombs for the parties that deal in them and the economic system. In our view, derivatives are financial weapons of mass destruction (WMD), carrying dangers that, while now latent, are potentially lethal" (Warren Buffett, Berkshire Hathaway's 2002 annual report).

As the Buffett indictment indicates, few areas of finance are more controversial than derivatives. Because derivatives are central to the strategy of (many) hedge funds, hedge funds have been placed at the center of this controversy. However, as with many things in finance, the risks and benefits of derivatives depend on the context and usage. In the right hands and the right reasons, they can be tremendously beneficial. At the same time, there have undoubtedly been cases of abuse and wrongful use of derivatives that have resulted in losses for individual hedge funds as well as creating problems for financial markets. The following discussion attempts to clarify some of the issues involving derivatives and their use by hedge funds.

DEFINITION

A *derivative* is a financial instrument whose price depends on, or is derived from, the price of an underlying asset, index, rate, or instrument. For example, the price of an option on IBM stock varies with the movement of the price of an IBM stock. The price of a futures contract on oil varies with the price of oil. The value of a fixed-for-floating interest rate swap depends on the relative movement of U.S. short-term and medium-/long-term interest rates, and a credit default swap (CDS) on Greek government debt derives its value from the risk of a default in Greek bonds.

Derivatives are broadly classified along the following criteria:

- The relationship between the underlying asset and the derivative. The major types are futures (and its variants, forwards and swaps) and options

- The type of underlying asset (i.e., equities and equity indices, foreign exchange, interest rate, commodity and credit)

- The market in which they trade, either exchange traded or over the counter

GROWTH OF DERIVATIVE MARKETS

The growth of the derivative markets is one of the most important developments in the financial world of the past 20 years. Figure 6–1 charts the explosion of derivatives from under $100 trillion in 1999 to more than $700 trillion in 2011. Following a slight decline after the credit crisis, derivatives are at new high levels and seem destined to continue to grow in the future. Hedge funds have served, and will continue to serve, as an important impetus to this growth.

Two points about the derivatives markets: First, 95% of this market is in the "over-the-counter" (OTC) market, defined as derivatives contracts that are not traded on a regulated market. Second, the statistics above refer to "nominal" or face values of these derivatives; the actual net amount is significantly lower, but still high.

The growth of derivatives and their central role in the rapid expansion and contraction of the subprime mortgage crisis have led to an outcry for reform, focusing on increased transparency and control of the credit risk contained in derivatives. The most immediate impact of these changes, described in the insert below, will be to move much of the derivatives' activity to exchanges, but would not lead to a reversal in the overall trends.

FIGURE 6-1

Derivatives, Total Notional Amount Outstanding in Billions

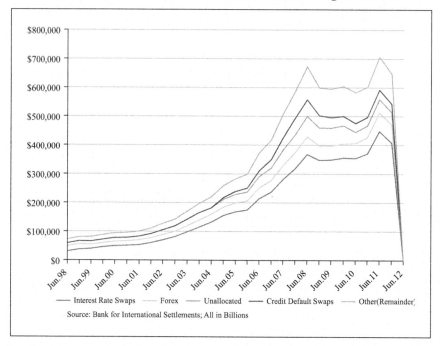

Source: Bank for International Settlements; All in Billions

Futures and Options

Derivatives are either futures (or similar instruments, such as forwards or swaps) or options, or a combination of the two. Futures and options are agreements to exchange cash for a fixed amount of an asset at a future date for a price that is decided today. The key difference between the two is that the parties to a futures deal *must* settle the transaction according to the terms of the deal (i.e., date, price, amount, delivery, etc.). Using this definition, futures-type contracts also include forwards, swaps, and futures.

In contrast, the buyer of an option has discretion and can decide whether to exercise the option or not. If the price of the asset moves in the wrong direction, the option buyers can "walk away" from the contract, limiting their loss to the premium paid. In contrast, futures contracts must be settled and therefore can experience unlimited losses. Of course, the case is different for the option seller whose loss is also theoretically unlimited.

REGULATION OF DERIVATIVES

In September 2009, at the G-20 Pittsburgh Summit, the leaders of the 19 biggest economies in the world and the European Union agreed that "all standard OTC derivative contracts should be traded on exchanges or electronic trading platforms, where appropriate, and cleared through *central counterparties* by end-2012 at the latest." Furthermore, they concluded that "OTC derivative contracts should be reported to *trade repositories* and that non-centrally cleared contracts should be subject to higher capital requirement."

The worldwide regulatory movement is centered on two features: having derivatives traded on organized exchanges, such as the Chicago Mercantile Exchange (CME), the world's largest; and having as much information on OTC derivatives captured by trade repositories. The benefit of clearing derivatives on an organized exchange is that it substitutes the bilateral counterparty risk of typical derivatives (i.e., between a hedge fund and a broker) for the risk of the exchange itself (or more correctly, a clearing house that has the backing of the combined capital of the exchange members).

In addition to providing a more significant capital backing for derivatives, exchanges typically require more collateral than OTC counterparties, and the sufficiency of the collateral is evaluated more frequently (usually on a daily basis), and any shortfalls must be covered in a short amount of time.

These regulations will not kill off the OTC market, which provides a flexibility and customization that is not possible on exchanges. However, it will move the great majority of standardized contracts onto exchanges.

There are also hybrid instruments—such as swaptions—that combine the characteristics of options and futures where some aspects of the contract must settle and others are discretionary.

Futures, Forwards, and Swaps

Futures, forwards, and swaps are contracts to buy or sell a given quantity of an asset on or before a future date at a price that is predetermined when the contract is initiated. A futures contract refers to a standardized contract written by a clearing house that operates an exchange where the contract can be bought and sold; the forward contract is a nonstandardized contract written by the parties themselves; for example, a hedge fund and a bank.

An example of a futures contract is as follows: a hedge fund purchases a gold futures contract in the expectation that the price of gold will increase before the contract expires. The gold futures contract trades on the CME for a fixed amount of 100 Troy ounces. Assume that the present price of gold is $1,000 and the one-year futures price of gold is $1,050. The equivalent contract amounts would then be $100,000 and $105,000. Assume further that the price of gold in one year is $1,200. A buyer of the futures contract will have made a profit of $15,000 by purchasing the gold via the futures contract at $1,050/oz. and selling the gold in the market at $1,200. The seller of gold futures would have lost the equivalent amount (Figure 6–2).

Swaps are contracts to exchange cash (flows) on or before a specified future date based on the underlying value of currencies exchange rates, bonds/interest rates, commodities exchange, stocks, or other assets (Figure 6–3). Swaps are related to futures in that they are often a series of futures with varying

FIGURE 6–2

Example of a Futures Contract

March 10, 2013 Gold Spot Price: $1,000 Futures Price (1yr): $1,050 Contract Size: 100 oz.	**March 10, 2014** Gold Spot Price: $1,200
Futures Contract Cost: $1,050 × 100 = $105,000	1yr Value of Futures Contract: $1,200 × 100 = $120,000
Profit: $105,000 (Cost) - $120,000 (Future Value) = $15,000	

FIGURE 6–3

Example of a Swap

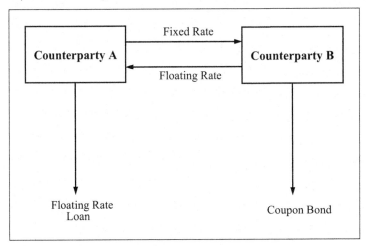

expiration dates strung together. There are three main types of swaps:

- *Interest rate swap:* These are far and away the most common swaps. The two parties to the swap agree on a nominal amount on which the cash flows will be exchanged. Then one party pays a fixed interest rate on that amount, and the other reciprocates with the payment based on a floating rate index—LIBOR, for example. If interest rates increase, the fixed-rate payer is in the best position, paying an interest rate that is below the market rate, and the floating-rate payer is the loser, paying the higher market interest rate while receiving a below-market fixed rate.

- *Currency swap:* In this kind of swap, the cash flow between the two parties includes both principal and interest. Also, the money that is being swapped or used as a reference is in two different currencies.

- *Credit default swap (CDS):* CDS cash flows are based on the credit condition of an underlying debt instrument, either corporate or government bonds, or an index based on groups of fixed-income instruments. CDS on mortgage-backed securities

FIGURE 6–4

Credit Default Swap Mechanics

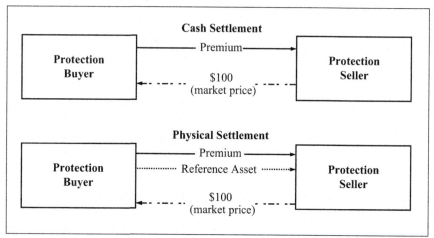

were a major factor in the onset of the credit crisis and losses incurred by many hedge funds.

In the example diagrammed in Figure 6–4, the counterparties decide on a nominal amount of a reference asset, say a Greek government bond. The price of the government bond when the swap is transacted is considered as par (100). The swap buyer pays the seller an annual "fee," normally in basis points on the nominal amount. If the price of the bond declines at the expiration dates of the swap, the protection seller either pays the buyer the difference between the par value and the market value (in a cash settlement) or pays the par value and receives the distressed bond. While this type of transaction has been compared to insurance, say on a house, the difference here is that the protection buyer does not need to own the bond. In addition, while insurance companies are highly regulated and required to have sufficient capital to meet future settlements, sellers of CDSs do not face these requirements. This was essentially the problem that caused tens of billions of dollars in losses for the AIG's London-based group, which sold CDSs without sufficient capital to pay off when the assets underlying the swaps (mostly subprime mortgage-backed securities) lost value. Hedge funds will often enter into CDSs to make speculative bets on the future credit condition of a bond or index without owning the asset.

Options

Options are contracts that give the owner the right, but not the obligation, to buy (in the case of a call option) or sell (in the case of a put option) a fixed amount of an asset at a future date. The price at which the future exchange takes place is known as the strike price, and is specified at the time the parties enter into the option. In the case of a European option, the owner has the right to require the sale to take place on (but not before) the maturity date; in the case of an American option, the owner can require the sale to take place at any time up to the maturity date. If the owner of the contract exercises this right, the counterparty has the obligation to carry out the transaction (Figure 6–5).

Options are of two types: call option and put option. The buyer of a call option has a right to buy a certain quantity of the underlying asset, at a specified price on or before a given date in the future; he or she, however, has no obligation to carry out this right. Similarly, the buyer of a put option has the right to sell a certain quantity of an underlying asset, at a specified price on or before a given date in the future, but has no obligation to carry out this right.

FIGURE 6–5

Payoff and Profit of Call Option at Expiration

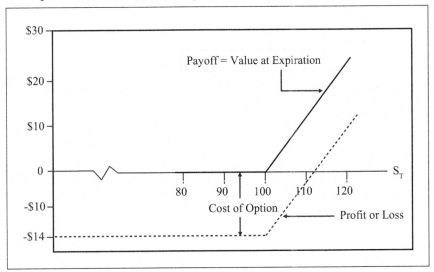

FIGURE 6–6

At Expiry Payoff for Long/Short Call-Put

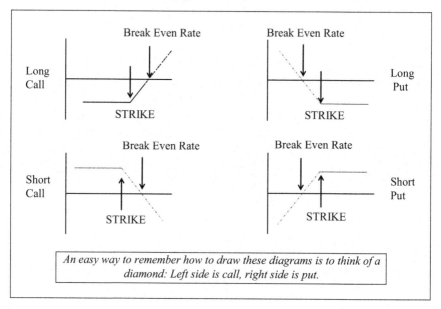

An easy way to remember how to draw these diagrams is to think of a
diamond: Left side is call, right side is put.

The payoff profiles of the four main variations of options
transactions are diagrammed above.

EXCHANGE-TRADED VERSUS OVER-THE-COUNTER DERIVATIVES

Exchange-traded derivatives

Exchange-traded derivatives are traded on specialized derivatives
exchanges, which act as an intermediary to all the transactions that
take place on the exchange. Examples of exchanges include Eurex
(which lists a wide range of European products such as interest
rate and index products) and the CME Group (made up of the 2007
merger of the CME and the Chicago Board of Trade and the 2008
acquisition of the New York Mercantile Exchange) (Table 6–1).

The key features of exchange-traded derivatives are as follows:

- Contracts are standardized as to size, settlement dates, and
  price increments.

TABLE 6-1   Common Examples of Derivatives

Some common examples of these derivatives are the following:

Underlying	Contract types				
	Exchange-traded futures	Exchange-traded options	OTC swap	OTC forward	OTC option
Equity	DJIA Index future Single future	Option on DJIA Index future Single-share option	Equity swap	Back-to-back Repurchase agreement	Stock option Warrant Turbo warrant
Interest rate	Eurodollar future Euribor future	Option on Eurodollar future Option on Euribor future	Interest swap	Forward rate agreement	Interest rate cap and Swaption Basis swap Bond option
Credit	Bond future	Option on Bond future	Credit default swap Total return swap	Repurchase agreement	Credit default option
Foreign exchange	Currency future	Option on currency future	Currency swap	Currency forward	Currency option
Commodity	WTI crude oil futures	Weather derivatives	Commodity swap	Iron ore forward	Gold option

71

- The counterparty to the derivative is the exchange itself. The exchange, in turn, is backed by the member firms, which include brokers, banks, and investment banks.
- All derivatives contracts are backed by collateral posted in margin accounts, providing a risk management tool. The amount of collateral fluctuates as the market price of the derivative fluctuates.

Over-the-Counter Derivatives

OTC derivatives are bilateral contracts that are privately negotiated directly between two parties (i.e., a hedge fund and a bank) rather than traded on an exchange. Products such as credit default swaps (CDSs), interest rate and currency swaps, total return swaps, equity derivatives, forward contracts on physical commodities and currencies are largely traded in this way.

The OTC derivative market is far larger than the exchange-traded market. According to the Bank for International Settlements, the total outstanding notional amount is US$638 trillion (as of June 2012). Of this total notional amount, 77% are interest rate contracts, 4% are CDSs, 10% are foreign exchange contracts, .4% are commodity contracts, .9% are equity contracts, and 7.7% are other. While the OTC market is the larger market, government regulation is pushing derivatives trading to exchanges, which provides greater transparency and a settlement mechanism that is not based on counterparty default.

Unlike derivatives exchanges, which are heavily regulated by the SEC, the OTC market is largely unregulated, relying on private agreements between two parties. The agreements are normally based on an industry standard established by the International Swaps Dealers Association (ISDA), an industry body composed largely of big banks. ISDA contracts lay out terms and conditions such as contract size, pricing, and settlement terms. Importantly, the agreement spells out the procedure to be followed if one of the parties to the agreement defaults on the contract. Because OTC contracts are only backed by the credit of the parties (as opposed to exchange-traded contracts that are backed by the exchange and all its members), this is a crucial provision. The ISDA agreement also describes the terms of the collateral that needs to be posted by the parties, and the changes in the collateral as market prices fluctuate.

Hedge funds favor the OTC market because of the flexibility it offers in terms of contract size, dates, terms, etc. For many derivatives, the OTC offers much greater liquidity and an easier access to leverage than exchanges. The OTC derivatives can be highly customized and are only limited by the imagination of the parties themselves. They can include hybrids that combine features of futures and options (i.e., swaptions, which combine features of interest rate swaps and options). They also include what are known as "exotic derivatives" such as knock-in options (whose exercise is triggered when the market price moves past a certain price) or Asian options whose exercise price is based on the average market rate over the period of the option contract.

Use of Derivatives by Hedge Funds

Derivatives are used by hedge funds in various ways:

- To speculate and make a profit if the value of the underlying asset moves the way they expect (e.g., moves in a given direction, stays in or out of a specified range, reaches a certain level)
- To provide leverage (or gearing), such that a small movement in the underlying value can cause a large difference in the value of the derivative
- To hedge or mitigate risk in the underlying asset, by entering into a derivative contract whose value moves in the opposite direction to their underlying position and cancels part or all of it out
- To obtain exposure to an asset where it is not possible to trade in the underlying (e.g., weather derivatives)
- To gain incremental premium income through the sale of options
- To create exposure where the value of the derivative is linked to a specific condition or event rather than a specific asset (e.g., weather derivatives)

Different types of hedge funds use derivatives in very different ways. The following illustrates the types of derivatives used by different types of hedge funds:

- *Long/short equity funds* use equity index futures or options—that is, S&P 500, Russell 2000, Nikkei, or FTSE—to hedge a portfolio of index positions or groups of stocks against movements in the overall equity market or a sector of that market. They also sell options against a portfolio of held stocks to generate income, and to purchase call or put options on individual stocks to gain from a directional move in the stock price.

- *Global macro funds* use a wide variety of exchange-traded and OTC derivatives to establish positions on macro markets such as currencies, commodities, interest rates, credit, and equities. These positions may be directional (i.e., speculating on the movement of the Japanese yen against the U.S. dollar) or as part of a spread strategy (i.e., long the Nikkei index and short the S&P 500) where the profit or loss depends on the relative movement of two assets. One of the reasons for using derivatives in this strategy is to gain leverage and thus amplify the possibility of profit. Global macro hedge funds are large users of OTC markets since they often enter into customized, leveraged trades in instruments that are not widely traded on exchanges.

- *Fixed-income arbitrage* funds are profligate users of interest rate derivatives (forward rate agreement, interest rate swaps, and swaptions) to hedge portfolios of underlying assets (bonds, mortgage-backed securities) or to take positions on interest rates either as a directional bet (i.e., a bet on the movement of U.S. Treasury bonds) or as part of a relative value strategy (i.e., long short-term Treasury bonds and short long-term Treasury bonds—known as a yield curve arbitrage, betting on the shape of the yield curve).

- *Credit hedge funds* use CDSs and total return swaps to take positions on the credit (i.e., probability of default) of a reference asset. Reference assets may include corporate or government bonds, mortgage- or asset-backed securities, and collateralized debt obligations (CDOs).

- *Convertible arbitrage* funds use equity options as part of a complicated transaction on convertible bonds that combine a corporate bond with an attached option that allows the bond holder to exchange the bond for stock shares.

Issues with OTC Derivatives

Derivatives, and especially OTC derivatives, have always been controversial. The controversy stems from the fact that the market is largely hidden from the government and from the public; the leverage contained in derivatives, which greatly magnifies losses that result from market movements; and the fact that derivatives rely on the credit of the individual counterparties makes them vulnerable to "counterparty credit risk." The bankruptcy of Lehman Brothers, for example, affected hundreds of billions of dollars of OTC contracts with thousands of counterparties, many of who suffered losses as a result. Different types of derivatives have different levels of counterparty risk. In OTC transactions, the parties will normally conduct due diligence on each other and often ask for collateral, which raises a host of problems, including valuation, margin calls, etc., and has been held responsible for the cascading sale of assets and redemption restrictions for certain hedge funds during the credit crisis.

VALUATION OF DERIVATIVES

The value of derivative contracts is ultimately decided in the market-place; it is the price someone is willing to buy or sell the position. In the case of exchange-traded derivatives, the prices are continuously available as transactions occur on the exchange. For exchange-traded derivatives, market price is usually transparent, making it relatively easy to automatically broadcast prices. In particular with OTC contracts, there is no central exchange to collate and disseminate prices. Mark to market may therefore be complex. For OTC contracts, prices are available on information networks (i.e., Bloomberg and Reuters), via brokers, and, ultimately by the derivative market makers, primarily large banks. (It is estimated that 80% of OTC derivatives are written by the five largest banks: Citi, J.P. Morgan, Bank of America, Barclays, and Societe Generale.)

However, futures and options values are also based on an "arbitrage free price," meaning a price at which no risk-free profits can be made by trading in these derivatives. There is elegance and logic to the arbitrage free pricing of derivatives. Software programs that calculate these values are widely available, although the user determines the inputs to the models so that two users may sometimes arrive at different values.

A common hedge fund strategy is to take a market position on the difference between the market price and the calculated arbitrage free price with the assumption that the two will eventually converge.

1. Arbitrage free pricing of futures

For futures/forwards, the arbitrage free price is relatively straightforward, involving the price of the underlying asset together with the cost of carry (income received less interest costs). The future price of an asset (let us use gold as an example) is equal to buying the asset today, storing it, and then selling it in the future. Thus, if we purchase gold today at $1,000/oz. and store it for a year, the value of the gold in one year will be the purchase price less the cost of acquiring the gold (i.e., the interest paid on the $1,000 over a year), plus the cost of storing and insuring the gold for a year. (In the case of some assets [i.e., bonds], there is also income that needs to be factored in the equation.)

In this hypothetical example, we know that we can own gold a year from now at the price of $1,000 (initial cost), plus the cost of interest (assume 3% or $300) and the cost of storage and insurance (assume $25) for a total of $1,325. The arbitrage free price for gold futures with a one-year expiration must therefore be exactly $1,325.

2. Black–Scholes: arbitrage free pricing of options

For options and more complex derivatives, pricing involves the use of complex pricing models. A key equation for the theoretical valuation of options is the Black–Scholes formula, which is based on the assumption that the cash flows from a European stock option can be replicated by a continuous buying and selling strategy using only the stock. While the mathematics of the model are complex, the elegance of the model is that it only requires five variables to come up with the price of an option:

- The current market price of the stock

- The "strike price" of the option, or the price at which the option buyer will be able to purchase the stock when the option is exercised

- The short-term interest rate in the market
- The volatility of the stock, which is measured using standard deviation of recent price movements in of the stock
- The expiration date of the option

With these five variables, we can calculate, for example, that a call option on IBM stock with a one-year expiration, prevailing one year interest rate of 3%, a market price of $100 per share, a volatility of IBM shares of 15% per annum, and a strike price of $105 (i.e., the call option buyer can purchase IBM from the seller for $105 in one year), will cost the buyer 3% of the face value of the option contract. If the option contract calls for $50,000 of IBM shares, the option buyer will pay $1,500 for the option.

This calculation also shows the extreme leverage contained in derivatives, where $1,500 allows the option buyer to have access to $50,000 of market positions.

PART THREE

History and Overview of the Hedge Fund Industry

CHAPTER 7

History of Hedge Funds

Now that the basics are behind us, we are ready to explore the hedge fund world in all its diversity and complexity. It makes sense to start with a history of hedge funds and a description of the evolution of the industry from its early days to the present. The story here is of an industry that grew from a seedling into a full-blown tree in a relatively short amount of time. It is also an industry that was literally invented from broadcloth in a manner that is more reminiscent of high technology companies than of financial institutions. As with high tech companies, it earned fortunes for those who helped build the industry.

One of the areas worth exploring is the reason that hedge funds became so successful and (some) hedge fund managers so wealthy. An interesting question to ponder is the economic basis for this growth. For example, when we contemplate the growth of Google or IBM, we can point to specific technological gains and productivity measures. Even mutual funds' rapid expansion in the 1980s came from the confluence of forces: the adoption of the modern portfolio theory by professional money managers and the rapid growth of savings in the form of pension funds and retirement savings.

As we trace the growth of hedge funds, we will be looking for the impetus for hedge fund growth, whether in the form of financial and economic benefits not available elsewhere or as a result of theoretical underpinnings for the hedge fund phenomena. To some extent, the search is hampered by the shortage of theorists able to articulate the basis for the industry's growth. However, there are a number of such people that we can look to, including practitioners such as George Soros and Ray Dalio, and academics such as Andrew Lo, Roger Ibbotson, and Burton Malkiel.

HEDGE FUNDS: THE EARLY DAYS

Modern-day hedge funds evolved from two precursors: first, a hedge fund started by Alfred Winslow Jones in 1949, which led to the development of the equity long/short and related equity hedge fund strategies; and second, a trading company called Commodities Corporation started in Princeton in the 1970s, which was the impetus for the development of fixed-income relative value, global macro and commodities trading strategies.

Alfred Winslow Jones

Alfred Winslow Jones, a sociologist and former *Fortune* magazine writer, is generally (if somewhat controversially) credited with developing the first hedge fund in 1949. (A *Fortune* article in 1966 titled "The Jones Nobody Keeps Up With" first used the term "hedge fund".) Jones' fund combined a number of characteristics that still define hedge funds. The fund:

- Sold short as many stocks as it bought
- Used leverage to purchase additional shares
- Avoided requirements of the Investment Company Act of 1940 by establishing a limited partnership limited to 99 investors

In addition, Jones took 20% of the fund's profits in addition to a management fee.

Jones's fund apparently did extremely well and was followed by a number of imitators that borrowed all or parts of his model, notably the limited partnership structure and the fee arrangement. Some of the later hedge funds followed long/short strategies based on fundamental research and relatively hedged portfolios. The success of Warren Buffett's value investing approach was also an impetus for the development of fundamental equity-based hedge funds, including those of Julian Robertson and George Soros in the early days of his hedge fund.

Another type of equities-oriented hedge fund in the early days was best exemplified by Michael Steinhardt's Steinhardt Capital Management, which traded on the basis of short-term market trends—especially those that stemmed from the placement of large market orders, which gave him access to short-term market information.

Each of these trading approaches to equities has hundreds of imitators in today's hedge fund world.

Commodities Corporation

A completely different approach to the marketplace was developed in the 1970s by Princeton-based Commodities Corporation. Commodities Corporation was founded in 1970 with the help of Paul Samuelson, the Nobel Prize–winning economist. The fund featured traders such as Bruce Kovner and Paul Tudor Jones—both of whom went on to found successful global macro hedge funds of their own. Launched in 1970, Commodities Corporation generated extremely high returns throughout the 1970s and early 1980s using both quantitative momentum models and fundamental economic analysis to take long and short positions in macro markets in bonds, stock market indices, currencies, and commodities. Commodities Corporation blazed the way for the global macro hedge fund strategy whose practitioners, in addition to Kovner and Jones, included George Soros.

However, hedge funds as an industry did not begin in earnest until the 1980s, when developments in technology allowed trading outside of bank dealing rooms. During the 1980s until the mid-1990s, the industry was dominated by oversized personalities and the most popular strategy was global macro in which managers took bets on the direction of currencies, interest rates, and commodities. The largest hedge funds during this period would barely meet the size of an average hedge fund today, and the investors were primarily wealthy individuals looking for outsized returns from hedge funds.

GEORGE SOROS TAKES ON THE BANK OF ENGLAND

George Soros's 1992 bet against the pound still stands as a center-piece of hedge fund lore. It is also a valuable lesson in how hedge fund global macro strategies are executed.

In 1992, the United Kingdom was part of the European Exchange Rate Mechanism, which maintained a range-bound parity between the member countries. Each member country was expected to maintain its currency with the range through a combination of fiscal and monetary policies, including raising interest rates and purchasing its own currency to prevent devaluation.

As 1992 wore on and speculative pressure against the pound increased, the Bank of England (BOE) both raised U.K. interest rates and used its foreign currency reserves to purchase the pound in the open market. (In fact, the BOE had to borrow from other countries to maintain its intervention.)

George Soros (together with his associate Stanley Druckenmiller, who went on to found the successful macro hedge fund, Duquesne Capital) decided that the BOE could not maintain its policies for long for fear of wrecking the British economy with high interest rates or running out of foreign currency reserves. Soros "went short" the pound to the tune of over $10 billion (the majority of which he borrowed to leverage his bet) and, when the BOE gave in and allowed the pound to depreciate on a day known as "Black Monday," Soros wound up with a profit of well over $1 billion.

In another common feature of global macro strategies, Soros also bought £350 million of British shares at the same time, gambling that equities often rise after a currency devalues.

Examples included Caxton (founded by Bruce Kovner), Moore Capital (founded by Louis Bacon), Paul Tudor Jones, Steven Cohen, Julian Robertson's Tiger Management, Leon Cooperman's Omega Advisors, and Michael Steinhardt's fund, although the latter resembled more a traditional equities trading room than a hedge fund. Although not technically a hedge fund, Warren Buffett's Berkshire Capital was representative of an investment firm with a fundamental approach to investing.[*]

---

[*]A fascinating history of the pioneers of the hedge fund world can be found in Sebastian Mallaby's *More Money Than God*.

In the 1990s, a new generation of hedge fund managers came to the fore as talented traders from the first group of hedge funds left to start their own, often with the backing of the "mother" fund. In the 1990s, the industry also consolidated and new strategies were developed, notably those linked to equities. This was logical since the equities market, which had been relatively inactive and directionless following the market crash of 1987, entered a multiyear boom, accompanied by the growth of other equity-linked strategies such as convertible arbitrage and merger arbitrage.

For investors, the main incentive for investing in hedge funds was to garner higher returns—indeed, at times spectacular returns—than were available from traditional investments in stocks and bonds. Investors for the most part assumed that these higher returns came from the ability of the hedge fund manager to time the markets or exploit niches that had not yet been arbitraged; in modern jargon, to add "alpha." Increased publicity for hedge fund managers such as George Soros and Michael Steinhardt facilitated this process.

THE GROWTH OF THE MODERN HEDGE FUND INDUSTRY

In 2000, a total of fewer than 1000 hedge funds managed less than $400 billion in assets, mostly provided by wealthy individuals, many based overseas. By 2008, the size of the industry had nearly quintupled with assets under management of nearly $2 trillion managed by nearly 10,000 hedge funds. Where hedge funds were once considered the playground of the rich, the majority of the inflow of funds was now garnered from institutions such as pension funds, endowments, insurance companies, or banks.

Hedge Fund of Funds

Another important development of this period was the spectacular growth of the fund of funds industry. In some ways a logical outgrowth of the growing number and complexity of the hedge funds, fund of funds acted as guides to investors, providing a roadmap to an exotic and private island. We will discuss fund of hedge funds in more detail below.

Hedge Fund Investors

Perhaps more than any other factor in the development of the hedge fund industry in the past 10 years, and into the future, has been the shift in the investors in hedge funds from wealthy individuals to institutions. We will have much more to say about this later, but at this point we note that 2009 was a landmark when institutions became the largest source of investment in hedge funds (Figure 7–1).

Hedge Fund Consolidation: Billion Dollar Club

One of the results of the inflow of institutional funds is the increased consolidation of the industry since institutions show a clear preference for larger hedge funds who they consider safer than smaller funds.

FIGURE 7—1

Hedge Fund Asset Evolution over Time

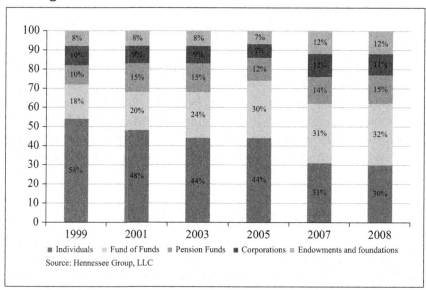

Source: Hennessee Group, LLC

FIGURE 7-2

Concentration of Investment in Large Scale Funds

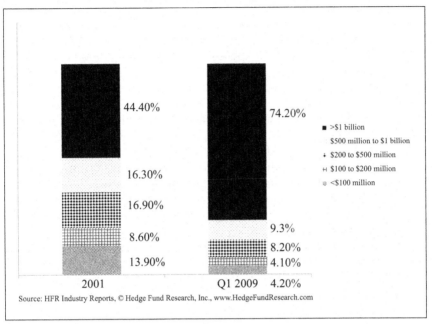

2001	44.40%
	16.30%
	16.90%
	8.60%
	13.90%
Q1 2009	74.20%
	9.3%
	8.20%
	4.10%
	4.20%

Legend:
- ■ >$1 billion
- $500 million to $1 billion
- ✦ $200 to $500 million
- H $100 to $200 million
- ⊛ <$100 million

Source: HFR Industry Reports, © Hedge Fund Research, Inc., www.HedgeFundResearch.com

While single-manager hedge funds with greater than $1 billion under management account for just 3.9% of reporting hedge funds, they control about 60% of the total single-manager hedge fund assets. In 2011, 322 single-manager hedge funds reported having assets under management of over $1 billion, for a total of $1.08 trillion in assets under management (Figure 7–2).

VALUATION OF HEDGE FUNDS

The consolidation of the hedge fund industry (as well as the formation of new hedge funds) has led to an increased interest in the valuation of hedge funds as entities. In an article titled "Hedge Funds: A Methodology for Hedge Fund Valuation" (*Journal of Alternative Investments*; winter 2000; pp. 43–46), I pointed out the complexity of this undertaking using traditional firm valuation methodology.

In typical M&A transactions, firms are valued using a combination of three tools: discounted cash flow, which takes future projected cash flows and discounts these flows to the present using a discount rate that reflects the risk associated with these flows; publicly quoted companies, which takes the multiple of earnings that are typical for comparable companies and applies them to the hedge fund being valued; and comparable transactions, which applies the same method but uses prices from comparable M&A transactions, rather than public prices.

The added complexity of applying this approach to hedge funds comes from problems in all three approaches. The discounted cash flow method is complicated by the fact that the greater amount of future cash flow will come from incentive compensation rather than management fees. Whereas the latter change in a way that can be predicted, at least to some extent, the former is much more open to various assumptions of future hedge fund performance and assets under management.

The other two valuation methods, comparable publicly quoted companies and comparable transactions, are difficult to apply for the simple fact that there are very few of either category, and even those that exist are so different as to make direct comparison formidable.

For these reasons, valuation of hedge funds depends on an in-depth knowledge of the dynamics of hedge funds and the particular strategy that is being valued.

HEDGE FUNDS AS THE NEW POWER BROKERS

McKinsey, the prestigious management consulting firm, has defined a group of "new power brokers," comprising investors and asset managers who together form an increasingly important part of the world's investment industry.

As shown in Figure 7–3, the traditional investment world is dominated by pension funds (with $25 trillion in assets under management in 2008), mutual funds (with around $20 trillion), and insurance companies (with $17 trillion). This group has dominated the financial system over the past three decades. The next group shown on the graph, the new power brokers, is significantly

FIGURE 7–3

Holding Steady: Assets Under Management ($ Trillion)

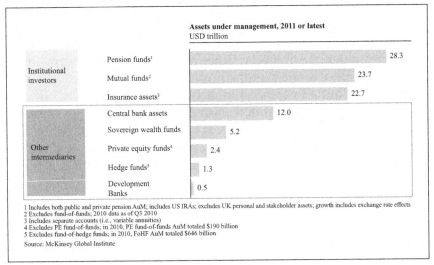

Assets under management, 2011 or latest
USD trillion

Institutional investors	Pension funds[1]	28.3
	Mutual funds[2]	23.7
	Insurance assets[3]	22.7
Other intermediaries	Central bank assets	12.0
	Sovereign wealth funds	5.2
	Private equity funds[4]	2.4
	Hedge funds[5]	1.3
	Development Banks	0.5

1 Includes both public and private pension AuM; includes US IRAs; excludes UK personal and stakeholder assets; growth includes exchange rate effects
2 Excludes fund-of-funds; 2010 data as of Q3 2010
3 Includes separate accounts (i.e., variable annuities)
4 Excludes PE fund-of-funds; in 2010, PE fund-of-funds AuM totaled $190 billion
5 Excludes fund-of-hedge funds; in 2010, FoHF AuM totaled $646 billion

Source: McKinsey Global Institute

smaller than the traditional investment firms in terms of size. This group is comprised of sovereign wealth funds (government-controlled pools of money from petrodollars and Asian export economies) with $10 trillion, hedge funds with $2 trillion, and private equity/buyout funds with $1 trillion.

As the term implies, however, McKinsey attributes power to the new group out of proportion to their size for two reasons: first, McKinsey predicts a greater degree of growth for the new sector than the established firms; second and perhaps more important, because the new power brokers are more active in their management of their assets and are therefore more likely to influence the movement of markets and perhaps economies. While the larger, traditional players invest greater amounts in companies and in markets such as bonds, their investment is largely passive and long term, with movement in and out of markets based on portfolio considerations. In contrast, the new power brokers make investment decisions with a view toward active management and at times control of companies, as we will see in the discussion of activist hedge funds.

Tax Issues

Because most hedge funds engage in more active trading, they generate significant realized gains and losses, leading to complicated tax reporting. In some of these funds, the limited partner may not receive his or her Schedule K-1 (Form 1065), which supplies all the information that the limited partner requires for a tax return—until a time very close to the standard April 15 filing deadline.

Since a limited partnership is a "pass-through entity" from a tax point of view, the limited partner pays taxes on her share of the partnership's realized return, at her own personal tax rate. The limited partner owes taxes whether or not she receives a distribution from the partnership. The underlying realized return is taxed as follows:

1. *Income and expenses.* Stock dividends and bond interest are taxed at the usual rates. Dividends owed on short positions are netted against dividends paid on long positions. Interest on short sale proceeds is part of income, and margin interest expense is netted against income.

2. *Realized gains and losses.* Realized gains and losses are taxed at the usual rates. Futures contracts and short sales receive special treatment. In each case, there is a tax advantage and a tax disadvantage. With futures, the disadvantage is that there is no such thing as an unrealized profit. All futures positions are marked to market at the end of the year, and they are taxed accordingly. The offsetting advantage is that all futures profits are taxed as if they were 60% long term and 40% short term. In the case of short selling, the disadvantage is that all profits from short sales are taxed as short-term gains, no matter how long the position is held. The advantage is that if a stock sold short goes to zero (e.g., in the case of bankruptcy), then there is no taxable gain if the short position is not covered.

Although it is common to criticize hedge funds for their tax inefficiency, this criticism is not completely fair. The recent preoccupation with tax efficiency is a by-product of a bull market that lasted almost 20 years. In an environment in which stocks are generally going up, appreciation is easy to earn and unrealized appreciation is better than realized appreciation. But if appreciation is harder to achieve or if unrealized appreciation suddenly evaporates into un-realized depreciation, then investors will place a higher premium on putting real after-tax money in their pockets.

There is a difference between annual and total taxes paid. Some studies suggest that the typical mutual fund investor has an investment horizon of only a few years. If you buy a tax-efficient fund and then sell it after three years, any unrealized appreciation in the fund becomes realized, and so you wipe out the tax advantage. To calculate the *total* tax efficiency of a fund, you have to take into account the tax impact of the final sale. Holding a low-turnover, tax-efficient fund is a smart way to *defer* taxes, but it is not a way to *avoid* taxes. In a highly tax-efficient fund, you pay less tax now, more later. In a high-turnover hedge fund, you pay more tax now, less later. The crucial question for the investor is how the two components add up, and that depends on the details of the situation.

Since hedge funds tend to be actively traded, the ideal hedge fund investor is a nontaxable investor. The main occupants of this category are U.S. tax-exempt institutions (pension funds, endowments, foundations, and so on) and offshore investors (the mythical Belgian dentist). These investors are able to take advantage of offshore hedge funds; and the offshore hedge fund also offers a major advantage to the manager of the fund. The fund is a corporation that is based in an offshore tax haven. The manager of the fund receives some percentage of the total return of the fund, but this allocation is an allocation to an offshore entity. If the profit allocation is not repatriated back to the United States, it is not yet taxable to the U.S. money manager. So the U.S.-based manager of an offshore fund has the ability to allow her performance fee to grow offshore in a tax-deferred fashion.

When U.S. tax-exempt institutions invest in hedge funds, they face a tax issue concerning what is known as *unrelated business taxable income* (UBTI). The basic idea behind the taxing of UBTI is that a pension fund, endowment, or foundation may invest in securities, but it may not conduct an operating business. If the General Electric pension plan opened a chain of clothing stores, other clothing stores would complain, justifiably, that they were competing against a new chain of stores that did not have to pay taxes. When a pension fund (or other tax-exempt institution) borrows money to take on a leveraged long position, this is viewed as a departure from "normal investing," a step toward behaving like an operating company. So the Internal Revenue Service penalizes this activity by imposing a tax. The tax is calculated at the normal corporate rate, and applies to that portion of the return attributable to the leverage.

Needless to say, most tax-exempt institutions prefer not to make investments that generate UBTI. The format of the offshore fund provides a convenient route around this problem. An offshore fund is a corporation. The corporation may employ debt in its activities, but that does not mean that the investing pension fund is employing debt. After all, pension funds make investments every day in companies that have debt on their balance sheets. But the pension fund is not borrowing the money; hence, there is no UBTI.

CHAPTER 8

Hedge Funds, Shadow Banking, and Systemic Risk

Hedge funds are often considered part of the "shadow banking" system—a group of firms that perform some of the same functions as banks, yet exist outside the regulated banking world. Examples include bank-sponsored intermediaries such as asset-backed commercial paper conduits, money market funds, collateralized loan obligations, finance companies, asset managers, private equity and venture capital funds, sovereign wealth funds, and hedge funds.

Entities in the shadow banking system perform some of the functions of a bank, particularly financing long-term loans with short-term borrowing. However, shadow banking players differ from traditional banks in a number important ways:

- They are highly leveraged, especially via securitization products

- They rely disproportionately on short-term financing, especially in the repo market

- They do not typically operate under bank regulatory supervision and thus often operate under differing capital, leverage, and liquidity guidelines

- They do not normally benefit from government capital support, such as deposit insurance

- They do not benefit from the liquidity support available to regulated banks, such as the ability to borrow from the Fed

The U.S. Nonbank Financial System

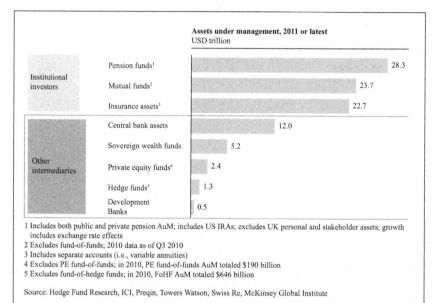

Assets under management, 2011 or latest
USD trillion

Institutional investors	Pension funds[1]	28.3
	Mutual funds[2]	23.7
	Insurance assets[3]	22.7
Other intermediaries	Central bank assets	12.0
	Sovereign wealth funds	5.2
	Private equity funds[4]	2.4
	Hedge funds[5]	1.3
	Development Banks	0.5

1 Includes both public and private pension AuM; includes US IRAs; excludes UK personal and stakeholder assets; growth includes exchange rate effects
2 Excludes fund-of-funds; 2010 data as of Q3 2010
3 Includes separate accounts (i.e., variable annuities)
4 Excludes PE fund-of-funds; in 2010, PE fund-of-funds AuM totaled $190 billion
5 Excludes fund-of-hedge funds; in 2010, FoHF AuM totaled $646 billion

Source: Hedge Fund Research, ICI, Preqin, Towers Watson, Swiss Re, McKinsey Global Institute

Post credit crisis, the shadow banking system shrank along with the overleveraged entities and conduits that were rampant before the crisis. However, it is still larger than the regulated banking system and is poised to resume its growth owing to the price advantages it retains compared with traditional banking (Figure 8–1).

SHADOW BANKING

The shadow banking system has come under increased scrutiny following the financial crisis of 2008 as regulators have sought to rein in what many believe were the high-risk, unregulated activities that underpinned the crisis itself, notably the extent of leverage and the interconnectedness of the shadow and regulated banking systems. Many of the activities of shadow banking were held to be largely responsible for the credit crisis (or at least the severity of the crisis) and are seen by some as likely to pose a future threat to the stability of the financial system.

A host of regulatory proposals have either come into effect or are planned to address this alleged threat, including moving securities loans to a central counterparty, requiring banks to retain "skin in the game"—that is, keep a portion of a deal on their books—for securitized deals, mandating minimum haircuts for repo transactions, and creating a trade repository for shadow banking. A related concern of regulators is the possibility that the practices and firms of shadow banking may pose a threat to the overall financial system—a threat known as "systemic risk."

In all these initiatives, the regulation of the shadow market will have important repercussions for hedge funds.

SYSTEMIC RISK

Systemic risk is the risk of instability arising across the entire financial system, or at least a significant portion of that system. Following the credit crisis, a number of U.S. and international governments and regulators—for example, the Financial Stability Forum, the U.K. Financial Services Authority, the U.S. Federal Reserve Board, the European Central Bank—have been exploring whether hedge funds are a potential source of systemic risk and, if they are, what steps can be taken to reduce the risk.

The arguments that hedge funds may be a potential source of systemic risk go as follows:

- Hedge funds have become increasingly important as traders and market makers in a number of markets, especially in fixed-income, convertible bond, and the massive derivatives market. The U.K. Financial Services Authority estimates that hedge funds hold in aggregate approximately "7% of the outstanding value of the global convertible bond market" and approximately "4% and 6% of the much larger and more systemically important interest rate and commodity derivative markets." As such, they could create instability if they exited these markets, either voluntarily or because they were forced to exit.

- A second source of systemic risk from hedge funds comes from their reliance on short-term financing, which, if suddenly reduced, could lead to the liquidation of their assets at fire sale prices, thereby upsetting markets. This argument points to the impact of the liquidation of mortgage-backed securities by hedge funds in 2007–2008, which undoubtedly contributed to the problems of the markets and the possibility of a replay in the future.

- A third argument focuses on the interrelationship in both credit and trading between hedge funds and a small number of brokers and banks, which could damage these firms if hedge funds become major credit risks or endanger the stability of markets.

THE INDUSTRY'S RESPONSE

The Managed Funds Association, the hedge fund industry association, has argued that hedge funds should not be grouped with other shadow banking firms and that they do not pose a systemic risk for the following reasons:

- *The size of the hedge funds industry:* The hedge fund industry—both in terms of the advisers/fund managers as well as the funds they manage—is relatively small in comparison with other financial market participants.

- *Low leverage:* Hedge funds generally do not employ a significant amount of leverage and typically post collateral in connection with any leverage employed.

- *Stable capital base:* Capital invested in hedge funds is subject to limited redemption rights; this provides a stable equity base and helps prevent runs on the fund's cash and assets.

- *Liquidity:* Hedge funds typically structure their borrowings to avoid a mismatch between their equity capital and investments on the one hand and their secured financing on the other hand.

- *Regulation:* Hedge fund advisers/managers are subject to regulatory supervision in many jurisdictions. Following the banking crisis, the regulation of hedge fund managers and the markets in which they operate has been enhanced.

Industry participants also point to the record of hedge funds during the credit crisis as proof that they do not contribute to systemic risk. According to Hedge Fund Research, for example, 1,471 hedge funds were liquidated in 2008, out of a total of 6,845. The industry's total capital plunged by $600 billion to $1.33 trillion as of the end of the first quarter of 2009. However, this large decline occurred quietly with no noticeable contribution to systemic risk, nor, pointedly, did it call for any government support or subsidy.

Some of the changes stemming from the credit crisis will also reduce the risk that hedge funds will cause systemic risk. For example, the Basel III accords of the Bank for International Settlements will impose higher capital requirements on banks, which will in turn reduce the amount of loans they make to hedge funds. In addition, the requirements of Dodd-Frank will obligate larger hedge funds to provide the Financial Stability Board with information about their positions and risks, allowing the board to take preventative action if a potential threat to the financial system arises.

BENEFITS OF HEDGE FUNDS IN THE FINANCIAL SYSTEM

Hedge funds have long been pilloried as a destabilizing influence in the financial markets. However, they also have their defenders among both academics and practitioners. This section describes some of the suggested benefits of hedge funds:

- *Sources of financial innovation:* Because hedge funds are not constrained in their use of strategies and tools, they are often the source of innovation in the development of new instruments and strategies, or new applications of instruments. As Andrew Lo, a leading theorist of hedge funds, puts it: "the hedge-fund industry is the Galapagos Islands—where Darwin [developed the idea of] evolution—of finance. Because of the lack of patents, speed of innovation, and the ruthlessness of competition, we can see evolution in the hedge-fund industry. It looks nothing like it did five years ago." (Quote in *Bloomberg Businessweek* magazine online, February 19, 2006)

- *Provide market liquidity:* Hedge funds are active traders in a variety of markets and instruments. They make markets and provide liquidity to markets, especially markets where liquidity is often missing (emerging markets, distressed debt, small cap stocks, structured products). By providing liquidity, hedge funds make these markets more efficient.

- *Assume market risks:* Hedge funds are willing to assume risks that other asset management entities will not or do not. In this regard, they serve as counterparts to hedgers by taking the other side of a transaction and facilitate the development of markets that may otherwise not exist or exist in a more limited form. In this role, they act out the function of the speculator in classic economic theory.

- *Encourage price discovery and market efficiency:* By adding liquidity to markets, by their ability to short markets, and by actively arbitraging markets, hedge funds add to the efficiency of markets. In addition, hedge funds add to the information available to investors by their focus on short selling, which makes them prone to look more closely at the weaknesses of stocks and other financial instruments.

THE FUTURE OF HEDGE FUNDS IN THE FINANCIAL SYSTEM

One of the results of the credit crisis has been the demise of the independent investment banking model. Investment banks were either taken over (Bear Stearns and Merrill Lynch), declared bankruptcy (Lehman Brothers), or converted to regulated bank holding companies (Goldman Sachs and Morgan Stanley) in order to take advantage of the benefits offered only to regulated banks, especially access to the cheap financing available from the Federal Reserve.

Commercial banks, too, have seen their activities in investment banking functions constrained through increased capital requirements and the implementation of the "Volcker Rule" in the Dodd-Frank legislation, which will force banks to vacate many investment banking activities, notably risk trading and direct participation in hedge funds and private equity.

Hedge funds are uniquely able to step in and fulfill some of the functions that were performed by investment banks and by the investment banking arms of commercial banks, notably trading, restructuring companies, distressed debt investment and financing, and some forms of specialized lending. The result may be nothing less radical than the evolution of hedge funds into the equivalent of investment banks or a new "investment bank/hedge fund" model.

Hedge Funds and Investment Banking

The functions of investment banking that are part of the hedge fund business model include:

- Trading in equity, currency, commodity, and fixed-income markets
- Provide specialized financing, including financing for merger and acquisition activities and private equity transactions
- "Merchant banking" through which investment banks place their own money to work in deals and equity investments
- Advise companies in restructuring transactions
- Provide investment and financial advisory services, especially to high-net-worth individuals and midsized institutional investors (in the case of fund of hedge funds)

The investment banking model described here is unique to the United States. In the rest of the world, traditional commercial or "universal" banks largely perform these functions. With the increased capital requirement imposed by Basel III, it is likely that international banks will also exit many investment banking and risk-trading activities and the U.S. and global banking models will converge. This trend is already evident with the exodus of traders from European banks to hedge funds, mirroring their American counterparts.

Hedge Fund Risk Trading

The logical implication of regulatory restrictions on bank trading is the migration of this activity to hedge funds, entities already skilled in trading and risk taking, but without the regulatory restrictions imposed on banks. In fact, the migration has begun in earnest with many traders leaving banks to either start new hedge funds or join existing hedge funds. Several reasons lie behind this exodus. First, the possibility of a passage of some form of the Volcker Rule would force banks to greatly reduce their trading—as well as their hedge fund and private equity—activities. Second, banks' increased capital requirements will likely put a brake on their ability to assume the type of risk positions needed to sustain a profitable trading desk. Finally, banks' compensation system is coming under increasing scrutiny and pressure, making hedge funds' compensation increasingly attractive.

Banks have been planning their future activities in so-called flow trading, which does not involve much capital but is hugely expensive in systems development. A handful of firms will dominate this activity with very large trading operations, highly mechanized and working on wafer-thin margins. Banks will also continue to have a role in over-the-counter trading, especially in derivatives. (Oliver Wyman, a consulting firm, estimates that while 75% of the derivatives activity will migrate to exchanges, only 25% of the profits will follow.)

In assuming a larger role in trading, hedge funds will need to adopt some of the organizational features of banks, including independent oversight and directors, internal audit functions, strong risk management and compliance functions, back office and systems capabilities, and personnel depth beyond the small group of decision makers. Many larger hedge funds have come to resemble—or will in the not too distant future—traditional investment bank trading rooms with multiple trading desks involved in multiple markets under a central management and organization.

As hedge funds grow larger in trading, they will inevitably face greater government scrutiny and the possibility of increased government regulation, especially in the areas of registration and disclosure, leverage, capital adequacy, and short selling. If the trend outlined above continues, it is easy to imagine a point in the future where hedge funds are required to have sufficient capital to support their risk-taking activities, in which case trading and regulation will have come a full circle.

Hedge Fund Corporate and Government Activism

While hedge funds have eschewed entering into such investment banking activities as M&A advisory and securities underwriting, they have become more actively involved as principals in the restructuring of companies and even governments. As large holders of equity and debt, hedge funds have gained increasing clout in influencing the strategy of companies, largely through the activist shareholder model discussed in chapter 17

As large holders of debt, including corporate and government debt, hedge funds have also become influential in the decision making of these entities, especially when they become distressed and need to restructure. Notable examples include the role of hedge funds in the Greek government's efforts to restructure its debt, as well as in several instances of emerging market debt crises.

Hedge Funds as Lenders and Merchant Bankers

Since the financial crisis in 2008, a combination of regulations—Basel III, Dodd-Frank, and the European Banking Authority's—and industry dynamics has led to a steady deleveraging of the banking sector as banks have been forced to sell assets and raise capital. There is no doubt that these regulations are driving banking and other financial activities into less-regulated entities, including hedge funds, that have the means and ability to lend funds.

Hedge funds have been important providers of liquidity in the secondary market as banks have shrunk their loan books. In this, they are competing with private equity firms who have long been providers of bridging finance. Distressed debt hedge funds have been proliferating and taking advantage of bank deleveraging by purchasing loans and bonds at a discount, looking to profit from a recovery in their value or by actively taking part in their restructuring.

A May 7, 2012, headline announced that a "$540M Debt Swap Gives Hedge Fund Majority Stake in Barneys." The article continues that Perry Capital LLC is the new majority owner of Barneys New York Inc., a financially troubled clothing company. This is an extreme form of a growing trend for hedge funds to provide financing to companies and security transactions including Initial Public Offerings (IPOs), mezzanine finance, structured products, distressed company debt and equity, and M&A activities.

The Good News for Regulators—
at Least for Now

While there is continuing controversy regarding hedge funds' expanded activities, one aspect should please supervisory authorities.

In the case or trading and lending activities, hedge funds have thus far only placed shareholder capital at risk. At least for now, hedge funds have no access to government guarantees or financing, a condition that should persist as long as hedge funds do not grow to the size of independent investment banks or assume the level of leverage that sank Long-Term Capital Management. In addition, hedge funds' leverage is dramatically lower than that of independent investment banks; lower even than that of commercial banks. Finally, hedge funds' assets and source of financing do not have the same mismatch between short-term capital supporting long-term investments that was responsible for the collapse of many vehicles during the credit crisis.

CHAPTER 9

Key Events in the Development of Hedge Funds: Long-Term Capital Management and the Credit and Liquidity Crisis

The hedge fund industry has been shaped by a number of events that led to changes in fundamental aspects of the way hedge funds conduct their business. This section discusses two such events: the collapse of Long-Term Capital Management and the Credit Crisis of 2007–2008.

THE ROLE OF HEDGE FUNDS IN THE CREDIT CRISIS

The credit crisis of 2007–2008 was a defining event for hedge funds, as for the rest of the financial world. The lessons that emerged from the crisis have fundamentally changed the way hedge funds conduct their business in such areas as risk management, redemption requirements, valuation of assets, prime brokerage relationships, leverage calculation, and operational and compliance functions.

Hedge funds were pilloried as one of the villains in the global credit and liquidity meltdown, and a number of steps, including restrictions on short selling of financial stocks, was taken by governments specifically to restrict the role of hedge funds. However, in the light of day, the causes of the crisis have been more evenly apportioned among many actors, and the role of hedge funds has been found to be more limited than portrayed by some of the more severe critics.

However, there are some areas where hedge funds did play a significant role. Hedge funds were instrumental in the growth of the market for certain mortgage-backed securities (MBSs) backed by subprime* mortgages, and in the growth of credit default swaps (CDSs). Both markets were central to the cause of the credit crisis. In both cases, investors, who normally would not have the knowledge or access to these instruments, poured many billions of dollars into these markets via hedge funds. By putting their money into hedge funds, investors were indirectly channeling investment funds into the MBS and collateralized debt obligation (CDO)† marketplace.

In addition, the reliance of hedge funds on short-term financing, especially repurchase agreements, as a source of leverage contributed to the crisis when hedge funds were forced to liquidate large amounts of structured mortgage products and unwind CDSs' into a market that was increasingly illiquid. The alternative step taken by many hedge funds was to avoid this liquidation by suspending investor redemptions.

A Brief Overview of the Credit Crisis

The causes of the credit crisis that swept the world starting in 2007 will be debated for years to come. However, few would dispute that the background to the credit crisis included a steep reduction in interest rates—between 2000 and 2003, the Federal Reserve reduced the federal funds rate target from 6.5% to 1%—which left investors scrambling for higher investment returns. This was especially true for institutions such as pension funds and endowments whose fixed obligations to pensioners and to educational and building expenses had increased in the previous decades.

Explosion in the price of housing

The price of housing increased so dramatically between 2002 and 2006 that the phenomena can only be described as a classic "bubble" (Figure 9–1). The inflated price of housing was key to the il-

---

*Mortgage Backed Securities are fixed income instruments that pool thousands of individual mortgages. The payment of interest and principal of the MBS comes from the cash flow of the mortgages. Subprime mortgages are mortgages provided to borrowers that have a history of credit impairment (i.e., defaults) and large debt compared to income or net worth.
†CDOs are fixed income instruments that pool together MBS and other assets.

FIGURE 9−1

The Housing Bubble

Low Interest Rates

- Low interest rates and the chase for yield.
- A steep discount in interest rates that left investors scrambling for investment returns. Between 2000 and 2003 the Federal Reserve reduced the federal funds rate target from 6.5% to 1%. This was true for individuals, but even more so for institutions such as pension funds and endowments whose fixed obligations to pensioners and to educational and building expenses had ramped up in the previous decades.

Increased Borrowing

- Investors encourage to borrow.
- Readily available financing and refinancing.

Subprime Lending

- Growth of subprime lending
- The loosening of borrowing standards and ease of money supply and ultra-cheap mortgages combined to dramatically increase the price of housing. As a result, US consumers greatly increased their debt. However, this was somewhat hidden by the explosion in house prices, which showed that the assets of home owning households was increasing at a faster rate than their borrowing. Lowered standards for mortgage underwriting lead to subprime mortgages.

Housing Bubble

- Explosion in the price of housing.

Slice and Dice Finance

- Decline in risk premium.

lusion that mortgages to high-credit-risk borrowers was safe since the increasing price houses, which was the collateral behind the loans, would guarantee the safety of these loans (Figure 9–2).

The great moderation and declining risk premiums
In the environment of easy money and financial innovation, investors acted as if risk had been greatly reduced, as reflected in the decline in credit spread (the difference in interest rates of assets with different risk profiles) (Figure 9–3). One of the theories propagated at the time by Wall Street, government officials, and academics was that financial innovation had caused a global dispersion of risk among many actors. In effect, risk was shuffled from actor to actor and instrument to instrument until it was no longer possible to identify where the risk actually resided.

The alchemy of "slice-and-dice" finance: hedge funds and CDOs
The financial system stepped up to fill the gap between the explosion of mortgages and the need of investors for increased returns. Financial intermediaries (mortgage providers, servicers, and banks) found a mechanism for turning a stream of mortgage payments into securities (bonds and bondlike investments) that could be presented to investors as relatively low risk and that provided returns higher than those available from other investments.

An extreme form of these structured products is known as collateralized debt obligations (CDOs), which pooled together MBSs, often backed by subprime loans, with other loans and then split the payment stream received from this debt into "tranches," each with a different priority in payments. As a result, CDOs' top tranches received credit ratings at times as high as AAA (the same credit risk as the U.S. government's), which made them tempting to investors that would never have considered investing in subprime mortgages (Figure 9–4).

Hedge funds, which were one of the largest purchasers of CDOs, played a key role as intermediaries between banks that created these high-yielding CDOs and investors seeking to eke out incremental returns in a low-interest-rate environment. Unfortunately, when the housing market collapsed, taking subprime

FIGURE 9-2

Housing Prices and Financial Crisis of 2007 – 2009

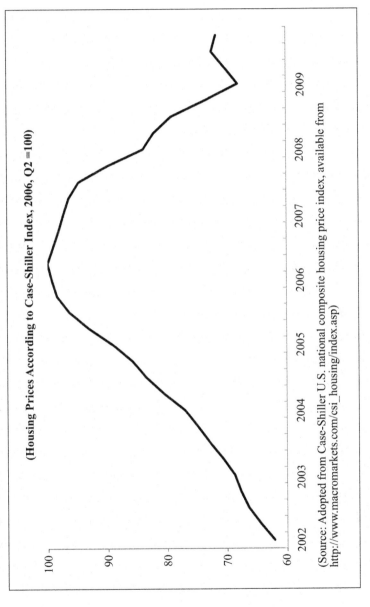

(Housing Prices According to Case-Shiller Index, 2006, Q2 =100)

(Source: Adopted from Case-Shiller U.S. national composite housing price index, available from http://www.macromarkets.com/csi_housing/index.asp)

FIGURE 9–3

Credit Spreads and the 2007 – 2009 Financial Crisis Baa–20 Year U.S. Treasury Spread (%)

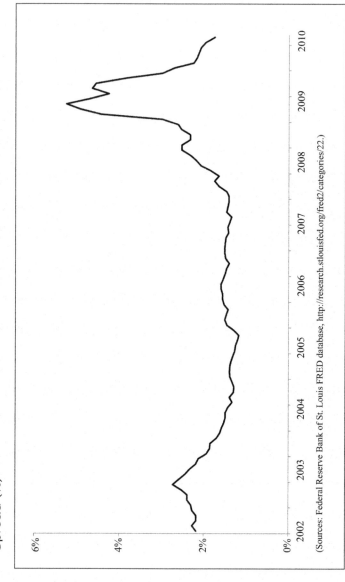

(Sources: Federal Reserve Bank of St. Louis FRED database, http://research.stlouisfed.org/fred2/categories/22.)

FIGURE 9-4

How CDOs Helped Transform Subprime Mortgages into AAA Credits

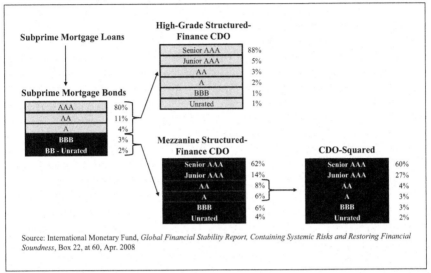

Source: International Monetary Fund, *Global Financial Stability Report, Containing Systemic Risks and Restoring Financial Soundness*, Box 22, at 60, Apr. 2008

mortgages down with it, CDOs suffered tremendous losses and their liquidation set in motion a chain reaction that helped spark the credit crisis.

In fact, two hedge funds owned by Bear Stearns and active in the CDO and CDS markets—the Bear Stearns High-Grade Structured Credit Fund and the Bear Stearns High-Grade Structured Credit Enhanced Leveraged Fund—served as "canaries in the coal mine" in regards to MBSs. Both funds collapsed in June of 2007—despite Bear Stearns's efforts to prop them up—as a result of a large concentration of subprime-backed CDOs and a high level of leverage, which made them vulnerable to margin calls as the mortgage market deteriorated. The margin calls in turn led them to liquidate illiquid securities at severe markdowns, finally leading the funds to lose virtually all its investors' money.

At the same time, however, other hedge funds prospered from the same market by going short or betting against the CDOs and other MBSs, anticipating that the housing market would collapse and cause these securities to lose value. The most famous case was the hedge fund managed by John Paulson, a former risk arbitrage manager who took massive bets against the mortgage market and ultimately earned billions of dollars for himself and his investors when the markets did deteriorate in 2007 and 2008.

Credit default swaps: financial weapons of mass destruction

Dubbed "weapons of mass destruction" by Warren Buffett, CDSs were the second leg (along with CDOs) that helped cause the extreme slide in the financial markets after the U.S. housing bubble burst. Like MBSs, they were devised to diffuse risk, but that diffusion ended up infecting the entire system when things went bad.

CDSs are agreements between two parties—often a hedge fund and a bank—involving bonds issued by a company or a government. On one side, a buyer purchases protection on that debt in the event the borrower should default by missing a bond payment, filing for bankruptcy, or restructuring the obligations. The seller agrees to cover the buyer's loses in the event of a default by paying the difference between a bond's par value and its ultimate recovery value. (Unlike insurance contracts, to which they are sometimes compared, CDS buyers need not own the bonds they are paying to protect.)

Because their prices can fluctuate, CDSs are also used as a trading vehicle by hedge funds and others looking to make bets not only on defaults but on directional movements of a bond issuer's credit quality. Hedge funds were active participants in this market, taking directional bets on CDOs. (CDSs have also played a central role in the recent European government debt crisis as hedge funds and other speculators used CDSs to bet on the direction of government bonds' credit quality.)

The culmination of the CDS crisis occurred when AIG revealed massive losses after selling $440 billion in CDS, mostly on MBSs' and CDOs. The U.S. government injected many billions of dollars into an insurer (AIG) at the height of the financial crises to cover AIG's losses. Federal Reserve Chairman Ben Bernanke described AIG contemptuously as a hedge fund attached to "a large and stable insurance company: A really, really bad hedge fund," a reminder, in case one was needed after the collapse of Lehman Brothers, that hedge funds do not own the patent on bets gone wrong.

The Credit Crisis: Unraveling of the Financial System

There is a widespread consensus that the proximate cause of the credit crisis was the decline in the price of housing, which led to an increase in mortgage delinquencies and defaults—especially in the case of subprime mortgages—which in turn drove down the value of MBSs and CDOs whose price depended on the cash flow from the underlying mortgages.

The deleveraging cycle

A crisis in a relatively small part of the financial world, subprime mortgages, led to a global financial meltdown because of the links in the chain that bound mortgages and financial derivatives. The decline in MBS and CDO prices need not by itself have caused a global credit crisis. However, the next link in the chain was the effect of these declining prices on banks and hedge funds who fund themselves (or leverage themselves) via such methods as repurchase agreements, issuance of debt backed by mortgages, and margin accounts. In all these forms of leverage, hedge funds pledged MBSs and CDOs as collateral. Once the value of this collateral declined, the lenders (investors in the case of bank-issued debt, and the banks and investment banks in the case of hedge funds) demanded additional collateral to support the same level of borrowing.

For example, whereas a $1 million CDO may have been used to support a hedge fund borrowing of $900,000, the decline in the price of the CDO to $800,000 meant that the bank required the hedge fund to post an additional $100,000 in collateral. If the hedge fund did not have sufficient cash to cover the margin call, they were forced to sell off parts of their holdings, often at prices that were considered to be a "fire sale," or well below their "market value."

If numerous hedge funds and other investors are forced to liquidate their holdings at the same time to meet margin calls or to escape a downward market, a self-fulfilling cycle sets in where each additional sale further depresses the price of the securities. This is effectively what happened in 2007 and 2008 in increasingly larger waves of selling. To complicate matters, once the price of these securities started to decline and the market became illiquid and prone to fire sales, the price or value of the securities became uncertain.

The liquidity crisis

This set in motion the next link in the chain: the liquidity crisis. Because market participants did not know the correct valuation of MBSs and CDOs and were ignorant of who held what security (and who might be next to liquidate their portfolios and suffer severe losses of even bankruptcy), banks became wary of lending to each other and to hedge funds. Counterparty risk became the watchword, and fear and uncertainty of counterparties caused markets to come to a virtual standstill, especially after the effective collapse of Bear Stearns and Lehman Brothers.

Hedge fund redemptions

Hedge funds faced an increasing problem during this time, as investors, nervous about the market meltdown or faced with their own need for liquidity to meet margin calls or investor redemptions (e.g., for fund of funds), attempted to redeem their shares in many credit-oriented hedge funds. Faced with the prospect of having to liquidate their structured products in an illiquid market at fire sale prices, dozens of hedge funds chose instead to exercise their power to suspend redemptions. Of course, increased calls for additional margin from banks only compounded their dilemma since they would need to sell securities to meet this margin on top of the redemption requests from customers. However, there is no way to suspend margin calls, so whatever liquidity hedge funds had first went to meet margin calls.

Issues Raised by the Credit Crisis

In addition to the trends noted above, the credit crisis led to at least four fundamental changes in the way hedge funds operate:

- First, the increased regulation of hedge funds and banks spurred by the credit crisis will have a profound influence on hedge funds.

- Second, the nexus between prime brokers and hedge funds has been permanently changed, with counterparty risk and repurchase agreements at the center of the change.

- Third, the risk management area has been revamped to take into account "fat tails" such as a future credit crisis.

- Fourth, the role of leverage combined with illiquid securities has once again become a focus of concern.

LONG-TERM CAPITAL MANAGEMENT: HUBRIS, FAILURE OF RISK MANAGEMENT, AND EXCESSIVE LEVERAGE

Long-Term Capital Management L.P. (LTCM) was formed in Greenwich, Connecticut, in 1994 by a distinguished group of money managers led by John Meriwether, former Vice Chairman of Goldman Sachs. This group raised several billion dollars from investors, then used borrowed money to take very large positions designed to exploit small price discrepancies in the financial markets. After several years of stellar returns, LTCM came apart in the late summer and early fall of 1998.

At the time it was launched, LTCM was considered the leading edge of hedge fund strategy and risk management. It utilized absolute-return and relative value trading strategies such as fixed-income arbitrage, statistical arbitrage, and pairs trading. The idea was to pursue hedged, market neutral positions with little exposure to overall stock and bond markets. LTCM relied on complex mathematical models to establish trading and risk management strategies. Some of the models followed the theories of LTCM consultants and Board of Directors members Myron Scholes and Robert C. Merton, who shared the 1997 Nobel Memorial Prize in Economic Sciences for a "new method to determine the value of derivatives."

Trading Strategies

Initially, LTCM focused on *convergence trades*, fixed-income arbitrage deals entailing U.S., Japanese, and European government bonds. An example of this strategy involved looking to exploit the price difference between 29-year Treasury bonds and 30-year Treasury bonds. The price differences between a 30-year-old Treasury bond and a 29-year-old Treasury bond should be minimal. However, small discrepancies arose between the two bonds because of a difference in liquidity as investors preferred "on the run" 30-year bonds. LTCM then purchased the 29-year bond and shorted the

30-year bond, looking for the liquidity effect to end and the price of the two bonds to converge.

Because these differences in value were minute, the fund needed to take highly leveraged positions to make a significant profit. At the beginning of 1998, the firm had an equity of $4.72 billion and had borrowed over $124.5 billion with assets of around $129 billion, for a debt-to-equity ratio of over 25:1. LTCM also had off-balance sheet derivative positions with a notional value of approximately $1.25 trillion, most of which were in interest rate derivatives such as interest rate swaps. The fund also invested in other derivatives, notably short positions in S&P 500 options, essentially betting that volatility in the stock market would decline in the near future.

Losses and Bailout

LTCM began to lose money on its position in 1998 as a series of crises—first in Asia and then in August and September 1998, when the Russian government defaulted on their government bonds. The largest losses in the portfolio were a result of two market reactions to these crises. First, a dramatic increase in market volatility led to large losses in LTCM's equity options positions. LTCM was "short volatility" (i.e., they sold options), which meant they lost money when market volatility increased. Second, a global panic led to a wholesale shift from Japanese and European bonds to U.S. Treasury bonds. Unfortunately, LTCM's convergence trades were designed to make money as the value of bonds converged; instead they diverged, causing large losses. Even the 29-/30-year convergence strategy, once thought to be immune to large losses, proved a drag as investors piled into the more liquid 30-year Treasury bonds, thereby widening the spread between the two bonds.

Because of LTCM's high leverage, small movements in the market caused amplified losses to its portfolio. In the first three weeks of September, LTCM's equity dropped from $2.3 billion at the start of the month to just $400 million by September 25. With liabilities still over $100 billion, this translated to an effective leverage ratio of more than 250:1.

In September 1998, the Federal Reserve Bank of New York organized a meeting of the heads of some of the largest investment firms of Wall Street to find a solution to LTCM's problems. The fear was that LTCM would need to liquidate huge positions in several markets to cover its debt, causing a chain reaction and severe losses through the financial marketplace. The meeting resulted in a bailout of LTCM by the leading Wall Street firms, in which the creditors seized control of the LTCM portfolio, thus essentially wiping out the equity investors, and organized a very gradual unwinding of the LTCM positions. Importantly, the government did not "bail out" the investors in the partnership: those who had money invested in LTCM lost their investment.

LTCM Influence on Hedge Funds

The LTCM experience had a profound influence on hedge funds (and the financial system in general); an influence that is still felt today. Among the lessons of LTCM:

- *Moral hazard:* The Federal Reserve Bank of New York's involvement in the rescue, although it did not involve the injection of public funds—or even guarantee of debt—created the possibility of a moral hazard whereby financial institutions would assume more risk with the likelihood that the government would bail them out.

- *Dangers of leveraged convergence trades:* LTCM's strategies were compared to "picking up nickels in front of a bulldozer"—a likely small gain (if the convergence worked) and a small chance of a large loss. Of course, by leveraging, the nickels became hundreds of millions and the large losses became billions of dollars.

- *Skepticism of risk models:* The theories of Merton and Scholes—and mathematical models in general—took a public beating. In its annual reports, Merrill Lynch observed that mathematical risk models "may provide a greater sense of security than warranted; therefore, reliance on these models should be limited."

- *Interconnectedness of financial markets and actors:* While there had been financial crises before LTCM, this was the first of a new type, where one firm threatened to bring down the financial system or at least a significant portion of the system. This interconnectedness was especially visible in the symbiotic relationship between LTCM and the Wall Street firms. The dangers of excessive leverage revealed during this event also changed the nature of this relationship, leading Wall Street firms to more closely monitor the leverage provided to hedge funds.

PART FOUR

Hedge Fund Performance: Mounting Criticism and Changing Benchmarks

CHAPTER 10

Mounting Criticism of Hedge Fund Performance

Some investors undoubtedly have nonfinancial reasons for investing in hedge funds—for example, the ego-enhancing thrill of being a member of an exclusive club. Probably a more important nonfinancial reason is that some hedge funds are so large and well established that they have become "brand names," much like some of the larger and better known mutual funds. However, for the majority of investors, the rationale for investing in hedge funds is that they will provide superior performance compared to mutual funds and long-only investments. Otherwise, why pay 2% management fees and 20% performance when you can pay 0.5% for a Vanguard mutual fund?

It therefore seems like a good idea to evaluate the claims that hedge funds offer superior performance, especially after fees are paid to their managers.

Unfortunately, we will not find a definitive answer to this question. We will find that performance measures are highly dependent on the time period we choose as a measure. Furthermore, various performance measures may point to different conclusions. An investment that is attractive by one measure may not be as attractive or may even be undesirable by another measure. Even more basic, we will find that the very data used to measure hedge fund performance is suspect.

The overarching questions that will guide the discussion are ones that are often lost in the debate over hedge fund performance:

- What is the realistic performance expectation of an average investor in hedge funds?

- Do the biases in hedge fund data make the data unusable in making hedge fund investment decisions?

- Do the hedge fund performance measures that are commonly used in the industry reflect the actual experience of a hedge fund investor?

- Can investors use common industry performance measures as a guide to future investment decisions?

While these seem like straightforward questions and certainly ones a potential investor in hedge funds would want answered, the overwhelming analysis of hedge fund performance has centered on the use of problematic data and reliance on a "hypothetical investor" that was able to invest an equal amount of money in every hedge fund during the time period under analysis.

DATA PROBLEMS IN MEASURING HEDGE FUND PERFORMANCE

Hedge fund performance data differ from mutual fund data. The differences stem largely from the fact that hedge funds are not required to divulge their performance to regulatory authorities, whereas mutual funds must disclose this information to the SEC. Additionally, while a mutual fund investor can normally enter and exit the fund on a daily basis, hedge funds have numerous liquidity restrictions on both investments and redemptions, which means that investors are usually not actually able to act on the performance data.

To illustrate this point, assume a mutual fund and a hedge fund that both report a gain of 3% during a certain quarter. Investors in the mutual fund that placed their money at the beginning of the quarter would have been able to redeem their investment with a 3% gain at quarter's end, while investors in the hedge fund may not have been able to redeem their shares for anywhere from one month to one year later at the price that exists when actual redemption takes place, by which time their investment may actually have a loss.

One of the most persistent critics of reported hedge fund data is Burt Malkiel, one of the leading efficient market theorists, who argues that these data problems are sufficiently serious as to make the claims of superior hedge fund performance meaningless. Of course, this is exactly what an efficient market theorist would expect since efficient market theory assumes that returns above the market are impossible over a sustained period of time.[*]

How Is Hedge Fund Data Collected?

Unlike mutual funds, hedge funds are not required to report their performance to any regulatory body or any other public forum. Instead, most hedge funds report their performance on a monthly basis to one or more of a handful of private information providers, the largest of whom are Hedge Fund Research, eVestment HFN, Lipper (formerly TASS), BarclayHedge, CISDM, and Eurekahedge. (See Table 10–1 for a listing of the major hedge fund data providers.) The data is then placed in a database that is made available to investors, typically for a fee.

A few key points about these databases: First, hedge fund reporting is entirely voluntary. Hedge funds decide how many vendors to report to (if any) and can start or stop reporting their performance at will. In addition, the data providers, who merely record the percentage gain or loss reported by the managers, do not confirm the data reported by the managers. Thus, there is no indication of whether the performance numbers are, for example, audited, final numbers, or merely estimates.

There are some checks on this reported data and some pressure for hedge funds to report their performance. Databases are a primary source of hedge fund information used by potential investors in making their investment decisions, which makes reporting a valuable marketing tool. In addition, there is some check on the validity of the reported data since investors in a particular fund expect to see performance numbers in the databases that match their own experience in a fund.

---

[*]Malkiel, B.G., Saha, A., 2005. "Hedge Funds: Risk and Return." *Financial Analysts Journal* 61, 80–88.

TABLE 10-1

Major Hedge Fund Database Providers

Database Provider	Funds in Universe	Also Has Index?	Website
BarclayHedge	6,000	Yes	www.barclayhedge.com
EurekaHedge	9,000	Yes	www.eurekahedge.com
eVestment	6,000	Yes	www.evestment.com
Hedge Fund Research	7,000	Yes	www.hedgefundresearch.com
HedgeFund Intelligence	13,000	Yes	www.hedgefundintelligence.com
Lipper-TASS	7,500	Yes	www.lipperweb.com
CISDM	5,000	Yes	www.isenberg.umass.edu/CISDM/
Morningstar	7,100	Yes	www.morningstar.com

Selective Reporting Bias

"Selective reporting" bias is a logical outcome of the voluntary nature of hedge fund reporting. There are a number of reasons hedge funds may choose not to report their performance, the two most common being poor performance or that they do not wish to attract investors by reporting to a common database.

Poor performance bias is self-evident; a hedge fund that is performing poorly does not wish to publicize the fact, hoping for an upturn in its performance or anticipating closing up shop. This type of bias artificially inflates hedge fund returns by omitting poorly performing funds.

On the other hand, there are some successful hedge funds that are either closed to investors or have no difficulty gathering assets and that do not report their performance data to the vendors. These include some well-known hedge funds such as Caxton, SAC, Renaissance, and Tudor. These funds are also among the largest and best performing in the industry, and their absence from the databases most likely causes a downward bias in overall hedge fund reported performance, especially in the asset-weighted measure discussed below.

A study by Burt Malkiel and others, "Why Do Hedge Funds Stop Reporting?," tests the two alternative reasons for nonreporting by hedge funds. Their evidence indicates that the overwhelming reason hedge funds stop reporting is because of poor performance and those hedge funds that did stop reporting had significantly poorer performance in the prior period.

Survivorship Bias

Hedge funds come and go. On average, 10–12% of hedge funds close up shop each year. This means that over the past 20 years, there are many more hedge funds that no longer exist than those that are now active. A recent survey of hedge fund databases conducted by PerTrac noted that there were upward of 50,000 "dead funds" compared with only 7,500 "live funds." However, the hedge fund returns that are normally published and used to analyze hedge fund performance, for example, in publicly available hedge fund indices, are based entirely on the performance of live hedge funds. Clearly, from an investor's point of view, it is important to know how the expired hedge funds performed because it is likely that he or she would have invested in one or more of these funds.

A number of studies have compared the performance characteristics of dead and live funds using data from data providers, several of who maintain records of dead funds in a "graveyard" database. Not surprisingly, they find that dead funds fared significantly worse than live funds on every measure of performance. The implications for investors are profound and disturbing: that the performance data commonly used to evaluate hedge funds is reporting performance that is substantially higher than the "real performance." The question is: How much higher?

Roger Ibbotson of Yale University and Peng Chen of Ibbotson Associates performed a widely cited analysis of hedge fund performance data problems in 2010. Using data from 1995 through December 2009 they find that survivorship bias may have added a full 5.21% annually to the performance of hedge fund as reported by the TASS database. Live hedge funds returned 12.84% annually during this time period, while the combined dead and live funds only returned 7.63% annually.

Admittedly, there is controversy over these results. Other studies that use different time periods, databases, and funds report a range of values for survivorship bias. However, it is widely accepted that survivorship bias does inflate the reported performance of hedge funds.

Backfill Bias

Backfill bias acts in the same way as survivorship bias, artificially inflating performance measures. The bias stems from the fact that new hedge funds can decide when to start reporting their returns to database vendors. In addition, when they do decide to start reporting, they are allowed to enter performance numbers from previous months, as many as they choose. It seems logical that hedge funds with good performance will give the databases their early performance, while funds with bad early performance will not. As would be expected, "backfilled" (i.e., noncontemporaneous) performance data is higher than contemporaneous data. Again, estimating the size of the backfill bias is controversial. Ibbotson and Chen report that the bias may be as high as 3.51%.

"End of Life" Reporting Bias

Hedge funds that are in the process of winding down their operations as a result of poor performance or the inability to gather sufficient assets to be economically viable have no incentive to report their performance results to the hedge fund data vendors. Because these funds tend to be poorer performers, their absence from the databases artificially enhances reported hedge fund performance. However, estimating the effect of this bias is obviously impossible.

HEDGE FUND INDICES AS A MEASURE OF HEDGE FUND PERFORMANCE

A number of database vendors publish monthly indices that attempt to measure the performance of hedge funds. (Table 10–1 lists the major vendors.) In much the same way that the S&P 500 is used as a broad gauge of the performance of the stock market, hedge fund indices are the most commonly used measure of hedge fund performance, relied on by investors, consultants, analysts, and academics. These indices are widely reported in the financial press and closely followed by industry participants.

However, there are difficulties in using hedge fund indices as measures of performance and, especially, as guideposts to making investment decisions.

First, hedge fund indices are plagued with all the issues we discussed above, including voluntary reporting of data, backfill, and survivorship bias. This is further complicated by the fact that many hedge funds may only report to one or two vendors, so that no one vendor has a complete picture of the industry. By one study, only 71% of hedge funds reported to only one database provider (Figure 10–1).

The most important limitation of hedge fund indices compared to, for example, the S&P 500 Index, is that an investor can actually invest in the S&P 500 Index and thus realize the performance of the index, a hedge fund investor cannot invest in a hedge fund index.

Investors can invest in an S&P 500 index through numerous mutual funds that offer this index. These funds offer investors daily liquidity and are open to any investor with no minimum investment requirement.

In contrast, hedge fund indices include hedge funds that are closed to investors. In addition, the indices do not take into account the minimum investment necessary to access the funds. These minimums are typically $1 million and may be much higher.

Finally, while the shares of companies in the S&P can be bought and sold on a continuous basis, investment in hedge funds are subject to time delays on withdrawals, some of which may last months or even years, so the prices used to construct the performance indices are not prices at which investors are actually able to redeem their shares.

WHAT DO WE LOOK FOR IN AN INDEX?

We look for at least three key characteristics that de define a useful index product:

- *Representativeness* means that an index should be as representative as possible of the investment the investor is attempting to evaluate.
- *Investability* means that the constituent hedge funds of the index are open to investment from prospective investors. This must also take into account any limitations such as minimum required amounts and limitations on redemptions and/or additional investments.
- *Minimum bias* refers to the absence (or near absence) of any practical or theoretical factors that may bias the index in an upward or downward direction from the actual performance of the investment universe.

FIGURE 10–1

Venn Diagram of the Overlap Between Select Hedge Fund Databases

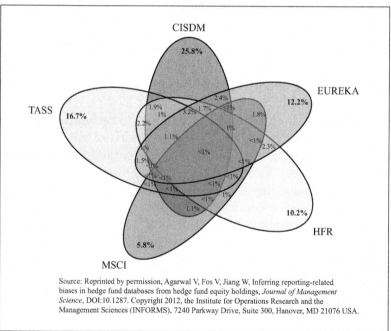

Source: Reprinted by permission, Agarwal V, Fos V, Jiang W, Inferring reporting-related biases in hedge fund databases from hedge fund equity holdings, *Journal of Management Science*, DOI:10.1287. Copyright 2012, the Institute for Operations Research and the Management Sciences (INFORMS), 7240 Parkway Drive, Suite 300, Hanover, MD 21076 USA.

INVESTABLE AND NONINVESTABLE HEDGE FUND INDICES

Performance of Investable Indices

In recognition of the numerous restrictions on hedge fund investments, a number of banks and companies have developed "investable" indices and investible index products that attempt to provide investors with a performance in line with the reported index. These products also typically offer lower minimum investments than individual hedge fund investments, allowing investors to invest in multiple hedge funds, as well as providing due diligence and managed account platforms that keep assets in a segregated account beyond the hedge fund managers' control.

The bad news for the hedge fund industry is that investable indices often underperform the noninvestable indices, often by substantial amounts (Table 10–2). The investable HFRX Global Hedge Fund Index, for example, has underperformed the noninvestable HFRI Fund Weighted Composite Index every year since 2003, by an average of 560 basis points.

Are Funds of Hedge Funds Better Indicators of Performance than Indices?

The argument has been made that funds of hedge funds (FoHFs) are a better gauge of hedge fund performance than either the investable or noninvestable indices.

TABLE 10-2

Investable and Noninvestable Hedge Fund Index Characteristics

Investable	Noninvestable
• Constituents must be open to new investments	• Constituents can include open or closed hedge funds
• Increased bias due to tougher selection criteria	• Suffer less from database biases than investable indices
• Poor estimators of the hedge fund universe	• Better estimator of the hedge fund universe
• More easily replicated	• More difficult to replicate

According to this argument, FoHFs by their nature overcome some of the biases of hedge fund data. For example, FoHFs only capture hedge fund data for hedge funds in which they are actually invested, thus effectively forming an investable hedge fund index. Furthermore, FoHFs have access to all the (normally audited) performance data of their underlying hedge funds, overcoming the selective reporting or hindsight biases. Also, FoHFs are often invested in hedge funds that are closed to new investors, diminishing the importance of the distinction between open and closed funds. Finally, FoHFs in aggregate reflect a form of asset weighting since fund of funds allocate more of their assets to larger funds.

CHAPTER 11

Is Smaller Better in Hedge Funds?

Much ink has been spilt about the relationship between hedge fund size and performance. As the claims for the superiority of hedge fund returns come under increasing attack, the superior performance of smaller funds has become a mantra, as witnessed by the dozens of investment programs geared toward this tiny niche of the hedge fund world.

The discussion is complicated by the fact that smaller funds tend to be "emerging" or "newer managers." The two designations often overlap, although there are small funds that have been in existence long enough so they are no longer considered emerging. However, in this book, we will use the two interchangeably unless there is a reason to treat them separately. While there is no consensus on the definition of small or emerging funds, a reasonable guideline is funds with less than $300 million in assets under management and less than 36 months of history.

There are three related issues about size and performance:

- First is whether newer and smaller funds do in fact offer better performance than more established (and typically larger) funds.

- Second, even if the answer turns out to be affirmative, can investors use this information to earn a higher return than otherwise?

- Third is whether hedge funds reach a size that becomes an impediment to their performance.

POSSIBLE ADVANTAGES OF SMALLER FUNDS

A number of well-publicized recent studies point to additional returns available by investing in smaller hedge funds. Some studies indicate that smaller or emerging hedge funds outperform their larger colleagues by as much as 5% a year, at least in the first few years of their existence.

There are several arguments as to why smaller and newer hedge funds may outperform their larger kin. Smaller funds are said to be:

- More flexible and nimble in their investment approach, therefore able to quickly exploit investment opportunities, strategies, and ideas. This is also because they are not weighed down by "legacy positions."

- Better at investing in niche and newly identified markets where larger funds may not be able to invest owing to their sheer size.

- Hungrier and more motivated to produce strong performance to gain investor recognition and investments.

Possible Disadvantages of Large Funds

The flip side of the size argument is that hedge funds' returns diminish as they grow large. The arguments put forth to support this view includes:

- Managers' motivation—As hedge funds grow larger, the revenue they get from management fees becomes increasingly significant, making managers more risk-averse in order to preserve their existing assets under management. In fact, they are said to resemble mutual funds in their economic motivation. The economics of managing a hedge fund reinforces this effect because expenses of managing more assets do not increase proportionately with the growth of assets; i.e., as assets double, the added expense in managing these assets may only grow by 20%—which means that profit grows more rapidly than revenues as assets under management increase.

- Unexploited markets—Many hedge funds started by investing in a relatively unexploited market; for example, small cap stocks or emerging market debt. However, these markets can only absorb a limited amount of assets. As funds grow larger, it becomes increasingly difficult to find these niche markets, forcing funds to invest in larger, more liquid markets where it may be more difficult to generate higher returns. In fact, for the largest hedge funds, only the largest equities, fixed income or commodities markets are viable, which does not bode well for these large funds being able to find arbitrage opportunities or differentiate themselves from each other—a situation mutual fund managers know very well. While a large fund may invest in a niche market, the investment may be insignificant as a percentage of the fund's assets and, even if the investment were successful, may hardly make a dent in the fund's overall performance.

Possible Disadvantages of Smaller Funds

Small funds as a group are also said to have some negative qualities that may influence their performance:

- There is a greater risk of a small or emerging fund having problems or even going out of business as a result of operational, personnel, or performance deficiencies, or the inability to gather sufficient assets to continue the fund.

- Emerging funds are sometimes created to exploit specific opportunities or market inefficiencies. However, this opportunity may be short lived and/or limited in the amount of assets a fund can deploy.

- Emerging managers underperform larger funds following market peaks and crisis periods, for example, in 1997–1998, 2002–2004, and 2009–2010.

INCREASED SIZE OF EMERGING MANAGERS

The most important difference between emerging hedge funds is their genesis and beginning size. The "emerging manager" or "small hedge fund" categories include a wide range of funds from small one- or two-person operations managing "family and friends" assets to a billion-dollar hedge fund formed by a team of traders that have left a bank or another hedge fund. Spin-off hedge funds have been a part of the industry since the early days. In fact, the "mother" fund often provides the seed money to the spin-off. However, over the past several years, there has been a pronounced move by teams of traders leaving banks to form hedge funds, a trend spurred by the Volcker Rule, which requires banks to divest themselves of hedge funds as well as to scale back their proprietary trading operations.

This has totally changed the dynamic of emerging managers. There is little or no similarity between a hedge fund starting with $500 million or a billion in assets, an experienced management team, and a full-blown operational infrastructure and a small $25 million hedge fund with a three to five people. The current average size of a small, medium, and large fund as provided by Per-Trac is as follows:

- Small: less than $100 million AUM
- Midsize: $100 million to $500 million AUM
- Large: more than $500 million AUM

The average size of a small or emerging manager has grown dramatically over the years, so comparing emerging managers of a decade ago to those operating today is not a comparison of apples to apples, or even apples to oranges.

How Do you Invest in Emerging/Small Managers?

Several studies find a "small fund effect"—somewhat comparative to the "small cap" effect in the equities market—whereby small-er hedge fund outperform larger funds. However, these studies have not addressed the issue of how an investor can actually take advantage of this supposed small fund advantage. The PerTrac study cited above, for example, finds that small funds outperform larger funds, although with more volatility. However, the database used for their analysis was composed of 3,262 "small funds," 967 midsized funds, and 340 large funds. There is no discussion in the study of how an investor can benefit from its findings.

Even taking advantage of the "small cap" effect in the equities world is highly problematic. First, there is a limitation on how much money can flow into the purchase of their stock without making the price unrealistic. Second, for many large mutual funds, the effect of a small investment on their overall portfolio is so marginal as to make the effort unrewarding. Finally, while the small cap universe of thousands of stock may indicate the possibility of higher returns, it is impossible to find a mutual fund that actually invests in all these stocks. At best, they select a sampling hoping they gain from this small cap effect. Finally, small cap stocks are also more likely to face sharp drops in price, illiquidity issues, and even bankruptcy.

And yet small cap stocks are publicly listed and regulated. Investing in small hedge funds is even more problematic.

We need to "operationalize" the knowledge that investing in a group of 3,262 small funds will give us a higher return than investing in a group of 1,300 midsized and large funds.

The first problem is actually finding this investment universe. The analogy to small cap stocks in not valid: Small cap stocks are a defined universe that investors can actually tap. Investors can look at their SEC filings, annual reports, etc. Small cap mutual funds are able to invest in a relatively large number of these stocks.

However, many small hedge funds do not report their returns for months or years, until they have established a sufficient track record. Even then, they may not have audited results for a period of time.

Since investing is all the small funds, or even a representative group of these funds is impossible, it becomes necessary to develop a strategy for choosing a group of these funds that will provide superior performance: a task comparable to identifying the next Microsoft from the thousands of start-up high tech funds. In practice, this is beyond the abilities of the great majority of investors. The fact that any group of funds will include many that will suffer large losses or close up their shop makes this even less likely.

Furthermore, there is the practical limitation in terms of time and expense in conducting due diligence on 3,262 hedge funds, especially since these funds are likely to have a very short track record, small staff, and limited infrastructure—all factors that would require more extensive due diligence than reading an annual report or audited financial statement.

The great majority of the money flowing into hedge funds the past decade has been to the largest hedge funds. Similarly, the majority of money flowing into emerging funds has been to the larger funds. It is true that there have been a number of fund of funds aimed at investing in small and emerging managers, notably by fund of funds seeking to find a niche and directly by some large institutional investors, notably CALPERS. However, these multi-fund entities have been small and are unlikely to make a significant difference in overall hedge fund returns for most investors. At any rate, most of these funds are relatively new and we do not have enough data to gauge their success.

Finally, it is important to note that for large institutional investors with many billions of dollars in assets, any incremental gain from investing in small funds is unlikely to make a material difference in their overall performance.

Statistical Measures of Performance

This section reviews the basic statistical measures used by investors in evaluating the performance of hedge funds and other investments. It is important to understand that no one measure by itself, or even a combination of measures, provides all the information needed to evaluate investments; each measure contributes a certain amount of information, but also has its limitations. Investors typically use as many measures as possible to make their investment decisions, in addition to using nonstatistical information.

STANDARD DEVIATION OF RETURNS AS A MEASURE OF RISK

The most basic performance measure is the mean or average return, which is calculated by summing up the periodic returns and dividing the result by the number of periods.

However, modern investment theory insists that return alone may present a misleading picture of the desirability of an investment since it ignores risk. A further tenet of investment theory is that increased return can only be achieved at the price of increased risk.

One of the most commonly used measures of a fund's investment risk is the standard deviation (SD) of its returns, which is also a measure of the fund's volatility. As a general rule, all other things being equal, the lower the SD the better for an investor. The formula for SD is as follows:

SD = [Σ (Return of Fund – Mean Return)^2 ÷ (Number of Periods – 1)]

Standard deviation is a statistical calculation derived from the assumption that hedge fund returns follow a "normal distribution" or a "bell jar" pattern of returns, as shown in Figure 12–1.

The figure shows a normal distribution of a hedge fund that has a 13.3% average annual return and an SD of 20.1%, with the SD calculated using the formula above. Using the assumptions of the normal distribution, the SD is interpreted to mean that there is a 68.26% probability that the fund's return will fall within 20.1% of the mean—that is, between –6.8% (13.3 – 20.1) and 33.4% (13.3 + 20.1). Clearly this is a wide range of probable outcomes, and indicates that this fund has a high volatility.

FIGURE 12–1

Normal Distribution

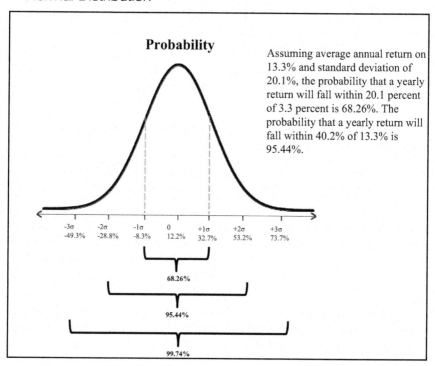

This is even more evident when we look at a two-SD measure of probable returns. Two SD, which measures the range of outcomes with a 95.44% probability, is 40.2% around the average return, which means that the return will be between –26.9% and 53.5% on any given year. Similarly, three SD is 60.3% (the SD of 20.1 times 3), which means that there is a 99.74% probability that the fund's annual returns will fall within the range of –47% to 63.3%.

A few things should be noted about the use of SD to measure a fund's performance or risk. A high SD indicates that a hedge fund is volatile; while a low SD indicates that a fund is generally consistent in producing returns close to the mean. It is important to note that SD is a statistic that measures predictability, and it does not necessarily indicate a fund's risk of losing money. A fund can have very low SD because it is losing small amounts of money on a consistent basis, or have a high standard deviation but without significant losses. With these caveats, SD is a good comparative measure available to investors.

SHARPE RATIO AND RISK-ADJUSTED RETURNS

A basic tenet in finance is the "risk-return" trade-off; that additional return on investment is only achievable by taking additional risk. One way to view this trade-off is with a risk-return graph, such as the one displayed in Figure 12–2. The most desirable investments are the ones that produce the highest return for any given level of risk.

The Sharpe ratio, one of the most widely used measures of performance for hedge funds, is a measure of the risk-return trade-off that allows for a statistical comparison between fund investments. The Sharpe ratio is a measure of the return of a hedge fund (adjusted by the risk free rate) divided by the SD of hedge fund returns.

The formula for the Sharpe ratio is very straightforward:

$$\text{Sharpe ratio} = (\text{Return}_{fund} - \text{Return}_{risk\ free}) / (\text{Volatility}_{fund})$$

Where $\text{Return}_{risk\ free}$ is equal to the prevailing market return of short-term investments, generally measured by three-month London Interbank Offered Rate or U.S. Treasury bills.

FIGURE 12-2

HFRI Index Risk Return Comparison 10-Year Annualized

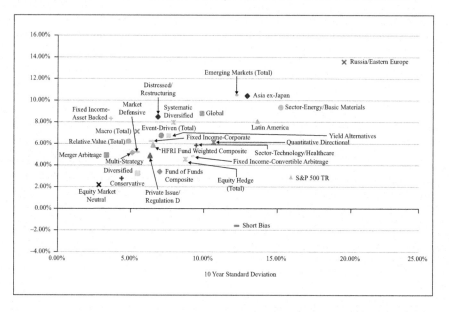

The Sharpe ratio has an appealing intuitive interpretation: the higher the Sharpe ratio, the more return is earned for each additional amount of risk. All other things being equal, a higher Sharpe ratio is preferable to a lower Sharpe ratio.

Another way to view the Sharpe ratio is as the statistical equivalent of the risk-return graph shown in Figure 12–2: Figure 12–3 shows the same risk-return graph expressed as Sharpe ratios.

SORTINO RATIO

The Sortino ratio is a variant of the Sharpe ratio. One problem with the Sharpe ratio is that its measure of volatility does not differentiate between volatility that results in a fund's returns moving up (upward or "good" volatility) and returns that are moving down (downward or "bad" volatility). Logically, there is no reason to penalize the performance of a manager for volatility that results in

FIGURE 12-3

HFRI Index Sharpe Ratio 10-Year Annualized

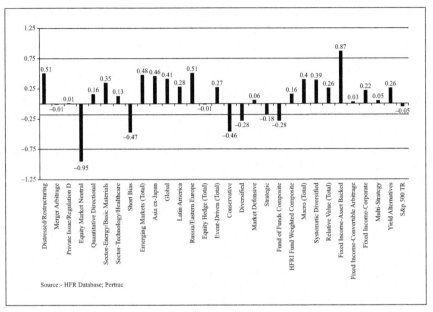

positive returns. The Sortino ratio differentiates between "good" and "bad" volatility. This differentiation of upward and downward volatility allows the calculation to provide a risk-adjusted measure of a fund's performance without penalizing it for upward price changes. The Sortino ratio is similar to the Sharpe ratio, except it uses downside deviation for the denominator instead of SD; it is calculated as follows:

$$\text{Sortino Ratio} = \frac{<R> - R_f}{\sigma_d}$$

$<R>$ = Expected Return
R_f = The Risk Free Rate of Return
σ_d = Standard Deviation of Negative Asset Returns

DRAWDOWN AND MAXIMUM DRAWDOWN

A drawdown is any losing period during a fund's investment record. The maximum drawdown is the largest decline in value from a peak to a trough in a fund's history. For example, in Figure 12–4, the HFRI Fund Weighted Composite experienced a 21.42% drawdown or decline that started in October 2007 and ended in February 2009. This is also the maximum (i.e., largest) drawdown experienced by the index during the period pictured here (i.e., December 1990 through December 2011). This drawdown took 16 months to unfold while the recovery period (i.e., the number of months until the index reached its pre-drawdown level) was 36 months. Normally an investor would prefer a recovery period with duration close to that of the drawdown period; in this case, 16 months.

The level that must be reached to recover from a drawdown is also known as the high-water mark; this level must be reached for most hedge funds before incentive pay for the manager kicks in.

FIGURE 12–4

HFRI Fund Weighted Composite Index Drawdown Analysis Since 1990

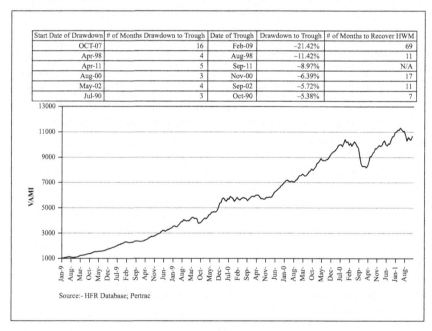

Start Date of Drawdown	# of Months Drawdown to Trough	Date of Trough	Drawdown to Trough	# of Months to Recover HWM
OCT-07	16	Feb-09	–21.42%	69
Apr-98	4	Aug-98	–11.42%	11
Apr-11	5	Sep-11	–8.97%	N/A
Aug-00	3	Nov-00	–6.39%	17
May-02	4	Sep-02	–5.72%	11
Jul-90	3	Oct-90	–5.38%	7

Source:- HFR Database; Pertrac

Investors use drawdown statistics to compare hedge funds with similar strategies to determine which fund is better able to preserve the investors assets. One of the most treacherous aspects of a drawdown is the asymmetry between the percentages of the drawdown compared with the percentage needed to recover from the drawdown. To take a simple example, a $1 million investment in the HFRI Fund Weighted Composite made in October 2007 would have been reduced by 30.58% to $694,200 by February 2009. The manager must earn a return of 44% (i.e., $305,800) to bring the investment to its original level (not counting the foregone interest that the investment could have made by placing funds in a money market account or Treasury bills).

Because hedge fund managers normally do not earn incentive fees until their fund has reached a new high-water mark (i.e., the fund has recouped the amount lost in the drawdown), they may be tempted to take excessive risks to regain the high-water mark. An alternative strategy pursued by some managers is to shutter the fund and open a new one that has no drawdown and earns incentive compensation immediately—unless, of course, the manager incurs another drawdown.

CORRELATION BETWEEN INVESTMENTS

Correlation measures the extent of linear association between the performances of two or more investments. Correlation is measured on a range from –1 to +1. A correlation value close to +1 indicates a high positive correlation, which means that the two investments will move in tandem in reaction to market movements. In general, a high correlation between hedge funds means that if one of the funds has positive returns during a certain period, it is highly probable that the other fund's returns will also be positive. If two funds have a correlation close to –1, one fund will experience positive returns during a period, while the other will sustain negative returns. If there is a correlation value of zero, the hedge funds' returns are uncorrelated and move independently.

$$\frac{\text{Covariance (Investment \#1 Returns, Investment \#2 Returns)}}{\text{StandardDev(Investment \#1 Returns)} \times \text{Standard Dev(Investment \#2 Returns)}}$$

TABLE 12–1

Correlation Between Hedge Funds and Major Asset Classes, 1990–2011

	Hedge Funds	Global Stocks	Global Bonds	Commodities
Hedge funds	1.00			
Global stocks	0.80	1.00		
Global bonds	−0.06	−0.03	1.00	
Commodities	0.41	0.33	0.00	1.00

Source: Centre for Hedge Fund Research

Investors often measure correlation to find return streams that are uncorrelated. Since diversifying investment allocations requires investing in assets that are not correlated with each other, investors find hedge funds that have low correlation with the main asset classes particularly attractive. Table 12–1, indicates that hedge funds have a very low correlation with bonds, a moderate correlation with commodities, and a relatively high correlation with stocks.

SKEWNESS AND KURTOSIS

The standard deviation and Sharpe ratio measures assume that hedge fund returns are normally distributed. In fact, they often are not. The distribution of return may be "biased" so that there is a higher probability than implied by the normal distribution that returns will be clustered to the left or right of the mean return, rather than evenly distributed around that mean. The measure of this bias is known as "skewness." As shown in Figure 12–5, a distribution of return can have a positive or negative skew, described as follows:

- *Negative skew:* The left tail is longer; the mass of the distribution is concentrated on the right of the figure. It has relatively few low values. The distribution is said to be *left-skewed, left-tailed,* or *skewed to the left.*

- *Positive skew:* The right tail is longer; the mass of the distribution is concentrated on the left of the figure. It has relatively few high values. The distribution is said to be *right-skewed, right-tailed,* or *skewed to the right.*

FIGURE 12–5

Skewness and Kurtosis

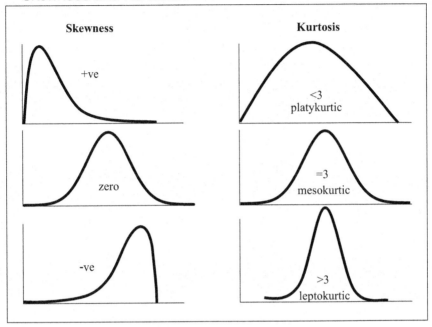

Kurtosis, another measure of the departure of a distribution of returns from the normal distribution, measures the steepness or flatness of a return distribution curve.

A normal distribution has a kurtosis of 3. A higher number indicates a higher probability of returns being concentrated near the mean, and also a higher probability of extreme returns at the negative and positive ends of the distribution curve (referred to as "fat tails"). On the other hand, lower kurtosis signifies returns are more disbursed around the mean, and that there is a lower probability of extreme movements.

Higher kurtosis, implying relatively few extreme movements, is normally preferred by investors. However, a low kurtosis, which indicates a higher frequency of extreme returns, may be desirable if combined with a right skew (i.e., that the extreme movements are most likely to be positive).

INFORMATION RATIO

Another risk-adjusted return measurement, the information ratio (IR), is the ratio of portfolio returns above the returns of a benchmark (usually an index) to the volatility of those returns. The IR measures a hedge fund manager's ability to generate excess returns relative to a benchmark and the consistency of the manager's returns. The IR is a measure of whether a manager has beaten the benchmark by a significant amount in a few months or by a small amount over many months; a higher IR implies a more consistent manager.

$$\text{Information Ratio} = \frac{(Rp - R_i)}{S_{p\text{-}i}}$$

where,

R_p = return of the portfolio
R_i = return of the index or benchmark
$S_{p\text{-}i}$ = tracking error (SD of the difference between returns of the portfolio and the returns of the index)

The IR is similar to the Sharpe ratio. However, whereas the Sharpe ratio is the "excess" return of an asset over the return of a risk free asset divided by the SD of returns, the information ratio is the "active" return (also known as alpha) to the most relevant benchmark index divided by the SD of the active return.

HEDGE FUND ALPHA AND BETA

Alpha is an outgrowth of modern portfolio theory, which separates the return of any investment into two components: beta, which is the return generated by movements in the overall markets (i.e., stock or bond markets), and alpha, which is the return above the beta returns, also known as "excess return" or "manager return."

Alpha is difficult to measure and to interpret. Ideally, a manager that shows significant alpha has a proven ability to time the market or otherwise exploit its inefficiencies. However, isolating the alpha of an investment means removing the other factors that can influence returns. These include betas, which come in many shapes and sizes and are sometimes difficult to identify, as well as random chance or luck (Figure 12–6).

Beta is typically measured as the correlation between investment returns and the movement in the major markets (stocks, bonds, commodities, etc.). A stock's beta is widely reported and used by investors. A stock with a beta of 0.50, for example, will move by 50% of the movement of the S&P 500. If the stock market moves by 10%, the stock will only move by 5%.

While beta was initially measured as sensitivity to the overall stock market, research by two University of Chicago academics—French and Fama—showed that stocks were also sensitive to (or had a beta exposure to) other factors, notably whether a stock was small cap or large cap, and whether it was a growth or value stock. This became known as the three-factor model, which dictated that these three market betas needed to be removed from the performance of a stock or portfolio of stocks before one can state that the portfolio generated alpha returns. (Then, of course, the alpha had to be shown to result for the efforts of the manager rather than random chance or luck.) Following on the work of French and Fama, the list of factors used to explain the returns of traditional invest-

FIGURE 12–6

Splitting the Components of Return

ments was expanded to include other markets such as commodities, real estate, credit spreads, emerging market debt, and many others.

Alternative Beta

Hedge fund managers often claim to generate alpha by removing the influence of the major stock and bond markets from their portfolios. However, hedge fund beta is much more complicated for three reasons: First, because hedge funds often include short positions, which is in a sense a negative beta. Second, because of the extensive use of derivatives by hedge funds. Derivatives often have a nonlinear relation to the large markets, and their beta is extremely difficult to measure. Third, hedge funds are involved in markets and pursue strategies that are not linked to the major markets. The discrete markets that are unique to hedge funds are said to comprise "alternative betas."

There is a long list of alternative betas because hedge funds are involved in so many markets and strategies. In fact, various strategies have their own unique betas. For example, the returns of M&A arbitrage hedge funds are driven by the level of M&A activity in the market; option strategies are driven by volatility in their marketplace as is convertible arbitrage (since convertibles include an option linked to a bond); and credit hedge funds' returns are based on the movement in credit spreads between various instruments.

What all this means is that before declaring that a hedge fund manager has produced alpha, an analysis needs to be performed to ensure that all possible betas have been removed from the returns.

Debate over Hedge Fund Alpha

Identifying the alpha component of a hedge fund's return has become the search for the grail in the investment world. Institutional investors especially have based their willingness to pay the hedge fund's normal two-and-twenty fees on evidence that hedge funds do provide alpha above market betas. The argument is that beta is easily available for very low fees. Stock or bond market beta, for example, can be obtained with an index mutual fund for under 1% in management fees and no incentive fee.

That hedge fund returns include a major market beta component is generally acknowledged. After all, most hedge funds invest in the same equity, fixed-income, real estate, and commodities markets as mutual funds.

It is the strategy and use of short selling and derivatives and (hopefully) manager skills that differentiate hedge funds from long-only managers. An influential study by Ibbotson and Chen, for example, finds that most hedge fund returns have significant beta to stock, bonds, and cash (short term interest rates). However, they also find that once the beta returns are removed, which they calculate at 7.63% per annum, the investor still receives an alpha of 3.01% (Table 12–2). Less appealing is that the amount of Alpha varies from strategy to strategy, with long/short equity strategies providing an annual alpha of 5.16% compared to a slim 1.17% for managed futures.

TABLE 12–2

Regression Results: Jan. 1995 – Dec. 2009*

Subcategory	Compound Annual Return	Annual Alpha	Betas (sun of betas = 1)			R^2
			Stocks	Bonds	Cash	
Convertible arbitrage	7.41%	2.79%	0.34	−0.21	0.87	0.35
Emerging market	8.81	4.66	0.65	−0.67	1.02	0.39
Equity market neutral	7.08	2.86*	0.08	0.04	0.87	0.17
Event driven	8.33	3.94*	0.31	−0.29	0.99	0.52
Fixed-income arbitrage	6.57	2.91*	0.11	−0.16	1.05	0.12
Global macro	7.67	2.54	0.16	0.26	0.58	0.09
Long¬–short equity	9.99	4.79*	0.49	−0.29	0.80	0.55
Managed futures	5.03	0.57	−0.05	0.59	0.46	0.10
Dedicated short	−0.34	1.91	−0.90	0.35	1.55	0.56
Overall equal weighted	7.70%	3.00%*	0.34	−0.21	0.87	0.48

Notes: This table reports regression results for equal-weighted indices' (live plus dead, no backfill) post-fee returns. The betas for stocks and bonds are the sums of their betas and their lagged betas.

*Significant at the 5 percent level.

CHAPTER 13

Aggregate Measures of Hedge Fund Performance

This chapter looks at various attempts to measure the performance at the aggregate level; that is the performance of all of substantially all hedge funds over time. It should be clear by now that the issue of hedge fund performance is not simple. There is no formula to help investors make decisions about which hedge fund to invest in. However, any potential investor in hedge funds needs to be well versed in at least the primary metrics of measuring hedge fund performance.

One effort to measure the aggregate performance of hedge funds is a 2012 study commissioned by the Alternative Investment Management Association and carried out by the Centre for Hedge Fund Research, Imperial College, London. The study, impartially named "The value of the hedge fund industry to investors, markets, and the broader economy," is based on monthly performance data for 3,822 "active" funds and 5,824 "inactive" funds between 1994 and 2011. As shown in Table 13–1, the study, which claims to have eliminated hindsight and survivorship bias from the data, concludes that:

- Hedge funds had higher returns than stocks, bonds, and commodities.
  - They achieved an average return of 9.07% in the period 1994–2011 after fees compared with 7.18% for stocks, 6.25% for bonds, and 7.27% for commodities.

TABLE 13-1

Statistics for Hedge Funds and Main Asset Classes,
1994-2011

Descriptive Statistics for Hedge Funds and Main Asset Classes				
	Hedge Funds	Global Stocks	Global Bonds	Commodities
Mean	9.07	7.18	6.25	7.27
Standard deviation	7.20	15.72	3.95	22.47
Sharpe ratio	0.76	0.23	0.68	0.16
Correlation Between Hedge Fund and Main Asset Classes				
	Hedge Funds	Global Stocks	Global Bonds	Commodities
Hedge funds	1.00			
Global stocks	0.80	1.00		
Global bonds	−0.06	−0.03	1.00	
Commodities	0.41	0.33	0.00	1.00

Source: Centre for Hedge Fund Research

- Hedge funds had lower volatility and risk than stocks and commodities.
  - They achieved these returns with considerably lower volatility and value-at-risk than stocks and commodities. In fact, their volatility was closer to that of bonds.
- Hedge funds were significant generators of "alpha."
  - The research also reported that hedge funds were significant generators of alpha, creating an average of 4.19% per year from 1994 to 2011.
- Investors received approximately 72% of all investment profits over this period compared with 28% for hedge fund managers.
- Hedge fund returns were relatively uncorrelated with those of stocks, bonds, and commodities (Table 13-1).

FIGURE 13-1

Hedge Fund Returns Compared to Stocks, Bonds, and
Commodities

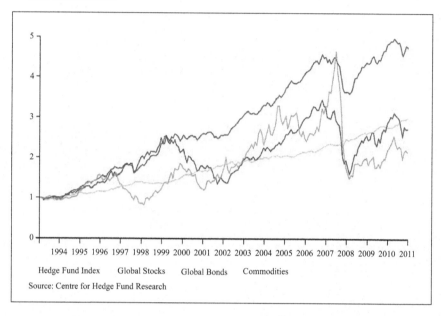

Hedge Fund Index   Global Stocks   Global Bonds   Commodities

Source: Centre for Hedge Fund Research

PERFORMANCE OF DIFFERENT HEDGE FUND STRATEGIES

Various hedge fund strategies show sharply different return and
other performance characteristics, as shown in Table 13–2. Indeed,
overall return during this time period ranged from 10.58% for equity hedge strategies to a low of 1.04% for short bias hedge funds.
Similarly, standard deviation measures differed markedly from a
low of 3.30% for market neutral to a high of 18.96% for short bias.

VARIATION IN HEDGE FUND PERFORMANCE OVER TIME

Any investment's performance will vary over time in response to
changing financial and economic conditions, business cycles, credit
market conditions, and other factors. Hedge funds are no exception. In addition, hedge fund performance has been effected by the

TABLE 13-2

Statistics for Hedge Fund Strategies: 1994–2011

	Equity Hedge	Emerging Markets	Event Driven	CTA and Macro	Relative Value	Market Neutral	Short Bias
Annualized mean	10.58	9.60	10.32	8.39	8.23	5.73	1.04
Annualized standard deviation	9.49	14.25	6.97	6.69	4.35	3.30	18.96
Annualized Sharpe ratio	0.74	0.42	0.97	0.72	1.06	0.65	−0.13

changes in the industry over time: changes in the number of hedge funds, the scale of the industry; strategies and instruments utilized; and the markets favored by hedge fund managers.

Table 13–3, which shows hedge fund performance—both in aggregate and by major strategies—for various periods since 1990 until 2011, clearly indicates the difference in performance for different time periods. The aggregate HFRI Fund Weighted Composite index, for example has an annual average return of 11.24% over the entire time period, but only 2.27% over the past five years and 5.80% in the past decade.

A similar situation is found when we look at individual strategies. Equity hedge, the largest hedge fund strategy, returned 12.89% over the entire 1990–2011 time period, but only 0.45% over the past five years and 4.57% over the past decade. Global macro, similarly, went from 12.7% for the entire time period to 4.79% for the past five years.

It is interesting to note that the stock market, as measured by the S&P 500, showed a similar sharp decline in returns over the time period, from 8.22% for the entire period to 2.92% for the past decade and a *negative* 0.25% over the past five years. Only bonds, whose returns have been helped by a general decline in interest rates over the past two decades, have maintained an even return keel, returning 8.03%, 6.09%, and 6.97% in the three periods.

TABLE 13–3

Hedge Fund Returns by Strategy and Major Asset Classes: 2011

Index	12-Month		3-Year Annualized		5-Year Annualized		10-Year Annualized		1990–2011	
	Return	SD	Return	SD	Return	SD	Return	SD	Return	SD
HFRI total	(5.02)	6.48	7.90	6.79	2.27	7.83	5.89	6.52	11.24	7.08
HFRI equity hedge	(8.25)	9.92	8.07	9.71	0.45	10.72	4.57	8.74	12.89	9.31
HFRI event-driven	(2.84)	7.08	10.77	6.81	2.53	8.15	6.82	7.08	11.70	6.95
HFRI macro	(9.73)	4.86	2.75	5.30	4.79	5.49	7.13	5.33	12.7	7.66
HFRI relative value	0.51	3.62	12.11	4.39	4.70	6.58	6.23	4.85	10.25	4.46
S&P 500	2.09	15.93	14.11	18.95	(0.25)	18.87	2.92	15.91	8.22	15.21
Aggregate bond	9.24	3.05	7.00	3.67	6.97	4.78	6.29	4.88	8.03	4.94
3-Month LIBOR	0.35	0.03	0.45	0.08	1.89	0.57	2.32	0.52	4.05	0.64

Hedge Fund Performance in Good and Bad Times

Hedge funds are described as "absolute return" vehicles that are meant to provide positive returns under all market conditions as well as provide protection against down markets. As Figure 13–2 shows, however, hedge funds have not been able to deliver this performance, especially during two major financial crises: the 1998 Asian/Russian crisis and the 2007–2008 credit crisis. Hedge funds lost significant amounts during both periods both in aggregate and for most strategies (Figure 13–2).

Between 2007 and 2011, for example, hedge funds in aggregate returned an average of 2.6% a year, less than the return on 10-year U.S. Treasury bonds during the same period. These disappointing results have led to an accelerating trend in the investment world—which we discuss later in the context of hedge funds in investors' portfolios: an increased scrutiny of hedge fund performance to determine if hedge funds do indeed offer absolute returns.

ARE HEDGE FUND RETURNS ALPHA OR A RISK PREMIUM?

Another supposed benefit of hedge funds over traditional investments in their ability to generate "alpha," of a premium return over that of traditional markets. This "alpha" is then considered to be a result of superior manager skills in outperforming the marketplace.

A recent academic study evaluated the extent to which hedge fund alpha (to the extent that it exists) is indeed a result of manager skill or instead a disguised form of premium given to investors because hedge funds are more susceptible to extreme losses (or "tail risk") during crisis times. The analysis found two results that may cast doubt on the traditional interpretation of hedge fund alpha. First, the study showed that hedge funds whose returns suffered the most during the 1998 crisis were also the ones that suffered the most during the 2007 credit crisis. A second finding was that the hedge funds with the largest losses during crises earned an average of 6% higher return over the 1998–2010 period than hedge funds that did not suffer as badly during the crisis periods.

The authors' conclusion is that the higher return earned by these funds was not really alpha, but a disguised form of disaster

FIGURE 13-2

HFRI Hedge Fund Index Quarterly Returns

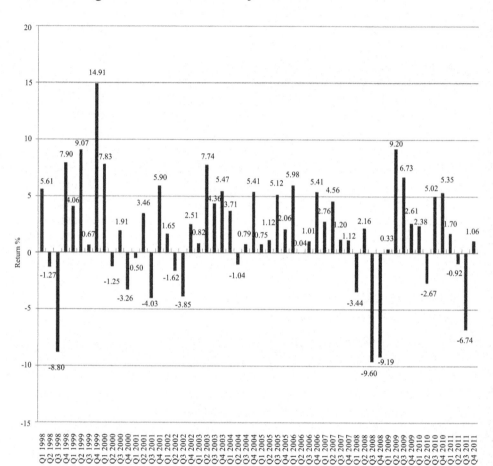

Source:- HFR Database; Pertrac

insurance where investors earned a 6% premium over the 1998–2010 because they suffered the most during the 1998 and 2007 financial crises.

Correlation Between Hedge Fund Strategies and Market Indices

The third leg of portfolio management (in addition to risk and return) is the correlation between the assets that are included in the portfolio. Diversification of portfolios is associated with lower portfolio risk, and is therefore desirable for investors. Tables 13–4 and 13–5 show that hedge fund strategies tend to have relatively high correlations with the stock markets (measured here by the MSCI World Index). However, they also have very low correlation with bond markets, and may therefore be useful especially in diversifying bond investments.

Also notable is the relatively low correlation of macro strategies with the major markets and other hedge fund strategies. Finally, it is noteworthy that all hedge funds' correlations, with the major markets and with each other, increased during the recent credit crisis, reinforcing the observations that markets tend to move together during times of market turmoil.

Hedge Fund Performance as a Moving Target

The definition or benchmarks of hedge fund performance has changed over the past 20 years along with the changing hedge fund industry and the economic environment. There are at least four distinct periods where different measures of performance held sway. The following are obviously generalizations, but I believe they are valid in a broad sense:

Period I: 1980s until mid-1990; investors used high returns as the key benchmark of hedge fund performance. Global macro funds such as Long-Term Capital Management (LTCM) and Soros were examples of success in this period.

Phase II: 1990 until mid-2000s; absolute returns were the key benchmark as hedge funds stemmed losses during the sharp market downturns in 1998 (Russian default; LTCM) and 2001 (Internet bubble bursts; 9/11), at least compared to stock market declines

Table 13–4

Correlation Matrix (January 1998 to December 2011)

	Barclays Aggregate Bond Index	MSCI World (MXWO Index)	HFRI Fund Weighted Composite Index	HFRX Global Hedge Fund Index	HFRI Equity Hedge (Total) Index	HFRI Event-Driven (Total) Index	HFRI Macro (Total) Index	HFRI Relative Value (Total) Index	HFRI Fund of Funds Composite Index
Barclays aggregate bond index	1.00								
MSCI world	-0.05	1.00							
HFRI fund weighted composite index	-0.06	0.82	1.00						
HFRX global hedge fund index	0.08	0.62	0.81	1.00					
HFRI equity hedge (total) index	-0.06	0.83	0.98	0.83	1.00				
HFRI event-driven (total) index	-0.09	0.79	0.93	0.78	0.89	1.00			
HFRI macro (total) index	0.08	0.35	0.65	0.62	0.59	0.51	1.00		
HFRI relative value (total) index	0.06	0.64	0.76	0.71	0.72	0.82	0.32	1.00	
HFRI fund of funds composite index	-0.06	0.67	0.94	0.84	0.89	0.87	0.69	0.78	1.00

Source: PerTrac

Table 13-5

Correlation Matrix (January 2007 to December 2011)

	Barclays Aggregate Bond Index	MSCI WORLD (MXWO Index)	HFRI Fund Weighted Composite Index	HFRX Global Hedge Fund Index	HFRI Equity Hedge (Total) Index	HFRI Event-Driven (Total) Index	HFRI Macro (Total) Index	HFRI Relative Value (Total) Index	HFRI Fund of Funds Composite Index
Barclays aggregate bond Index	1.00								
MSCI WORLD (MXWO index)	0.15	1.00							
HFRI fund weighted composite index	0.05	0.89	1.00						
HFRX global hedge fund index	0.07	0.78	0.94	1.00					
HFRI equity hedge (total) index	0.03	0.92	0.99	0.90	1.00				
HFRI event-driven (total) index	0.01	0.87	0.96	0.94	0.95	1.00			
HFRI macro (total) index	0.00	0.31	0.52	0.47	0.44	0.34	1.00		
HFRI relative value (total) index	0.14	0.77	0.89	0.94	0.88	0.94	0.23	1.00	
HFRI fund of funds composite index	0.01	0.77	0.96	0.96	0.93	0.93	0.54	0.90	1.00

Source: PerTrac

The idea here is straightforward: that hedge funds, with their ability to short markets and find excess returns, would turn in positive performance even during periods of sharp downturn in the major (stock, bond, commodities, currencies) markets.

Period III: mid-2000s to 2007; risk-adjusted return; alpha. One of the supposed benefits of hedge fund investing is their ability to protect investors during a sharp market downturn or extremely high market volatility. This turns out to be true for three of the two extreme periods of the past two decades; the Russian debt crisis and collapse of LTCM (1998–1999), and the "high tech bubble" collapse and 9/11 (2001–2003). However, it failed miserably in the "credit crisis" of 2007–2009.

Period IV: 2008–present; portfolio diversifier. The disappointing results of most hedge fund strategies during and following the credit crisis have undermined some their previous alleged performance benefits, including absolute return, alpha, and downside protection. As a result, the strongest claim for hedge fund performance today is perhaps its role in providing diversification in traditional investment portfolios, and thus reducing portfolio risk. We will return to this theme in the discussion of hedge fund in investors' portfolios.

FROM ALPHA TO SMART BETA

The following tongue-in-cheek "letter" from a hedge fund to an investor, published in the *Economist* magazine on February 8, 2012, captures the changing nature of hedge fund performance measures and, unfortunately, also captures the cynicism with which some hedge funds have been able to change their "objectives" with changing times.

"The Lexicon of Hedge Funds: From Alpha to Smart Beta"

Dear Investor,

. . . Zilch Capital used to refer to itself as a "hedge fund" but 2008 made it embarrassingly clear we didn't know how to hedge . . . So like many others, we have embraced the title of "alternative asset manager". . .

We know we used to promise "absolute returns" (i.e., that you would make money regardless of market conditions) but this pledge has proved impossible to honour. Instead we're going to give you "risk-adjusted" returns or, failing that, "relative" returns . . .

It is also time to move on from the concept of delivering "alpha . . . ," we have decided that we're actually much better at giving you "smart beta." . . .

Some parts of the lexicon will not see style drift. We are still trying to keep alive "two and twenty," the industry's shorthand for 2% management fees and 20% performance fees. It is, we're sure you'll agree, important to keep up some traditions. Thank you for your continued partnership.

Zilch Capital

Hedge Fund Returns from the Investors' Viewpoint

This chapter examines three important aspects of hedge fund performance that directly address the experience of hedge fund investors. First, we examine the dispersion of hedge fund returns around the average. Second, we examine the persistence of hedge fund returns. Both factors need to be taken into account by investors in selecting hedge funds. Finally, the book's section on performance ends with an attempt to analyze hedge fund returns from an average hedge fund investor's perspective.

DISPERSION OF HEDGE FUND RETURNS

The hedge fund indices that are most commonly used to illustrate hedge fund performance provide average returns for all the funds in a specific series designated by an index provider. However, hedge fund returns are widely dispersed around that average, which means that an investor's hedge fund returns will be highly dependent on selecting managers that are in the top grouping.

The dispersion of hedge fund returns is much greater than is true for mutual funds. Figure 14–1 shows the performance of the top and bottom 20% of hedge fund managers between 2000 and 2009. Hedge funds in the top decile provided an average annual return of 42.61% and a cumulative return of 421.87% over the decade, while those in the bottom decile

FIGURE 14-1

Average Return of Top Quintile Funds versus Bottom Quintile Funds

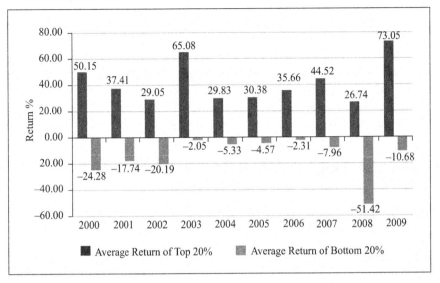

provided an average annual return of *negative* 14.7% a year and a cumulative *loss* of 147%. Clearly, an investor's experience will be profoundly different depending on specific hedge funds in his or her portfolio.

PERSISTENCE OF HEDGE FUND RETURNS

This brings up a related issue: To what extent can an investor use historical performance of individual managers as a predictor of future performance? In the investment jargon, this is known as the "persistence" of hedge fund performance. For example, would a portfolio comprising hedge funds selected from the top quintile from Figure 14–1 continue to do well in the future?

Unfortunately, there is no definitive answer to this question, despite considerable research. The same difficulty exists in finding whether or not there is persistence in the returns of mutual fund managers. The issue is complicated because persistent returns (i.e., a hedge fund that shows continuous positive returns) may be caused by temporary factors and even from sheer luck. For example, a fixed income hedge fund may perform well for a long period of time because of a sustained trend in interest rates, but perform poorly when the trend reverses. The only way to gauge whether the fund's performance was caused by skill in timing the market or by luck is to monitor its performance over several interest rate cycles.

To the extent that there is evidence available, it points to a lack of positive persistence among most hedge funds. In other words, a period of positive performance for most hedge funds is not necessarily followed by another positive performance period. In fact, the evidence is stronger for the existence of negative persistence , meaning that hedge funds that perform below their peers are likely to continue to underperform in the future.

MOMENTUM INVESTING MEETS MEAN REVERTING HEDGE FUNDS

There is strong evidence that hedge fund investors, along with mutual fund investors, have a tendency to invest in funds that have done well in the recent past on the assumption that they will continue to do well in the future. This is known as "momentum investing" or "chasing returns" or, in a less favorable characterization, following a "herd mentality."

If, as we indicated above, superior performance does not persist, momentum investing is bound to fail as a strategy. Matters may be worst yet: there is evidence that hedge fund returns are "mean reverting," which means that a fund's overperformance during one period is likely to be followed by an underperformance in the subsequent period.

When we combine the two notions—that investors tend to follow momentum and hedge funds tend to be mean reverting—the result is that investors pile money into a hedge fund when it has done well and is about to revert to mean (i.e., underperform and possibly lose money).

Needless to say, this is a general analysis and does not preclude individual investors identifying true positive persistence or hedge funds displaying this characteristic. However, in the aggregate, it does make sense and explains some of the results reported below indicating that the average hedge fund investor has not fared well over time.

HEDGE FUND RETURNS FROM THE INVESTORS' VIEWPOINT

A recent analysis by Simon Lack, formerly a managing director at J.P. Morgan, has created a stir in the hedge fund industry by claiming that investors as a whole have actually lost money over the past 16 years in their hedge fund investments, while hedge fund managers have walked off with the great majority of any hedge fund returns. While Lack's methodology has been questioned and criticized, his analysis brings up important issues for investors.

Lack's analysis is reminiscent of the conclusions reached by Fred Schwed, Jr., famous in his classic book, *Where Are the Customers' Yachts? or A Good Hard Look at Wall Street*, originally published in 1940. Lack makes the similar point that while there are many individuals who became extremely wealthy by managing hedge funds, one would be hard put to find a comparable number of individuals who became extremely wealthy by investing in hedge funds.

Lack's analysis is relatively straightforward. He starts with the HFR Global Hedge Fund Index (the HFRX), an asset-weighted index comprising thousands of hedge funds. The reason for choosing this index is described by Lack as follows:

> . . . In assessing how the industry has done, what seems absolutely clear is that you have to use an index that reflects the experience of the average investor. While individual hedge investors may have portfolios of hedge funds that are equally weighted so as to provide better diversification, clearly the investors in aggregate are more heavily invested in the larger funds. Calculating industry returns therefore requires using an asset-weighted index (just as the S&P500 Index is market-cap weighted (p. 6).)

As Lack notes, there is a fundamental problem with the standard formula for calculating hedge fund returns used by most of the hedge fund indices. Known as "time weighted returns," this method merely takes annual returns of all the hedge funds in a given database and averages the funds' annual returns, assigning an equal weight to each hedge fund no matter how large or small. An example shows how misleading this calculation can be. Assuming an investor that invests $1 million in a hedge fund that achieves a

50% gain during the first year, leaving the investor with a profit of $500,000. On the basis of the success, and assuming the manager will continue to perform well, the investor placed another $1 million at the start of the second year, bringing the total assets in his account to $2.5 million.

However, the manager hits a rough patch in the second year and loses 40% of the hedge fund's assets, bringing the investor's assets down to $1.5 million. The investor has thus lost $500,000 (or 25%) of his out-of-pocket $2 million investment. From the hedge fund manager's viewpoint, however, and the way he will report the fund's "performance," the fund had an average annual return over two years of +5%. The simple example clearly shows the difference between the time-weighted return method, which shows an average annual gain of +5%, and the investor's actual return of –25%, a whopping 30% difference between reported performance and the investor's actual investment experience.

Of course, the situation is even worse than this example shows once we include the manager's fees. Assuming a standard two-and-twenty fees structure, the manager took a management fee of $20,000 and a performance fee of $100,000 in the fund's first year, which means that the fund starts year 2 with $2.38 million, which declines to $1.428 million owing to the fund's 40% loss. To add insult to injury, the fund's manager will charge an additional $47,600 in management fees for year 2 (2% of $2.38 million), bringing the investor's assets down to $1.38 million and bringing the loss on his investment to 31% or 36% below the fund's reported +5% performance.

Lack then proceeds to measure the hedge fund industry's performance from the investors' viewpoint (i.e., their actual investment experience—negative 31% or a loss of $620,000 in our example) compared with the reported performance of the industry (+5% in our example) and compared with the compensation earned by the hedge fund manager ($197,600 in our example). The results are presented in Table 14–1.

Lack finds that in total, hedge funds had total profits of $449 billion between 1998 and 2010, a reported annual return of 7.3%, and a cumulative return of 94.9%; a near doubling of investors' money. However, he finds that $379 billion (or 84%) went to hedge fund managers as fees while only 16% ($70 billion) wound up with investors, making their real return a tiny fraction of the reported performance, and well behind returns in stocks or bonds.

TABLE 14-1

Hedge Fund Performance and Compensation

Year	Average AUM (BNs)	HFRX	Real Investor Profits (BNs)	Estimated Total Fees (BNs)	Fees as Percentage of AUM	Total Profits	Industry Share of Total Profits
1998	$142	12.9%	$10	$7	5%	$17	40%
1999	$189	26.7%	$36	$14	9%	$51	28%
2000	$237	14.3%	$17	$12	6%	$29	41%
2001	$322	8.7%	$13	$12	4%	$25	47%
2002	$505	4.7%	$12	$13	3%	$26	51%
2003	$826	13.4%	$82	$36	5%	$118	30%
2004	$1,229	2.7%	$14	$27	3%	$42	66%
2005	$1,361	2.7%	-$6	$35	3%	$29	119%
2006	$1,713	9.3%	$67	$66	4%	$133	50%
2007	$2,137	4.2%	–$11	$59	3%	$48	122%
2008	$1,458	–23.3%	–$448	$36	2%	–$412	NM
2009	$1,554	13.4%	$200	$30	2%	$230	13%
2010	$1,694	5.2%	$83	$32	2%	$115	28%
			$70	$379		$449	84%

Source: Simon Lack, *The Hedge Fund Mirage: The Illusion of Big Money and Why It's too Good to Be True*. Hoboken, NJ: John Wiley & Sons, Inc. 2012. Reprinted by permission.

PART FIVE

Hedge Fund Strategies

CHAPTER 15

Overview of Hedge Fund Strategies

The following chapters will describe the myriad strategies pursued by hedge funds. Each strategy is described in detail, along with its performance and the "drivers" or factors that explain the strategy's risk and return during different time periods and under various market conditions.

CLASSIFYING HEDGE FUNDS

There are a number of classification schemes that attempt to place hedge funds into useful categories for analysis. Arguably the most commonly used category scheme is that of Hedge Fund Research (HFR). Since we use HFR's database for much of our analysis of hedge fund performance, it makes sense to reproduce its strategy categories in Figures 15–1 and 15–2. Each of the major categories are described in the sections below.

Distribution of Hedge Fund Strategies

Figures 15–3 and 15–4 show the evolution of the distribution of hedge fund strategies by asset size between 1990 and 2011. The changes during this period are striking. The dominant strategy

FIGURE 15–1

HFR Strategy Classification

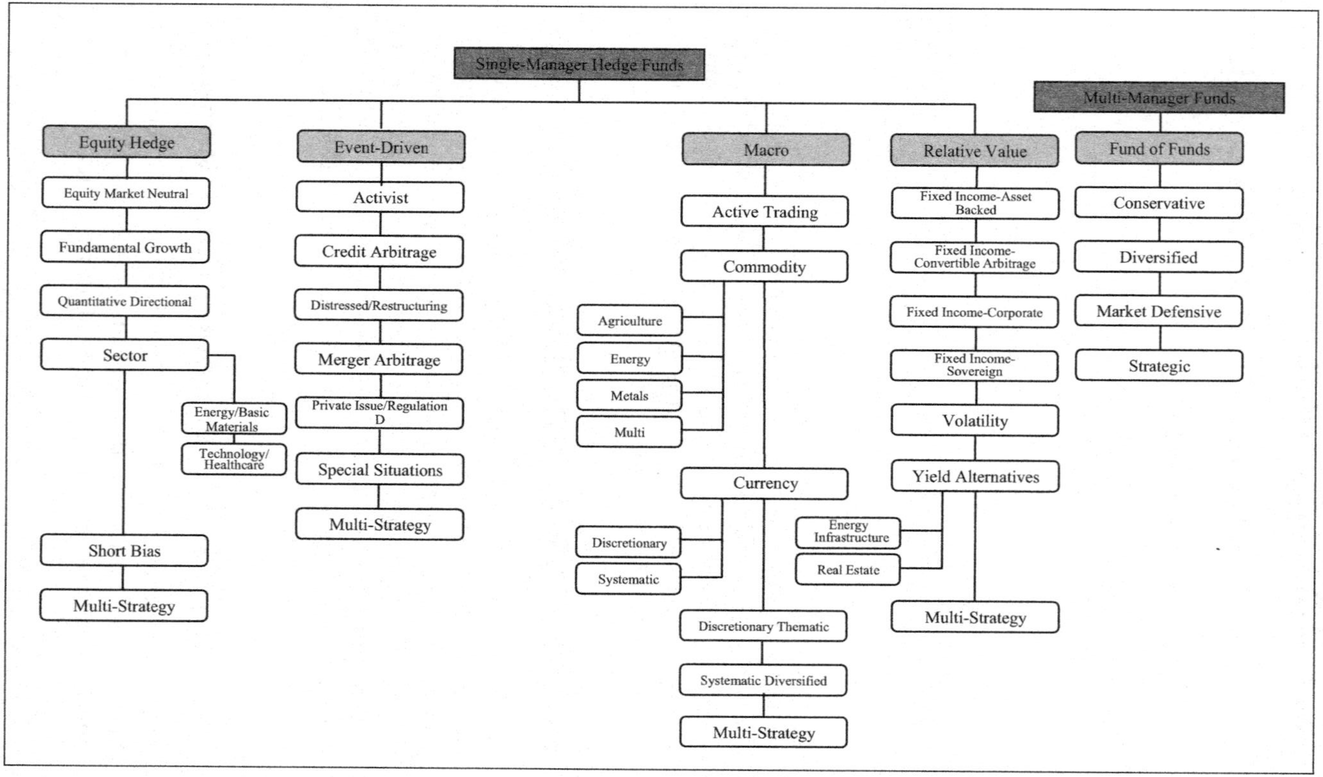

FIGURE 15-2

Hedge Fund Regions of Focus

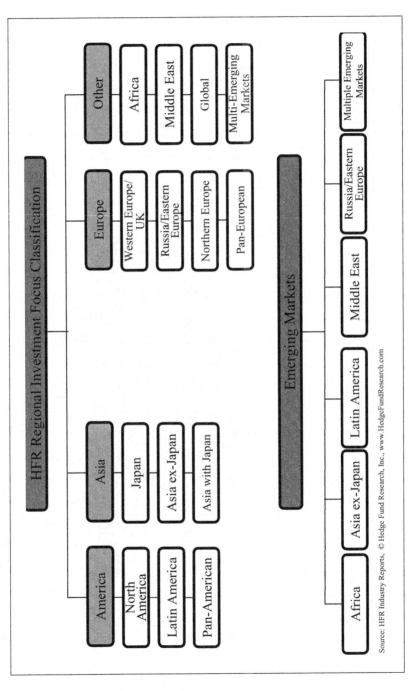

Source: HFR Industry Reports, © Hedge Fund Research, Inc., www.HedgeFundResearch.com

FIGURE 15-3

Asset Distribution by Strategy—1990

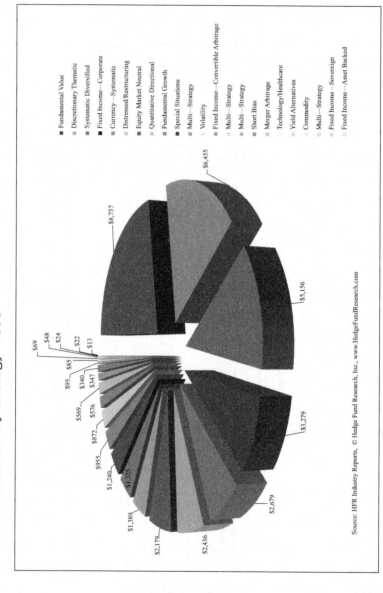

Souce: HFR Industry Reports, © Hedge Fund Research, Inc., www.HedgeFundResearch.com

FIGURE 15-4

Asset Distribution by Strategy—2011

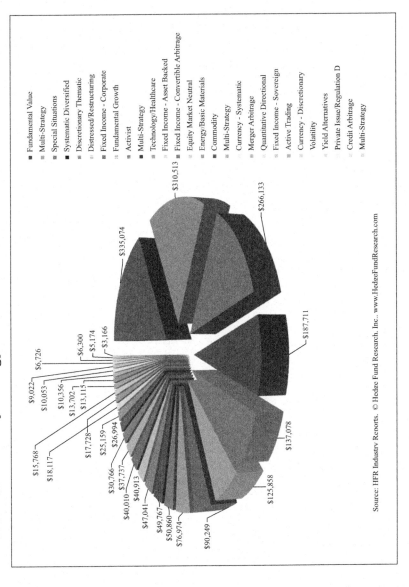

- Fundamental Value
- Multi-Strategy
- Special Situations
- Systematic Diversified
- Discretionary Thematic
- Distressed/Restructuring
- Fixed Income - Corporate
- Fundamental Growth
- Activist
- Multi-Strategy
- Technology/Healthcare
- Fixed Income - Asset Backed
- Fixed Income - Convertible Arbitrage
- Equity Market Neutral
- Energy/Basic Materials
- Commodity
- Multi-Strategy
- Currency - Systematic
- Merger Arbitrage
- Quantitative Directional
- Fixed Income - Sovereign
- Active Trading
- Currency - Discretionary
- Volatility
- Yield Alternatives
- Private Issue/Regulation D
- Credit Arbitrage
- Multi-Strategy

$310,513
$335,074
$266,133
$187,711
$137,078
$125,858
$90,249
$76,974
$50,860
$49,767
$47,041
$40,913
$40,010
$37,737
$30,766
$26,994
$25,159
$17,728
$18,117
$15,768
$13,115
$13,702
$10,356
$10,053
$9,022
$6,726
$6,300
$5,174
$3,166

Source: HFR Industry Reports. © Hedge Fund Research, Inc.. www.HedgeFundResearch.com

in 1990 was global macro, accounting for nearly 40% of the industry's assets under management. By 2011, equity strategies were the largest category, followed by relative value, which also includes equity strategies. Also worth noting is the proliferation of strategies in the intervening years, including energy/basic materials, credit arbitrage, currency—systematic, special situations, active trading, and activist.

CHAPTER 16

Equity Hedge Strategies

Equity strategies account for over one-third of all the assets managed by hedge funds, more than any other strategy. Hedge funds in this group trade a wide range of instruments—individual stocks, stock market indices, and equity derivatives—with the common feature that they are all equity based. The major strategies in this group are equity long/short, equity market neutral, and short-biased strategies.

A common feature of these strategies is their correlation to the stock market. Most of these strategies focus either on taking long positions in undervalued stocks, short positions in overvalued stocks, or a combination of the two. While hedge fund managers are adroit at taking steps to mitigate market risk by portfolio diversification, derivatives, and shorting, there are limitations. As a result, every strategy in this group—with the possible exception of equity market neutral—contains a significant amount of risk from fluctuations in stock market prices and volatility, as evidenced by the high correlation of these strategies with equity market factors.

EQUITY LONG/SHORT

Equity long/short managers structure their portfolios around a core group of long equity positions, which are combined with short sales of individual stocks and/or short positions in stock index options or futures. Long/short hedge funds tend to be net long (meaning that their portfolios have a positive exposure to the stock markets) under the assumption that stocks increase in value over time.

Long/short equity managers use one of two major approaches in making their portfolio selection: top down and bottom up. In reality, most hedge funds use a blend of the two styles, but do tend to favor one or the other.

Top down starts with one or more investment theses—for example, that global economic growth will slow—and then chooses stocks that will be most affected by this view. Bottom up starts with the selection of stocks that the manager feels are undervalued (for long positions) or overvalued (for short positions) based on their intrinsic characteristics. The bottom up approach is similar to that used by mutual fund managers. However, while mutual fund managers merely fail to include overvalued stocks in their portfolio, hedge fund managers will use them to create short positions.

Characteristics of Long/Short Equity Funds

Again, in broad-brush strokes, long/short equity funds differ from each other in a number of ways, including:

Quantitative vs. qualitative analysis
Hedge funds differ in the extent to which they rely on quantitative techniques in selecting stocks to purchase or short. Quantitative long/short hedge fund managers evaluate and select stocks using quantitative measures to identify overvalued or undervalued stocks. These measures may include price to earnings, price to book value, return on equity, free cash flow, dividend yield, sales growth, etc. While qualitative approaches to stock selection may use the statistical tools described above, they also incorporate such factors as a company's strategic plan, technology, competitor information, economic environment, etc. These managers typically meet with company managers, competitors, vendors, and service providers during the stock selection process.

Investment universe
Long/short equity hedge funds differ by the emphasis they place on particular sectors, countries, and regions. Common sector

strategies include healthcare, technology, financial service, and natural resources. Most country funds focus on the largest and most liquid stock markets, including the United States, Japan, and the United Kingdom. However, there are many niche funds that focus on emerging market stocks, especially those of the so-called BRIC countries (Brazil, Russia, India, and China). Europe and Asia are the most common focus of regional funds. The number of hedge funds that invest in Asian stocks, many of them based in Hong Kong, Singapore, and, increasingly, Shanghai, has been growing rapidly in keeping with Asia's growing economic importance.

Funds that invest in smaller markets, especially emerging markets, face a number of unique issues. These markets tend to be relatively illiquid, which makes getting in and out of positions difficult. The markets are often dominated by a small number of stocks. Transparency is also an issue, especially if accounting standards differ from the international norm. Finally, shorting stocks or even stock indices may be extremely difficult or nearly impossible. These funds therefore tend to have a significant long bias and their performance is very sensitive to stock market movements.

Investment style

Investment style refers to the extent that a hedge fund is focused on small versus large cap and growth versus value stocks. Value managers, for example, look for stocks that trade a low price relative to their fundamentals, betting that they will outperform stocks that trade at high prices relative to fundamentals. Value stocks tend to be those of established companies in relatively mature industries such as consumer goods or healthcare. Growth managers will accept weak fundamentals (i.e., low profits) if they feel the stock price will appreciate over time. The classic example here is high technology stocks that may not show a profit for years but whose stock price may appreciate quickly. Experts debate the relative attractiveness of growth versus value stocks. However, the real issue may be a matter of timing: growth stocks tend to do especially well during stock market rallies and/or bubbles, but are also vulnerable to sharp declines. Value stocks often pay dividends, which can be reinvested by shareholders. Over time, dividends are a significant source of income to investors.

Another investment style is the extent to which a hedge fund is focused on micro-, small-, medium-, and/or large-cap stocks. There are distinct advantages and disadvantages to each. Large-cap stocks are highly liquid and can absorb the growing assets of hedge funds. However, they are also widely followed and traded by investors, which makes it difficult for any one investor to gain an information advantage over others. Small- and medium-cap stocks may offer higher returns than large-cap stocks. However, this comes at the expense of potential liquidity constraints and, perhaps more important, limitation on the amount that can be invested by hedge funds.

Portfolio turnover

Hedge funds vary in how often they trade their positions. Statistical arbitrage funds may only hold a stock for seconds and high-frequency funds may do thousands of trades in split seconds, while value managers may hold a stock for months; however, most hedge funds' average position is weeks. The hedge fund's investment approach determines the frequency of trading. Managers that trade frequently are looking to take advantage of price trends in the marketplace or surprises such as unexpected earning announcements. Slow turnover hedge funds are more focused on selecting portfolios of overvalued and undervalued stocks, which may take months to reach their price objective.

Use of derivatives and leverage

Funds vary widely in their use of derivatives and leverage. The Federal Reserve, via Regulation T, limits the leverage of purchasing individual stocks since 50% of the stock price needs to be kept as margin. However, there is no regulatory limit on leverage gained through derivatives, including the use of futures and options on stock market indices, total return swaps linked to stock market indices, and options on individual stocks. Some hedge funds are prolific in their use of options and futures strategies, including the sale of options.

A key difference between hedge funds is the manner in which they establish their short positions, with some funds relying largely or exclusively on short sale of individual stocks while others use futures and options on stock market indices, such as the S&P 500 or

NASDAQ. The advantage of the latter approach is that these derivatives are highly liquid. However, they do not allow hedge funds to take advantage of a decline in the price of an individual stock. Some derivatives allow managers to short sectors of the stock market such as health care or high tech.

Net and gross market exposure

Net and gross market exposures are measures of the extent to which a hedge fund is exposed to the movement of the overall stock market and to individual stocks. The gross market exposure of a fund is the sum of both its long and short positions, while the net market exposure is the long position minus the short position. For example, a fund with $10 million in long position and $5 million in short positions would have a gross market exposure of $15 million and a net market exposure of $5 million.

Both the net exposure and the gross exposure numbers are important. Net exposure reflects the extent of a manager's exposure to overall up or down market movements. In the example above, the net market exposure of $5 million, which is the unhedged exposure to market movement, is derived from netting out the long and short positions. Hedge funds that choose to have significant net exposures are taking a directional view of the market, also referred to as market timing, a difficult and risky strategy. For example, managers that feel the stock market has been oversold and is due for a rebound would increase their net long exposure.

Gross exposure gives an indication of the degree of stock-specific risk the manager is undertaking. For example, take two managers (manager A and manager B) with the same stock holdings and the same net exposure of zero. Now assume that manager A has gross exposure of $15 million while manager B has a gross exposure of $5 million. Because manager A has $15 million worth of stocks in his or her portfolio while manager B only has $5 million, manager A has $10 million more exposure to stock-specific movements. In general, quantitative managers (e.g., statistical arbitrage funds) tend to have relatively high gross exposures. Hedge funds that have relatively large gross exposures are looking to profit from stock selection. If a manager feels that they have a method that is effective in selecting overvalued and undervalued stocks, then having a larger position in stocks makes sense. It is important to point out, however, that exposure to multiple individual stocks is generally less of a risk than exposure to the overall stock market.

Stock Selection Methods

There are numerous approaches to the selection of stocks. Here we can only touch on some of the major approaches.

Balance sheet models

A popular selection method involves an analysis of a stock's "price-to-book (P/B) ratio," which compares the stock market's valuation of a company to the company's value as based on its assets and liabilities. The ratio is calculated by dividing the current closing price of the stock by the latest quarter's book value per share:

$$P/B \text{ ratio} = \frac{\text{Stock price}}{\text{Total assets} - \text{Intangible assets and liabilities}}$$

A lower P/B ratio could mean that the stock is undervalued. In theory, the market is valuing the company at less than its sale value. However, it could also mean that something is fundamentally wrong with the company. As with most ratios, this ratio varies by industry and by overall market conditions.

Dividend discount models

The dividend discount model (DDM) values the price of stocks that pay dividends by using predicted dividends and discounting them back to their present value; much the same manner in which the price of bonds is determined. The idea is that if the value obtained from the DDM is higher than what the shares are currently trading at, the stock is undervalued and should be purchased. The value of a stock is calculated as follows:

$$\text{Value of stock} = \frac{\text{Dividend per share}}{\text{Discount rate} - \text{growth rate}}$$

Price-to-earnings ratios

Also known as price multiple or earnings multiple, the price-to-earnings (P/E) ratio is a valuation of a company's current share price compared with its per-share earnings. P/E is calculated as market value per share/earnings per share. For example, a company trading at $40 a share with earnings over the last 12 months of $2.00 per share would have a P/E ratio of 20 ($40/$2). In general, a high P/E suggests that investors are expecting higher earnings growth in the future. The P/E is sometimes referred to as the "multiple," because it shows how much investors are willing to pay per dollar of earnings.

Free cash flow approach

Free cash flow (FCF), which is calculated as operating cash flow minus capital expenditures, represents the cash that a company is able to generate after laying out the money required maintaining or expanding its asset base. It is calculated as follows:

$$\text{EBIDTA } (1 - \text{Tax rate}) + \text{Depreciation and amortization} - \text{Change in net working capital} - \text{Capital expenditure}$$

Where EBIDTA is "Earnings before Interest, Taxes, Depreciation, and Amortization." Some managers believe that investors focus myopically on earnings while ignoring the "real" cash that a firm generates. However, earnings are influenced by accounting treatment, but it is tougher to manipulate cash flow. For this reason, these investors believe that FCF gives a clearer view of a company's ability to generate cash (and thus, eventually dividends and profits).

Capturing equity risk premium

The equity risk premium is the excess return of an individual stock or the overall stock market above the risk-free interest rate. This excess return compensates investors for taking on the relatively higher risk of the equity market. The size of the equity risk premium varies dramatically over time (see Figure 16–1) and provides a signal to some investors to purchase stocks when the risk premium is low and sell when it is high.

Earnings yield of S&P 500 versus 10-year Treasury bond yield

Earnings yield (EY) is the inverse of the P/E ratio and is calculated as the earnings of a company divided by its market price. EY is the

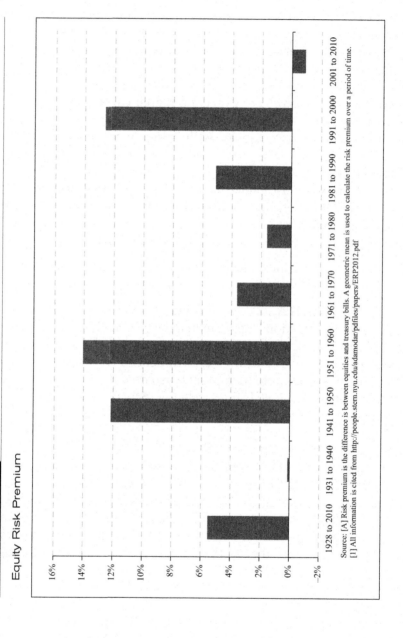

FIGURE 16-1

Equity Risk Premium

Source: [A] Risk premium is the difference is between equities and treasury bills. A geometric mean is used to calculate the risk premium over a period of time.
[1] All information is cited from http://people.stern.nyu.edu/adamodar/pdfiles/papers/ERP2012.pdf

yield anticipated by the market for investing in a stock, and can therefore be compared to other market yields, such as bond yields. EY is normally calculated for the entire market (or the S&P 500) and compared to the yield on current 10-year Treasury bonds.

Decisions based on EY are related to the equity risk premium because stocks are expected to provide higher rates than Treasuries to compensate investors for the additional risk of holding stocks. However, as shown in Figure 16–2, there are times when the spread over Treasuries becomes large enough to tempt some managers into selling shares with the expectation that the EY will come down (i.e., market prices will decline) and buying shares when the spread is low.

EXPLOITING MARKET INEFFICIENCIES

Efficient market theory dictates that there are no exploitable market inefficiencies (i.e., ones that can provide a profit for any sustained period). In fact, any inefficiency that actually does allow some to profit will be quickly erased as investors pour into the strategies. However, managers do seek to exploit actual or assumed inefficiencies. Some of the more often used equity strategies are based on the following theories:

- That the stock market does not give sufficient weight to earnings announcements in their valuation of stock prices. The theory here is that earnings announcements provide information about the longer-term prospects of the company while most investors treat them as short-term factors.

- That the market overreacts to bad news by pushing down the price of a stock too far, and underreacts to good news.

- That individual stocks and the stock market as a whole have a momentum that can be exploited to make a profit. Momentum means that the direction of a stock's movement is likely to last long enough to allow for a profitable position.

- That value stocks outperform growth stocks and small-cap stocks outperform large-cap stocks.

- That the stock market trends upward over time, and maintaining an overall long position is a profitable strategy.

FIGURE 16-2

Earnings Yield of S&P 500 Versus 10-Year Treasury-Bond Yield

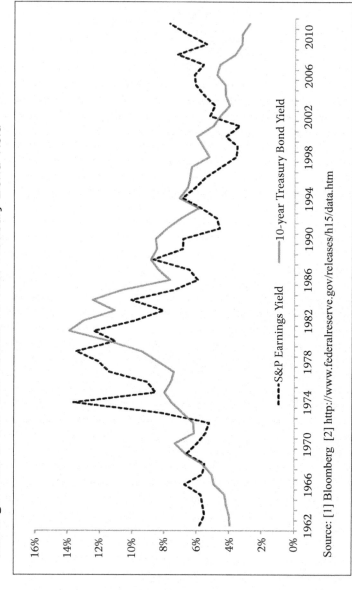

Source: [1] Bloomberg [2] http://www.federalreserve.gov/releases/h15/data.htm

Sean O'Shaughnessy, in a popular book entitled *What Works on Wall Street*, provided empirical tests of many of the supposed market inefficiencies and reaches the following conclusions:

- Small capitalization strategies owe their superior returns to microcap stocks with market capitalization below $25 million. However, these stocks have very limited capacity, and can be used by a limited number of smaller hedge funds.

- Buying stocks with low P/E ratios is most profitable when you stick to larger, better known issues, including such "brand names" as Coca-Cola and IBM.

- Price-to-sales ratio is the best value ratio to use for buying market-beating stocks.

- Last year's biggest losers are the worst stocks to buy this year, a refutation of the so-called dogs of the Dow theory, which claims that last year's losers will outperform the market.

- Last year's earnings gains are worthless in determining what the stock will do this year.

- Using several factors dramatically improves investment performance.

- You can beat the S&P 500 by four times if you concentrate on large, well-known stocks with high dividend yields.

- Buying the most popular issues with the highest P/E ratios is one of the worst approaches.

- Combining growth and value strategies is the best way to improve investment performance.

- Relative strength (a measure of market momentum) is the only growth variable that consistently beats the market.

Portfolio Construction Method

Long/short equity funds typically have a set of limits that impose constraints on portfolio construction. These constraints, which are designed to reduce portfolio risk, are often described in hedge funds' marketing material and/or offering documents. A typical set of these limits might read as follows:

- A maximum of 35 to 40 long positions. And 50 to 60 short positions.
- No long position will be allowed to exceed 5% at market.
- No short position will be allowed to exceed 3% at market.
- Gross long position will be between 75% and 150%.
- Gross short position will be between 30% and 50%.
- Maximum sector exposure, 25%.
- Maximum group exposure, 15%.
- Maximum gross exposure not to exceed 200%.

EQUITY MARKET NEUTRAL

Equity market neutral hedge funds use computerized modeling to construct portfolios holding dozens of long and short stock positions. The portfolio is designed to be neutral or largely immune to fluctuations in the larger marketplace as well as to other factors such as economic growth and interest rates. As such, their return is entirely dependent on the correct selection of the long and short individual stock positions.

Equity market neutral hedge funds typically hold long and short positions of the same dollar amount—or, for some managers, beta equivalent amounts—which means that their gross exposure tends toward 200%. Because the proceeds of their short sales can be used to fund their long purchases, they tend to be highly leveraged. However, the risk is offset, at least in theory, by the attempt of market neutral managers to remain neutral to a variety of market exposures, including overall market beta, sector or industry, country, currency, market capitalization, style (value/growth and large cap/small cap), and other factors.

Market neutral managers differ in the time horizon for their stock selection, trading frequency, sector or country limitations, the number and type of factors that are neutralized, and the extent to which human discretion is allowed to override the model, for example, in the face of news announcements.

There are two steps to constructing a market neutral portfolio: stock selection and portfolio construction.

Stock Selection Process*

There are 8,000 publicly traded stocks in the United States alone. The first step in stock selection is to screen stocks on the basis of their liquidity and ability to be shorted. This process may also include the exclusion of some sectors (i.e., high tech, natural resources) and stocks of distressed companies or those undergoing corporate restructuring. This process yields the universe of investable stocks, which is then used to select the long and short positions.

While models vary, the selection of stocks is often based on three types of factors: *fundamental factors*, which seek to exploit the market's overvaluation or undervaluation of a stock compared to its fundamentals; *price momentum* or technical factors, which seek to exploit the tendency of stocks to trend up or down; and *expectation factors*, which exploit the differing expectations that market participants have of forecasted and actual earnings. A typical model for stock selection includes the following factors:

- Fundamental factors
    - Dividend yield
    - Earnings yield
    - Price to book ratio
    - Price to earnings ratio
    - Change in return on equity
    - Revenue growth
    - Rate of reinvestment
    - Return on equity
- Price momentum/technical factors†
    - One month/one year price momentum
    - One year historical earnings growth/momentum

---

* An excellent resource that discusses the stock selection and portfolio construction process in a real world setting is a Harvard Business School Case Study, Maverick Capital.

† Technical factors refer to "technical analysis" which measures the direction of market movements irrespective of market fundamentals. We will discuss this in greater detail in the section on Global Macro and Commodities Trading Adviser strategies below.

- Relative strength indicators

- Mean reversion (trend line)

- Expectation factors

  - Change in consensus FY1 estimate—last three or six months

  - Consensus FY2 to FY1 estimate change

  - Consensus forecast earnings estimate revision ratio

  - Twelve months prospective earnings growth rate

  - Three-year prospective earnings growth rate

  - Twelve months prospective earnings yield

Portfolio Construction and Optimization

Market neutral portfolios are often constructed using sophisticated optimizers, for example, those offered by vendors such as APT, BARRA, and Northfield. These optimizers use multifactor models to model the expected returns, risk, and correlation between the stocks and various market factors, as well as transaction costs. The portfolio is constructed to minimize or eliminate exposure stock market betas and economic factors such as interest rates, commodity prices, and currencies.

Problems with Market Neutral

Market neutral strategies tend to live up to their name and deliver low-volatility portfolios that are largely immune to large market shocks. They also tend to have low correlations with the stock market, making them valuable for diversification in investment portfolios. The problem with this hedge fund strategy has been disappointing returns, which is a result of the difficulty of finding stock-specific anomalies that can be profitably exploited.

Some concerns that are specific to market neutral strategy include:

- Value trap—underperforming (overperforming) stocks may be underperforming (overperforming) for a reason, such as a change in long-term fundamentals or sector or regulatory issues that are not picked up in the model.

- Model risk—historical correlations may break down leading to unanticipated and unpredictable stock price movements.

- Reduced income from short selling in a low-interest-rate economy.

- Difficulty in finding liquid short stocks.

- Vulnerability to event risk (earnings reports; M&A).

- Increases in hedge fund activity limits the time period during which stocks remain overpriced or underpriced; since market neutral funds tend to rebalance their portfolios on a monthly basis, they may miss the window of opportunity.

PAIRS TRADING AND STATISTICAL ARBITRAGE

Pairs trading has evolved over the past 20 years from a medium term, fundamentally driven long/short equity strategy to the building block of highly computerized, super short-term trading programs known as "algorithmic trading" and "statistical arbitrage."

In theory, pairs trading is simple; it consists of matching a long position with a short position in two stocks that have a high historical correlation. The stocks are typically in the same sector, which creates a hedge against movement in that sector as well as the overall market. By neutralizing much of the influence of the sector and overall stock market, the success or failure of the strategy depends entirely on the selection of the two stocks.

Historically, these trades are based on fundamentally driven, longer-term investment decisions. The basic thesis is that one of the stocks is temporarily undervalued compared with the other, but that their value will converge in the direction that will make the pair profitable. Examples of pairs trade might include Coca-Cola and Pepsi; Walmart and Target Corporation; Dell and Hewlett-Packard; Ford and General Motors.

Pairs trading in its classic form is no longer a widely used strategy. However, it forms the basis for statistical arbitrage strategies that use quantitative methods, technical analysis, and complex computer models to identify very short-term trading opportunities. Statistical arbitrages strategies are often referred to as "black box" strategies, a reflection of their complexity, and the secrecy with which hedge funds shroud and vigorously protect their trading models. In fact, one of the largest statistical arbitrage hedge funds, Citadel, sued a former employee for allegedly stealing the fund's statistical arbitrage model.

The three most common forms of statistical arbitrage trading techniques are as follows: *pairs trading*, the simultaneous buying and shorting of companies in the same sector or peer group; *stub trading*, the simultaneous buying and shorting of stocks of a parent company and its subsidiaries to exploit imbalances in the market valuations of a company, the classic example being Shell and Royal Dutch Shell; and *multiclass trading*, the simultaneous buying and shorting of different classes of stocks of the same company (e.g., common and preferred) to exploit anomalies in how these shares trade.

Statistical arbitrage trading begins by identifying pairs of stocks that have exhibited a close correlation in price movement for a sustained period, often stocks in the same industry. Sophisticated computer systems then identify situations where formerly highly correlated pairs of stock diverge in price. The bet in this strategy is that the widening of the spread between the two stock prices is caused by temporary factors and that the spread will revert to its historical norm, so purchasing the stock that went down in value and shorting the stock that went up in value will profit when stocks return to their historical spread.

Of course, the trade will only be profitable if there is no fundamental reason for the price divergence but that the divergence is a result of short-term supply and demand factors, or a news announcement, or some form of "crowd behavior" that leads to a short-term aberration, typically because the "crowd" tends to overreact and push prices higher or lower than can be sustained over time. At any rate, the risk of any one divergence being a result of a structural change is minimized by entering in to numerous trades a day, often looking for very short term (seconds, minutes, or hours) divergence and convergence periods.

Statistical arbitrage programs require fast reaction and execution time to take advantage of tighter spreads before other similarly situated trading groups can. To get to the market quickly with large trades, they use algorithmic trading programs that facilitate trading large amounts of stock in very short time periods (sometimes less than a second) with minimal disruption in the marketplace. In fact, these strategies have become so reliant on trading prowess that they are classified as a segment of "high-frequency trading." The requirements of this type of trading have become so large that they are increasingly limited to a small number of large proprietary trading firms, both hedge funds (i.e., D.E. Shaw, Citadel, and Renaissance) and banks such as Goldman Sachs and Deutsche Bank who view it as a profitable replacement for their proprietary trading desks.

The "Flash Crash"

The sheer scale of high-frequency trading, which sometimes accounts for over 50% of the stock trading in the United States, has led to concern about the practice and its possible disruption of stock markets. (However, others argue that this type of trading actually provides liquidity and narrows the trading spread for individual and institutional traders.) One concern is that as more actors enter this field, the arbitrage opportunities become harder to identify and disappear more quickly, forcing participants to trade ever larger amounts for ever shorter time periods.

While not necessarily linked to statistical arbitrage programs, two notable market disruptions (the quant fund crisis on August 6, 2007, and the other, known as the "Flash Crash," on May 6, 2010) did cause market disruption and led to losses for many hedge funds. The causes of both have not been fully identified, but it does indicate that high-frequency trading is susceptible to systemic risk, which could adversely influence hedge funds pursuing this strategy.

Short-Biased Hedge Funds

Short-biased hedge funds take short positions in stocks that they feel are overvalued and will fall in value more than the over-all stock market index. As with long-biased funds, these funds use fundamental and quantitative techniques to find shortable stocks. Because of the complexities involved in shorting stocks, they also have more experience than most hedge funds in managing risks such as margin calls, and the potentially unlimited risk of holding a short position in a stock whose value can rise indefinitely.

Portfolio managers often include some short-bias managers in their portfolio as an insurance against market declines. The appropriate benchmark for these funds is the S&P 500 since shorting the S&P is relatively simple and inexpensive. The best-known short-bias hedge fund is Kynikos Associates, founded by James Chanos in 1985.

HISTORICAL PERFORMANCE OF EQUITY HEDGE STRATEGIES

Tables 16–1 to 16–3 contain statistics for the main equity hedge strategies (equity market neutral, short bias, equity hedge [total]) for three time periods: 1990–2011, 1998–2011, and 2007–2011. We will also use the same periods in analyzing the performance of all the strategies. The reason for analyzing the strategies' performance in this manner is because of the changes in both the hedge fund and the larger financial and economic world that occurred during these periods; changes that make comparison of different time periods relevant.

The first time period, 1990–2011, is commonly used largely because the hedge fund databases of the major data vendors start with 1990. Also, it is arguable that the hedge fund industry entered its adulthood at that

TABLE 16–1

Equity Hedge Performance From 1/1990 To 12/2011

	CASAM/ CISDM Equity Long / Short Index	HFRI EH: Equity Market Neutral Index	HFRI EH: Short Bias Index	HFRI Equity Hedge (Total) Index	MSCI WORLD (MXWO Index)	Barclays Aggregate Bond Index
Yearly average return	11.87%	7.14%	1.88%	14.03%	5.23%	7.13%
Annualized standard deviation	8.16%	3.31%	19.01%	9.31%	15.67%	3.76%
Sharpe ratio	0.75	0.58	-0.15	0.83	−0.02	0.53
Max draw-down	−17.22%	−9.15%	−53.36%	−30.59%	−55.37%	−5.15%
Skewness	−0.29	−0.29	0.19	−0.25	−0.61	−0.3
Kurtosis	2.00	1.50	2.10	1.76	1.22	0.75

TABLE 16-2

Equity Hedge Performance From 1/1998 To 12/2011

	CASAM/ CISDM Equity Long / Short Index	HFRI EH: Equity Market Neutral Index	HFRI EH: Short Bias Index	HFRI Equity Hedge (Total) Index	MSCI WORLD (MXWO Index)	Barclays Aggregate Bond Index
Yearly average return	8.15%	4.24%	1.31%	9.00%	4.04%	6.14%
Annualized standard deviation	7.91%	3.34%	19.23%	10.00%	16.85%	3.56%
Sharpe ratio	0.35	−0.23	−0.18	0.31	−0.11	0.31
Max draw-down	−17.22%	−9.15%	−51.05%	−30.59%	−55.37%	−3.82%
Skewness	−0.21	−0.23	0.32	−0.15	−0.67	−0.4
Kurtosis	3.02	2.14	3.22	1.90	1.17	1.40

TABLE 16-3

Equity Hedge Performance From 1/2007 To 12/2011

	CASAM/ CISDM Equity Long / Short Index	HFRI EH: Equity Market Neutral Index	HFRI EH: Short Bias Index	HFRI Equity Hedge (Total) Index	MSCI WORLD (MXWO Index)	Barclays Aggrexgate Bond Index
Yearly average return	3.44%	0.31%	−1.71%	2.09%	−1.22%	6.51%
Annualized standard deviation	7.35%	3.48%	13.64%	10.72%	20.42%	3.60%
Sharpe ratio	−0.25	−1.32	−0.55	−0.36	−0.36	0.42
Max draw-down	−17.22%	−9.15%	−46.66%	−30.59%	−55.37%	−3.82%
Skewness	−0.65	−1.12	0.02	−0.73	−0.55	0.15
Kurtosis	0.10	1.50	−0.28	1.02	0.74	1.58

time. However, the hedge fund and financial world of 1990 has little resemblance to today's; hence the analysis of hedge fund strategy performance from 1998 to 2011. The starting point, 1998, is somewhat arbitrary. However, it also coincides with the diversification of hedge fund strategies, especially into the equity space, and the rise in institutional investors. Finally, the period 2007–2011, which covers the credit crisis and its aftermath, takes into account the changes in the financial and hedge fund world caused by the credit crisis. This period may well be a better indication of future trends. The data in the tables indicates a number of salient points:

1. The yearly average return of all four equity hedge strategies declined sharply over the three time periods. The equity hedge (total) index, for example, had an average annual return of 14.03% for the entire time period, but only 9.00% between 1998 and 2011 and a meager 2.09% during 2007–2011.

2. A similar trend is shown in the deterioration of the Sharpe ratio for equity funds overall from a robust 0.83 for the entire period to 0.31 since 1998 and –0.31 since 2007. This decline, which indicates a worsening of the risk return trade-off, was largely caused by a decline in equity hedge fund returns. Annual standard deviation was relatively constant in all three periods.

3. With a maximum drawdown of –30.59%, equity hedge as a strategy clearly did not provide the downside protection or absolute return that is often claimed for hedge funds. While the maximum drawdown for equity markets was –55.37%, the relatively smaller drawdown for equity hedge funds is not a valid comparison if we take hedge funds at their word that their goal is to produce positive returns in all market environments.

4. Market neutral funds provided a sharp contrast to equity hedge funds in general. As we would expect, their volatility was much lower than equity hedge funds. However, their returns were lower yet, resulting in Sharpe ratios well below those of equity hedge funds in all three periods. These funds did live up to their "market neutral" label to some extent with a maximum drawdown of –9.15%.

CHAPTER 17

Event-Driven Strategies

Event-driven hedge funds take positions on discrete events such as mergers, bankruptcies, and corporate restructurings. They include activist hedge funds, which take significant shares in a company in order to actively change the company's management, strategy, and/or organization; merger arbitrage funds, also called risk arbitrage funds, which take a long position in a company about to be acquired and a short position on the acquiring company seeking to profit from the convergence of the shares' prices; and distressed investment funds, which take positions in the stock and fixed-income instruments of companies that are undergoing financial distress or may be about to become bankrupt or are coming out of bankruptcy.

ACTIVIST HEDGE FUNDS

Activist hedge funds take a significant minority position in a publicly traded company with the goal of effecting changes that will increase the company's value and share price. A key hypothesis underlying this strategy is that the target company is undervalued and is generating earnings below its potential, but is not necessarily distressed. The strategy is primarily equity-focused with a six-month to two-year investment horizon.

Activist Strategy

Activist hedge funds rely on changing one or more of the following aspects of a target company: financial restructuring, operational turnarounds, strategic initiatives, and corporate governance (Figure 17–1).

- *Financial restructuring:* Restructuring a company's balance sheet to increase the valuation of the company by reducing excess cash (accomplished by increasing the dividend payout or initiating share buyback programs) and/or changing the leverage structure by retiring outstanding debt or restructuring debt.

- *Operational turnaround:* Increasing operating margins either by implementing revenue-enhancing techniques or by reducing operating costs.

- *Strategic turnaround:* Including making strategic moves such as M&A transactions, joint ventures, and/or the spin-off of incompatible divisions or product lines.

- *Corporate governance:* Change the composition or incentive of board and/or management team.

FIGURE 17-1

Activist Toolbox Value Creation Capabilities

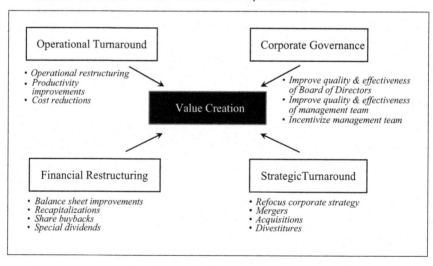

Activist Tactics

Activist hedge funds start by buying a small position in a target company, which provides the investor with access to information and creates an incentive for the company's managers to enter into discussions. Subsequent increases in stock purchases are made in order to exert increasing influence over the governance of the target company. In the process, the hedge fund may obtain representation on a target company's board of directors. In the United States, a shareholder who acquires more than a 5% share in a public company is required to file a Schedule 13D with the SEC within 10 days.

Once a significant position is established, the investor typically approaches the company's management with a plan to improve the company's valuation using one or a combination of the four tactics described above. Communication can be conducted in either a hostile or a non-hostile manner. Hostile situations usually involve proxy fights, competition for board seats, and/or takeover bids, and not infrequently results in publicity.

Activist investing can span the equity market capitalization spectrum, but lends itself more readily to small- and mid-cap companies where they are likely to face relatively inexperienced managers and where a smaller investment will gain them the status of a significant minority shareholder.

Activist Hedge Fund Structures

Activist funds typically have a concentrated portfolio with 8 to 15 core positions. They tend to invest with a longer-term time horizon of six months to two years, longer than a typical hedge fund but much shorter than a private equity fund. Many activist investors try to match their fund's liquidity terms to this investment horizon. Therefore, although activist funds are generally invested in liquid positions, they may have longer lockup periods to match the investment horizon of the strategy. Some activist investors also offer funds with capital commitments and a drawdown structure similar to a private equity fund.

Activist funds generally have a long bias, although some funds may hedge the overall market or a particular industry or sector with short position in an index or basket of stocks. Examples of activist hedge funds include:

- Shamrock Holdings formerly run by Stanley Gold and Roy Disney.

- Barrington Capital Group, which has not had a losing investment since 2001.

- Third Point, LLC, run by Daniel Loeb, who is known for his sharp and public criticisms of company management. Third Point is probably the highest returning fund on the list.

- Jana Partners LLC.

- Icahn Enterprises LP—Carl Icahn's recent success, believe it or not, includes Time Warner.

- Chapman Capital—Chapman is an extreme activist and usually files very detailed 13Ds.

- Steel Partners, which tried to bring the activist strategy to Japan.

- Pershing Square, managed by William Ackman, may have set a new standard for activist funds by going after the giant Procter & Gamble.

- Newcastle Partners.

MERGER (RISK) ARBITRAGE

Merger arbitrage is a popular event-driven strategy involving a hedge fund manager buying the stock of a company that is expected to be acquired, while shorting the stock of the acquiring company. The manager's aim is to capture the spread between the current market prices that the stocks trade at, and the value of these shares once an expected merger is completed.

As an example, company A trades at $50 and company B trades at $75. Company A makes a bid to purchase company B for two shares of its own stock for one share of company A's. Typically, company A's stock will decline to $45 and company B's will rise to $87 immediately after the announcement. The hedge fund would purchase one share of company B and sells short two shares of company A. If the deal goes through at the initial terms, the fund will make $3 for every transaction. However, if the terms of the deal change, this could become less or more. If the deal falls apart and the price of the shares revert to their prebid levels, the hedge fund will lose $15.

Because the profit or loss on deals is dependent on the relative price of the share in each transaction, the correlation between merger arbitrage and the general market is relatively low. However, the profit generated by these funds is a direct function of the level of M&A activity, which is in turn a function of the state of the economy and the stock market. This does result in an indirect relationship between the stock market and this hedge fund strategy.

The risk in this strategy is that the transaction does not go through, in which case the prices of the stocks tend to revert to pre-deal announcement levels. This means that the price of the to-be-acquired company will decline, causing losses in the hedge fund's long position.

At this point in time, M&A funds and corporations have record cash holds; however, the depressed economic environment has discouraged M&A activity. As a result, the performance of M&A funds has been disappointing.

DISTRESSED SECURITIES

Distressed debt hedge funds invest in the securities of companies that are in financial distress, including companies that are in bankruptcy, are expected to enter bankruptcy, or are coming out of bankruptcy. Hedge funds invest in a wide range of types of debt and equity issued by distressed companies. Unlike private equity firms, which often invest in similar situations, hedge funds are less concerned with the fundamental value that can be recognized by a company, and more interested in how that company's securities trade.

There are a number of ways hedge funds invest in distressed situations. One strategy is an outright long or short position in the company's equities or debt, depending on the manager's view of the prospects of the company. This strategy often works because investors tend to avoid distressed company securities, which means that they are often priced at levels below their economic value.

An alternative approach is often referred to as "capital structure arbitrage," which involves taking long and short positions that attempt to exploit mispricing between a company's debt and its other securities (such as equity or different tranches of debt). This form of investing is based on the principal that a company's various forms of debt and equity have varying levels of risk and that the market price of their relative risks are mispriced. For example, a company may have, in descending levels of risk, senior secured debt, junior subordinated debt, preferred stock, and common stock that may present relative value opportunities.

To reduce the risk of holding this type of security, a hedge fund manager may go long in one type of a company's securities, while shorting another. For example, a typical strategy may be to go long senior secured debt and short the junior subordinated debt; another would entail buying the preferred stock and short the common stock.

The growth of the credit default swap (CDS) market, essentially insurance contracts against the default of a company, has also led to distressed debt strategies that involve CDS as a hedge against owning a security of a distressed company. A hedge fund may purchase the debt of a distressed company, but also purchase a CDS on the company. The CDS would pay the hedge fund if the company defaulted on its debt.

PRIVATE ISSUE/REGULATION D

Private issue/Regulation D hedge funds invest in privately issued securities of companies that also have publicly traded securities. The Securities Act of 1933 allows public companies to issue private securities, which are not traded on an exchange, but are rather offered, and traded, privately.

These securities are only offered to the most sophisticated investors, and are restricted from being advertised. Known as "Reg D" securities, these issues may trade at a discount to the publicly traded securities of a company, or, on occasion, Reg D securities offer hedge funds an arbitrage opportunity when they can buy the Reg D securities and short the public securities, in a form of capital structure arbitrage.

The level of activity by hedge funds using this strategy has stagnated since 2007, as returns diminished for a number of reasons, including the manipulation of these securities by hedge funds.

HISTORICAL PERFORMANCE OF EVENT-DRIVEN STRATEGIES

Overall, event-driven hedge fund returns exhibit a similar pattern to those of equity hedge funds, with a decline in returns and Sharpe ratio over the three time periods. Other salient conclusions can be drawn from Tables 17–1 to 17–3.

TABLE 17–1

Event-Driven Performance From 1/1990 To 12/2011

	HFRX Activist Index	HFRI ED: Merger Arbitrage Index	HFRI ED: Distressed/ Restructur- ing Index	HFRI ED: Private Issue/ Regulation D Index	HFRI Event- Driven (Total) Index	MSCI WORLD (MXWO Index)	Barclays Aggregate Bond Index	Barclays High Yield Credit Bond Index
Yearly Average Return	N/A	9.05%	12.94%	N/A	12.45%	5.23%	7.13%	10.13%
Annualized Standard Deviation	N/A	4.12%	6.67%	N/A	6.96%	15.67%	3.76%	9.45%
Sharpe Ratio	N/A	0.89	1.02	N/A	0.93	−0.02	0.53	0.43
Max Drawdown	N/A	−8.06%	−27.41%	N/A	−24.79%	−55.37%	−5.15%	−33.31%
Skewness	N/A	−2.13	−1.02	N/A	−1.3	−0.61	−0.3	−0.92
Kurtosis	N/A	8.81	4.7	N/A	3.89	1.22	0.75	7.75

TABLE 17-2

Event-Driven Performance 1/1998 To 12/2011

	HFRX Activist Index	HFRI ED: Merger Arbitrage Index	HFRI ED: Distressed/ Restructur- ing Index	HFRI ED: Private Issue/ Regulation D Index	HFRI Event- Driven (Total) Index	MSCI WORLD (MXWO Index)	Barclays Aggregate Bond Index	Barclays High Yield Credit Bond Index
Yearly Average Return	N/A	6.64%	8.93%	8.99%	8.71%	4.04%	6.14%	7.93%
Annualized Standard Deviation	N/A	3.83%	6.92%	7.04%	7.32%	16.85%	3.56%	10.42%
Sharpe Ratio	N/A	0.38	0.45	0.48	0.42	−0.11	0.31	0.19
Max Drawdown	N/A	−8.06%	−27.41%	−15.28%	−24.79%	−55.37%	−3.82%	−33.31%
Skewness	N/A	−1.58	−1.44	0.88	−1.3	−0.67	−0.4	−0.96
Kurtosis	N/A	5.95	4.66	2.28	3.71	1.17	1.4	6.84

TABLE 17-3

Event-Driven Performance From 1/2007 To 12/2011

	HFRX Activist Index	HFRI ED: Merger Arbitrage Index	HFRI ED: Distressed/ Restructuring Index	HFRI ED: Private Issue/ Regulation D Index	HFRI Event-Driven (Total) Index	MSCI WORLD (MXWO Index)	Barclays Aggregate Bond Index	Barclays High Yield Credit Bond Index
Yearly Average Return	3.31%	3.89%	3.67%	2.46%	3.68%	-1.22%	6.51%	10.81%
Annualized Standard Deviation	17.33%	3.57%	8.40%	5.86%	8.16%	20.42%	3.60%	14.22%
Sharpe Ratio	-0.19	-0.33	-0.29	-0.45	-0.26	-0.36	0.42	0.24
Max Drawdown	-37.37%	-8.06%	-27.41%	-15.28%	-24.79%	-55.37%	-3.82%	-33.31%
Skewness	-0.67	-0.94	-1.02	0.44	-1.09	-0.55	0.15	-1
Kurtosis	1.13	1.11	1.83	1.11	2.05	0.74	1.58	4.62

While the distressed/restructuring hedge funds outper-
formed fixed-income indices in terms of both performance and
volatility in the first two periods, they greatly underperformed
in the 2007–2011 period. This was most likely a result of the flight
from illiquid securities in the wake of the credit crisis. This would
also help explain the higher negative skew of this strategy, which
indicates that a large number of distressed securities hedge funds
lost money.

As was the case with equity hedge funds, the distressed/
restructuring funds' maximum drawdown of –27.41% was out
of line with their stated goals of absolute return and downside
protection.

The merger arbitrage index has also shown a dramatic decline
in returns and Sharpe ratio over the past few years as a result of the
slowdown in M&A activity worldwide. However, the strategy's
maximum drawdown of –8.06% was much lower than the dis-
tressed/restructuring funds.

Relative Value Strategies

Relative value hedge funds seek to profit by exploiting irregularities or discrepancies in the pricing of stocks, bonds, currencies, or interest rates, as well as derivatives. The term *relative value* refers to the fact that these strategies look to take advantage of the price relationship between two securities, rather than making bets on single instruments or markets.

RELATIVE VALUE AND ARBITRAGE

While relative value have some structural similarities to arbitrage transactions, and the two terms are often used interchangeably, there are some key differences. Both strategies take advantage of a price difference between two securities. However, relative value strategies look for a convergence of the price of these instruments to some fundamental value and accept the fact that the outcome— whether a profit or a loss—is not guaranteed and depends on the movement of market factors.

An arbitrage strategy also takes advantage of the price difference between two or more instruments. When used by academics, an arbitrage is a transaction that involves no negative cash flow and a guarantee that the instruments will converge and yield a profit; in simple terms, it is the possibility of a risk-free profit at zero cost.

The confusion comes in when some attempt to equate the academic definition of arbitrage and relative value as used in the hedge fund industry. Hedge fund managers recognize that there are no risk-free arbitrage opportunities in the financial markets. However, they do take positions that seek to take advantage of relative prices of instruments and attempt to reduce as many extraneous risks as possible, and thus label their strategies as "arbitrage."

Fixed-income arbitrage is a form of relative value investing that entails the purchase of one fixed-income security and simultaneous sale of a similar security with the expectation that the prices of the two instruments will converge over the investment-holding period.

Fixed-income relative value strategies were made famous by the failure of Long-Term Capital Management, whose bets included a number of relative value and fixed-income arbitrage trades, notably the 29-/30-year Treasury yield curve strategy. These strategies are sometimes described as "picking up nickels in front of a steam-roller," a reference to the high leverage they often employ, and the risk of a major market move that can cause large losses. As the profit comes from a relatively small yield differential that needs to be leveraged to reach acceptable levels of return. It is noteworthy that many of the large trading losses incurred by hedge funds over the years came from fixed-income arbitrage strategies, including the losses recently incurred in the mortgage-backed securities market.

Yield Curve Arbitrage

Yield curves are constructed by charting the interest rates of securities of varying maturities. Yield curve arbitrage strategies take long and short positions at different points along the yield curve, hoping to benefit from the interest rate differential and any subsequent movement in relative rates. For example, in a positive yield curve environment, a manager may borrow three-month U.S. Treasury bills to invest in five-year Treasury notes, hoping to earn the interest rate difference between the two. However, the strategy may lose money if the three-month rates increase compared with the five-year rates. More complex strategies with the same basic structure would entail yield curves of differing instruments (i.e., U.S. Treasuries vs. U.S. corporates) or different countries (i.e., U.S. Treasuries vs. German bunds). In the latter, currency risk would accompany interest rate risk.

High-Yield and Emerging-Market Debt

Strategies that invest in higher-yielding instruments are always appealing, especially in a low-interest-rate environment when other investment opportunities are relatively few. Two markets that attract this type of investment because of their relatively high yield, large size, and relatively high liquidity are high-yield bonds and emerging-markets bonds.

Long-only mutual funds also invest in these markets. What makes hedge funds different is their attempt to hedge out some of the risks of these instruments by finding a lower-yielding yet correlated security. For example, a trade entailing owning a high-yield corporate bond may be offset by an (imperfect) hedge of a short position in a high-grade bond or, at greater risk, with a U.S. Treasury bond.

Whether the strategy gains or loses depends on whether the interest earned from the spread between the long and short is sufficient to cover the risk that the spread will diverge (i.e., short-term rates increase relative to longer-term rates). Because these strategies depend on the relationship between two instruments, they are also referred to as "spread" strategies.

Figure 18–1, which shows the spread between corporate high-yield bonds and U.S. Treasuries of similar duration, clearly demonstrates the cyclical narrowing and widening of the spreads. The high-yield default rates indicate the percentage of high-yield bonds that default on their debt. A profitable strategy would consist of purchasing high-yield bonds when spreads are "rich" (i.e., wide) yet default rates are relatively low.

Asset-Backed/Mortgage-Backed Securities Arbitrage

Asset-backed or mortgage-backed securities (ABSs or MBSs) normally provide interest rates higher than U.S. Treasuries or high-grade corporate bonds of similar duration, and are therefore tempting investments for fixed-income hedge funds. The complexity of these instruments calls for elaborate mathematical and statistical models, limiting their use to relatively few hedge funds that specialize in these markets.

FIGURE 18-1

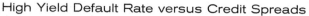

High Yield Default Rate versus Credit Spreads

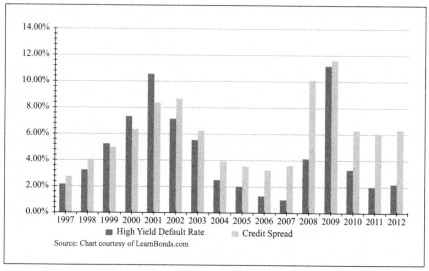

The common strategy here is to invest in ABSs/MBSs and short U.S. Treasuries or corporate bonds as a hedge. Another variation is to purchase Credit Default Swaps on these securities to hedge the risks. The risk in this strategy, which led to large losses during the credit crisis, is that the long position and the hedge do not move in opposite directions. During the credit crisis, investors flocked to U.S. Treasuries, seeking safety and driving up the price of these bonds. Unfortunately, hedge funds pursuing this strategy were short Treasuries and lost on the supposed hedge part of the transaction. (They also lost on ABSs/MBSs, which declined in value at the same time.)

Another strategy in MBSs attempts to exploit relative mispricing between MBS and other securities, such as Treasuries based on an optionality feature contained in MBS. These bonds contain a prepayment feature, which means that mortgage holders can prepay their mortgages if interest rates decline. This is essentially an option for the mortgage holder and is priced using an option-adjusted spread model. Hedge funds take positions based on the spreads between fixed-income securities with an embedded prepayment option (i.e., ABSs and MBSs) and bonds without these features.

Convertible Arbitrage

Convertible bonds are issued by companies and contain an embedded option to convert the bonds into shares of the underlying company's stock. This option feature is provided as an added incentive for investors to purchase the bonds at lower interest rate.

Convertible arbitrage hedge funds establish long positions in the convertible bonds of a company, while selling the company's stock (or options on the stock), thus removing the exposure of the equity component of the investment. This hedge ratio is known as "delta," and reflects the sensitivity of the convertible bond value to movements in the underlying stock. They also use swaps to hedge out the interest rate risk component of the bond.

Convertible bonds may trade as more like stocks or like bonds depending on their conversion value relative to the market price. Because hedge fund managers are able to use stocks, bonds, and swaps to hedge the various sources of risk and return within the convertible bond, they attempt to identify arbitrage opportunities where there is a discrepancy between a convertible bond and its component parts, or alternatively, they hedge away the risk of each individual component, leaving only the embedded option.

Because convertible bond arbitrageurs short stocks, this strategy inherently involves leverage. Leverage for this strategy ranges from two to six times the amount of invested capital.

Volatility Arbitrage

Volatility arbitrage is a popular strategy that seeks to profit from the difference between the historical volatility of an asset—frequently the S&P 500—and the volatility implied by the market price of an option on that asset/instrument.

Options prices are determined by a number of factors, one of which is the volatility of the underlying instrument. The market price of an option on the S&P 500 is based on an implied volatility that is determined by supply and demand among market participants. However, it is also possible to calculate the historical volatility of the S&P 500 by calculating its standard deviation. If the fund manager feels that the implied volatility is too high compared with the actual volatility, then the price of the option is overvalued, in which case the manager would sell the option (receiving the "rich" premium), and then delta hedge the option position.

Delta hedging entails buying and selling futures on the S&P 500 to hedge the risk of the sold option. In the course of delta hedging this type of position, the hedge fund will lose money. The size of the loss will largely depend on the volatility of the S&P 500. If the manager's forecast was correct, the fund will lose less money from the delta hedge than it took in from selling the option.

A riskier type of volatility arbitrage is to take an unhedged view of the future direction of volatility, a strategy made popular with the introduction of the VIX contract, which is based on the volatility of the S&P 500. Managers that feel that the volatility implied in the S&P 500 is too high and will come down can go short the VIX either with futures or options. Their position will profit if the volatility does come down. Hedge funds that purchase the VIX at troughs and sell the contract at peaks will realize a profit. Figure 18–2 shows the volatility of the S&P 500 as captured in the VIX contract.

HISTORICAL PERFORMANCE OF RELATIVE VALUE FUNDS

Relative value hedge funds have produced moderately higher returns than stocks and bonds (including high-yield bonds) during the 1990–2011 period. These strategies do, however, have a negative skew and positive excess kurtosis, reflecting their tendency to suffer large drawdowns during times of stress. This was especially pronounced during the 1998 market crisis when relative value strategies suffered large losses, as exemplified by Long-Term Capital Management (Tables 18–1 to 18–3).

The convertible arbitrage strategy has also come under significant pressure in the wake of the credit crisis, as the high leverage employed by this strategy has become harder for funds to obtain.

In the past several months, strategies that involve long positions in mortgage backed securities have generated considerable interest among hedge funds, and a number of funds dedicated to this strategy have been launched. The strategy is based on the assumption that the price of these securities has been driven down to levels that make them an attractive investment. The results of this

FIGURE 18–2

Illustration of the Volatility of S&P 500–CBOE VIX

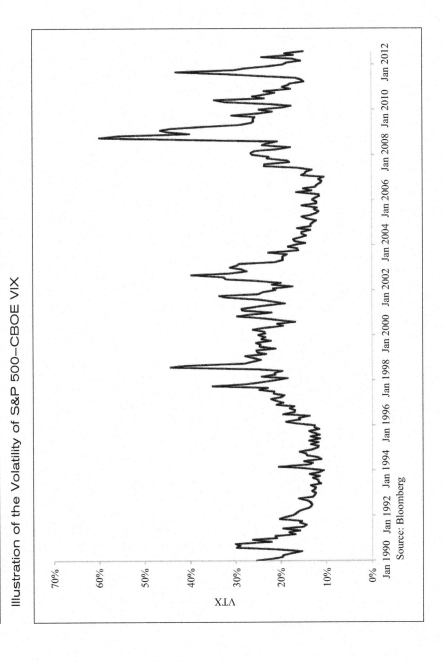

Source: Bloomberg

TABLE 18-1

Relative Value Performance From 1/2007 To 12/2011

	HFRI RV: Fixed Income- Asset Backed	HFRI RV: Fixed Income- Corporate Index	HFRI RV: Fixed Income- Convertible Arbitrage Index	HFRX Volatility Index	HFRI Relative Value (Total) Index	MSCI WORLD (MXWO Index)	Barclays Aggregate Bond Index	Barclays High Yield Credit Bond Index
Yearly Average Return	N/A	8.76%	9.78%	N/A	10.64%	5.23%	7.13%	10.13%
Annualized Standard Deviation	N/A	6.71%	6.74%	N/A	4.46%	15.67%	3.76%	9.45%
Sharpe Ratio	N/A	0.44	0.54	N/A	1.12	-0.02	0.53	0.43
Max Drawdown	N/A	-28.16%	-35.32%	N/A	-18.04%	-55.37%	-5.15%	-33.31%
Skewness	N/A	-1.32	-3.05	N/A	-2.13	-0.61	-0.3	-0.92
Kurtosis	N/A	7.63	28.15	N/A	13.4	1.22	0.75	7.75

TABLE 18−2

Relative Value Performance From 1/1990 To 12/2011

	HFRI RV: Fixed Income-Asset Backed	HFRI RV: Fixed Income-Corporate Index	HFRI RV: Fixed Income-Convertible Arbitrage Index	HFRX Volatility Index	HFRI Relative Value (Total) Index	MSCI WORLD (MXWO Index)	Barclays Aggregate Bond Index	Barclays High Yield Credit Bond Index
Yearly Average Return	7.66%	5.46%	8.61%	N/A	7.66%	4.04%	6.14%	7.93%
Annualized Standard Deviation	4.64%	6.28%	8.06%	N/A	4.72%	16.85%	3.56%	10.42%
Sharpe Ratio	0.5	−0.01	0.27	N/A	0.47	−0.11	0.31	0.19
Max Drawdown	−13.48%	−28.16%	−35.32%	N/A	−18.04%	−55.37%	−3.82%	−33.31%
Skewness	−3.11	−2.15	−2.63	N/A	−2.8	−0.67	−0.4	−0.96
Kurtosis	18.78	9.66	20.63	N/A	14.32	1.17	1.4	6.84

TABLE 18-3

Relative Value Performance From 1/2007 To 12/2011

	HFRI RV: Fixed Income-Asset Backed	HFRI RV: Fixed Income-Corporate Index	HFRI RV: Fixed Income-Convertible Arbitrage Index	HFRX Volatility Index	HFRI Relative Value (Total) Index	MSCI WORLD (MXWO Index)	Barclays Aggregate Bond Index	Barclays High Yield Credit Bond Index
Yearly Average Return	8.11%	3.68%	7.99%	-0.59%	5.66%	-1.22%	6.51%	10.81%
Annualized Standard Deviation	4.02%	8.55%	12.63%	6.69%	6.59%	20.42%	3.60%	14.22%
Sharpe Ratio	0.65	-0.29	-0.03	-0.79	-0.02	-0.36	0.42	0.24
Max Drawdown	-6.27%	-28.16%	-35.32%	-15.37%	-18.04%	-55.37%	-3.82%	-33.31%
Skewness	-0.45	-1.64	-1.78	-1.45	-2.08	-0.55	0.15	-1.00
Kurtosis	1.25	5.40	8.20	3.24	7.11	0.74	1.58	4.62

strategy have been positive, and this may well be a growth sector in the future. If the strategy does succeed, it reinforces the fact that even high risk strategies may be priced at levels that make the risk worth taking.

CHAPTER 19

Global Macro and Commodity Trading Adviser Strategies

WHAT IS GLOBAL MACRO?

Global macro hedge funds use a wide variety of strategies and instruments to take long and short positions in the global markets for equities, commodities, fixed income, and currencies. Global macro strategies differ from other hedge fund strategies by their extensive use of stock market and bond market indices rather than individual stocks and bonds to implement their views. This approach is consistent with global macro's focus on broad economic and financial trends.

The decision-making process starts with forecasts of trends in broad economic variables such as inflation, economic growth, and interest rate movements. Global macro managers will take positions that reflect the impact these economic trends will have on financial markets. Examples would be taking a position on the U.S. dollar/euro exchange rate on the basis of a prediction of the relative economic growth of the United States and Europe; taking a position in certain commodities on the basis of the anticipation of Chinese economic growth and the influence this will have for global demand on commodities; and taking a position in the relative value of U.K. versus European bonds on the basis of expectations of inflation in the two markets.

Global macro hedge funds normally have wide discretion as to the markets they trade and the instruments they utilize. This discretion is considered necessary to allow the managers to respond to changes in the economic environment and use the best strategy for any given opportunity. Thus, global macro managers are active across market sectors, including equities, fixed income, foreign exchange, and commodity asset classes; they utilize cash, futures, and/or options; trade in all geographical regions; employ both discretionary and systematic analysis; and frequently use leverage.

HEDGE FUND ASSET FLOWS

Global macro investing came of age in the 1980s, when managers like George Soros, Julian Robertson, and Paul Tudor Jones established their hedge funds. As their asset grew, they increasingly entered larger and more liquid markets such as bonds, currencies, and commodities. These markets were also marked by the extensive use of derivatives (futures, forwards, swaps, and options) and the relative ease of taking short positions. In addition, these markets were global in nature and had relatively few regulatory constraints. This allowed global macro managers to respond quickly to changing economic conditions, and marks a distinct characteristic of most global macro managers: they are, for the most part, active traders rather than buy-and-hold investors.

Hedge fund assets flowed from global macro to equity hedge funds throughout the 1990s and early 2000s as the bull market in equities led investors to stocks. Thousands of hedge funds devoted to equity strategies were formed during this time, and the share of hedge fund assets in global macro shrank from over 60% in 1990 to around 30% by 2010.

However, this trend has reversed in recent years. The volatility and lack of direction in the stock market (which ended the 2000s essentially at the same level as the beginning of the decade) has caused disenchantment among investors in this asset class. At the same time, the pronounced trends and dramatic events in the currency, interest rate, and commodities markets has convinced many investors that they need to be invested in global macro funds. The results are striking. Between 2007 and 2011, the share of hedge fund assets in equity hedge fund strategies declined from 37% to 27%, while the assets in macro strategies rose from 15% to 22%. In addition, there was a sharp rise in the number of macro hedge funds launched during this period, notably by traders leaving bank trading operations.

DISCRETIONARY VERSUS SYSTEMATIC (TECHNICAL) STRATEGIES

Global macro strategies are usually classified as either discretionary or systematic. In reality, many global macro managers use both approaches. However, there is a group of hedge funds, commodities trading advisers (CTAs) that are almost exclusively systematic in their approach.

Discretionary Global Macro

As the name implies, discretionary global macro strategies are based on decisions that are made at the discretion of the manager or investment team. While the manager may use quantitative analysis and models as aids to take positions, at the end of the day decisions are made on the basis of the manager's own interpretations and convictions about the financial markets and typically involve intensive fundamental research. Discretionary managers pore over economic data such as growth indicators, production indexes, central bank publications, and other data sources, to derive trading ideas. They may also have economic models that quantify the impact of fundamental economic data on financial market prices; for example, the impact of GDP changes on equity market prices or the sensitivity of inflation to global interest rates. Discretionary managers tend to take a "top-down" approach that first identifies broad economic trends and then determines how these trends will affect individual markets. The next step is to decide the specific strategy and instrument that are best suited to implement the thesis in these markets.

For example, the manager's world view could conclude that China's robust growth will continue for the foreseeable future, which in turn would inspire the theme of rising commodity prices. The manager would then focus on the markets that would be most influenced by long-term Chinese growth; for example, the oil and copper markets (two of China's largest imports). Several other markets could be affected by this broad theme, including the currencies of commodity-driven economies (e.g., the Australian dollar) or the equity indices of large oil-exporting countries like Canada.

Discretionary managers use their own judgment about the timing of their trades in entering or exiting a position. The price of markets can be affected very quickly by political or economic events, and discretionary traders typically have complete flexibility if changing, or even reversing, their positions. Thus, the manager's positions could be held for days or months depending on market developments and the manager's trading style. This need for flexibility and quick response is another reason these managers trade in large and liquid markets.

GEORGE SOROS' BRITISH POUND STRATEGY

The classic example of a global macro discretionary trade was that taken by George Soros (and his protégé Stanley Druckenmiller) in 1993. European currencies were under continual pressure in the early 1990s, and competitive devaluations became the norm adopted by countries to solve their balance of trade crises. One tactic adopted by governments was to increase their domestic interest rates as a way of attracting foreign capital to their currencies (and discouraging domestic capital from fleeing their currency).

This was the situation in 1993 as the British pound came under intense selling pressure and the government proceeded to raise interest rates as a defense tactic. However, Soros shorted the pound in (at the time) massive amounts, betting that the U.K. government was limited in its ability to raise interest rates or at least keep them high for sufficiently long to discourage the short sellers, who had to pay these high interest rates in order to short the currency. In this case, Soros was correct. The U.K. government lowered interest rates, the pound devalued, and Soros made a billion in profit, becoming a legend in the process.

Interestingly, there is a variation of this strategy that is more widely used today: investing in low-interest-rate, strong currencies such as the Swiss franc, Danish krona, and Singapore dollar. These currencies are under pressure from an inflow of capital seeking safe haven from the volatility of the currency markets. However, the governments, not wanting to see their currencies strengthen and acting as a drag on exports, have driven their interest rates down to zero, or even below on an inflation-adjusted basis. Yet, hedge funds still plow money into these currencies, speculating that the governments will not be able to stem their appreciation.

Carry Trades

A carry trade involves borrowing or selling a financial instrument with a low interest rate, then using the proceeds to purchase a financial instrument with a higher interest rate. The strategy attempts to capture the difference between the interest it pays on the borrowed funds and the interest it receives from the invested funds. The carry of an asset is the returns obtained from holding it (if positive), or the cost of holding it (if negative). Thus, a manager's profit is the money he collects from the interest rate differential. Carry trades are not arbitrages, which, at least in theory, make money no matter what happens; carry trades make money only if nothing changes against the carry's favor.

Interest rate carry trade

Interest rate carry trades entail borrowing a low-interest-rate instrument (e.g., 3-month U.S. Treasuries) and investing the proceeds in a higher-interest-rate instrument (e.g., 10-year Treasury bonds or corporate bonds), hoping to benefit from the interest rate difference between the two. This extremely common strategy is discussed in detail in the relative value chapter above. However, it is worth noting that interest rate carry trades are not restricted to hedge funds, but are commonly used by banks, although they do not refer to it as a carry trade.

The traditional income stream from commercial banks is to borrow cheap (at low rates, i.e., the rate at which they pay depositors) and lend expensive (at the long-term rate, which is usually higher than the short-term rate). This mismatch is known as "maturity transformation" by economists. However, this strategy entails considerable risk. Many hedge funds and investment banks, such as Bear Stearns, have failed because they borrowed cheap short-term money to fund higher-interest-bearing long-term positions. When the long-term positions declined in value or defaulted, or the short-term interest rate increased, the hedge fund or bank was unable to meet its short-term liabilities and goes under.

Currency carry trade

The term *carry trade*, without further modification, often refers to currency carry trade: investors borrow low-yielding currency and lend high-yielding currencies. As with futures on physical commodities, investors earn the carry but also bear the risk of potential adverse movements in the exchange rate.

JAPANESE YEN CARRY TRADE

An example of a carry trade involves the Japanese yen and Australian dollar. The relative annual interest rates between the two (1% for Japan and 5% for Australia) makes this attractive for hedge funds at various times.

In this trade, a hedge fund would borrow Japanese yen and convert the proceeds to Australian dollars. (Actually, the transaction would involve a currency forward contract, but the economics are identical because of an arbitrage known as the "covered interest rate arbitrage.") If all goes well, the hedge fund would have realized a 4% profit in one year. Because of the leverage available in currency trading, this profit can be increased by multiples.

However, the hedge fund needs to convert the proceeds of the loans at the end of the year to realize its profits. In other words, the Australian dollars (the initial investment plus the 5% interest) must be converted to Japanese yen to repay the loan plus the 1% interest. If the yen appreciated (strengthened) against the Australian dollar in the intervening year, the hedge fund will need to pay more Australian dollars to repay the loan. In fact, a Japanese yen appreciation of 4% would have wiped out the interest differential "profit," while any greater appreciation would cause an outright loss.

So why do hedge funds open themselves to this risk? Clearly because they project that the "carry" (i.e., 4% in this case) is sufficient to protect them from the risk of currency depreciation. However, the hedge fund in this case is facing serious risk in the form of the "uncovered interest rate parity theory," which states that currencies with low interest rates (i.e., Japanese yen) will appreciate against currencies with higher interest rates (i.e., Australian dollar).

So let us go back to early 2007 when it was estimated that some US$1 trillion might have been staked on the Japanese yen carry trade. Since the mid-1990s, the Bank of Japan has set Japanese interest rates at very low levels, making it a favorite carry trade borrowing currency not only for hedge funds but also for Japanese investors. The proceeds of the borrowing were invested throughout the world in activities that included subprime lending in the United States, emerging-market countries, and resource-rich countries, including Australia.

However, the trade collapsed in 2008 as the credit crisis led to the global liquidation of risky positions and the Japanese hurried to bring their assets home. At the same time, the Japanese yen strengthened dramatically against most currencies, resulting in large losses for many global macro hedge funds.

However, this did not eliminate the carry trade, which is currently alive and well with favored borrowing currencies being the U.S. dollar, the British pound, and the Japanese yen, and investing currencies including the euro, some emerging-market currencies, high-yield bonds, and resource-rich currencies such as the Australian dollar. These carry trades may be riskier than in past times for two reasons: first, because of the increased volatility in the currency markets caused by the euro crisis; second, the lower level of interest rates around the world has made the interest rate spread in carry trades precariously narrow, leading hedge funds to either increase their leverage (and risk) or accept a lower expected rate of return.

TREND-FOLLOWING STRATEGIES, MANAGED FUTURES, AND CTAs

In sharp contrast to discretionary global macro, systematic or trend-following global macro strategies use computerized models to analyze market price movement to discern trending or momentum patterns and generate buy and sell "recommendations." The distinguishing characteristic of systematic programs is that the hedge fund manager's role in establishing positions ends once the model is developed. The hedge fund then automatically follows the model's recommendations without human intervention except for exceptional cases of market disruption. These programs typically focus on highly liquid, exchange-traded futures and options and typically maintain shorter holding periods than discretionary programs. Although some strategies seek to employ counter trend or mean reverting models, these strategies benefit most from an environment characterized by persistent, discernible trending behavior.

Trend-following systems are commonly used by discretionary managers, but only as another tool in reaching their trading decisions. Hedge funds that rely exclusively on trend-following systems are known as "managed futures" hedge funds. Since U.S. government regulation requires hedge funds that trade in the futures markets to register as commodities trading advisers with the Commodities Futures Trading Commission, these funds are also known as CTAs.

Systematic global macro attempts to capture trends in various markets by the use of statistical techniques such as momentum or moving averages. A trend exists when the future direction of a market is based on the present direction. Thus, if the U.S. dollar is appreciating against the Japanese yen, the model would project the trend forward, generating a buy signal on the U.S. dollar.

It is interesting to note that systematic trend-following systems are based on the assumption that the price movement of a market provides sufficient information to form a trading strategy, without any additional information such as supply and demand or economic trends. This is because trend following is based on the assumption that all the information about a market is embodied in the price movement, and no further information is needed.

Managed futures hedge funds vary in the number of markets they cover, the statistical systems they utilize, their use of leverage, the duration of their average trade (short, medium, and long term), and the levels at which they set their entrance and exit levels. The latter is important in defining the risk and return profile of the program. Some programs are established to take advantage of longer-term trends by setting exit levels far away from the market price. These funds can rack up very large losses when the market goes through a correction as they wait for the trend to reassert itself. John Henry is a CTA that is known for this approach, and his investors have had to endure drawdowns of 20% and 30%.

Other programs try to benefit from shorter-term trends (normally days or weeks) by setting their exit levels relatively close to the market price. While they avoid the types of large drawdowns of long-term programs, they are vulnerable to "whipsaw" markets—markets that do have a pronounced trend but lurches up and down, causing the program to repeatedly enter and exit the market, each time at a loss.

Many trend-following hedge funds will use a combination of short, medium and long-term models in making trading decisions.

The results of a systematic program are obviously dependent on the assumptions and methods incorporated in their models. As with all such models, there is always the risk of "curve fitting," which means building a model that will produce very attractive results when based onto a historical price series, but will not perform as well going forward.

Some of the larger CTAs include Winton Capital ($29 billion), Man AHL Diversified ($16.3 billion), TransTrend ($9.4 billion), BlueTrend ($13.6 billion), Graham Capital ($7.5 billion), Altis ($1.1 billion), and Aspect ($7 billion).

DISCRETIONARY GLOBAL MACRO PERFORMANCE

The suggested benefits of global macro hedge funds change from time to time but basically follow three lines: first, they provide superior absolute return to investors; second, they act as insurance because of their ability to preserve capital or profit during times of crisis; and, third, they act as diversifiers in an investment portfolio because of their low correlation with the equity and fixed-income markets.

Global macro performance has changed from the early days when they delivered outsized returns. This is probably partially because of the inflow of assets into the markets favored by hedge funds, meaning that are fewer inefficiencies that may be exploited. It is also a function of the increasing complexity and interconnectedness of the global economic and financial system, making it more difficult to identify and segregate cause and effect. Finally, the increased government intervention in financial markets has made them less predictable and more susceptible to sudden changes and reversals.

As mentioned above, money flooded into the global macro arena in 2009–2010 on the basis of their performance during the credit crisis. However, in a classic instance of chasing a trend, these funds have not lived up to investors' expectations. While global macro hedge funds in aggregate made 8% in 2010, they lost 4.88% in 2011, well behind their hedge fund peers. Many global macro funds found the markets increasingly difficult to navigate: investing based on relative value became more difficult as market volatility skyrocketed. Market trends (in currencies, commodities, rates, equities, etc.) kept reversing direction (sometimes several times a month), often rendering fundamental economic analysis completely useless. Matter became so bad that Stanley Druckenmiller, protégé of Soros, closed his fund Duquesne Capital Management because of poor performance.

The hedge funds that performed well during these types of markets were the ones that held concentrated positions that had pronounced trends. Passport Capital, a $3.4 billion macro hedge fund based in San Francisco, rose 18% last year, partly because it piled more than half its assets into commodity-related equities such as Riversdale, an Australian mining company. Bridgewater, a large macro fund, gained nearly 45%, aided by its bets on gold and American and European bonds. Autonomy Capital was up 26%, partly because it shorted the euro and European credit and went long on various Asian currencies. Owning commodity currencies, such as the Canadian dollar, also proved lucrative for some funds.

DIVERSIFICATION BENEFITS OF MANAGED FUTURES

A typical proponent of the benefits of managed futures phrased them as follows: "Managed futures provide direct exposure to globally traded futures contracts on physical commodities such as grains, livestock, metals, energies and soft commodities (coffee, cotton, sugar, cocoa), and financial assets such as equity market indices, government bonds and currencies. In addition, often the same economic and market shocks that negatively impact traditional assets create opportunities in commodity markets; managed futures thus offer the potential for true portfolio diversification."

There is extensive literature going back to the 1980s that argues that managed futures programs are ideal for inclusion in investment portfolios because of their diversification benefits and because they tend to perform well in a crisis *if* markets present a trend that is sustained long enough for their models to profit. This indeed occurred during the Russian debt crisis in 1998, when this strategy rose nearly 20% while the hedge fund index lost money and the major markets lost even more. The performance during the credit crisis and its aftermath has been more uneven, as shown in Tables 19–1 to 19–3, which has tarnished the strategies' reputation.

There is also contrary analysis that casts doubt on the usefulness of managed futures. This doubt is perhaps best expressed in the title of a recent paper: "Fooling Some of the People All of the Time: The Inefficient Performance and Persistence of Commodity Trading Advisers."[*]

HISTORICAL PERFORMANCE OF MACRO AND CTA STRATEGIES

The most notable feature of Macro/CTA is their significantly lower maximum drawdown than equity, event-driven, or relative value strategies. This strategy comes closest to the hedge fund model's goal of absolute returns and downside protection, and helps explain the increase in assets managed by these hedge funds (Tables 19–1 to 19–3).

TABLE 19–1

Macro and CTA Performance 1990–2011

	HFRI Macro: Systematic Diversified Index	HFRI Macro (Total) Index	MSCI World (MXWO Index)	Barclays Aggregate Bond Index	Barclays High-Yield Credit Bond Index	S&P GSCI Tot Return Index (SPGSCITR Index)
Yearly average return	11.88%	13.55%	5.23%	7.13%	10.13%	7.80%
Annualized standard deviation	7.45%	7.66%	15.67%	3.76%	9.45%	21.70%
Sharpe ratio	0.85	0.97	−0.02	0.53	0.43	0.08
Max drawdown	−6.23%	−10.70%	−55.37%	−5.15%	−33.31%	−67.65%
Skewness	0.12	0.49	−0.61	−0.3	−0.92	−0.14
Kurtosis	−0.3	0.88	1.22	0.75	7.75	2.02

---

[*] Yale ICF Working Paper, October 2008, Geetesh Bahardwaj et. al.

TABLE 19–2

Macro and CTA Performance 1998–2011

	HFRI Macro: Systematic Diversified Index	HFRI Macro (Total) Index	MSCI World (MXWO Index)	Barclays Aggregate Bond Index	Barclays High-Yield Credit Bond Index	S&P GSCI Total Return Index (SPGSCITR Index)
Yearly average return	10.69%	7.52%	4.04%	6.14%	7.93%	7.93%
Annualized standard deviation	8.19%	5.94%	16.85%	3.56%	10.42%	24.39%
Sharpe ratio	0.65	0.4	−0.11	0.31	0.19	0.06
Max drawdown	−6.23%	−7.32%	−55.37%	−3.82%	−33.31%	−67.65%
Skewness	0.18	0.44	−0.67	−0.4	−0.96	−0.36
Kurtosis	−0.43	0.87	1.17	1.4	6.84	1.03

TABLE 19-3

Macro and CTA Performance 2007–2011

	HFRI Macro: Systematic Diversified Index	HFRI Macro (Total) Index	MSCI World (MXWO Index)	Barclays Aggregate Bond Index	Barclays High-Yield Credit Bond Index	S&P GSCI Total Return Index (SPGSCITR Index)
Yearly average return	6.59%	4.84%	-1.22%	6.51%	10.81%	1.50%
Annualized standard deviation	9.10%	5.50%	20.42%	3.60%	14.22%	27.51%
Sharpe ratio	0.18	-0.02	-0.36	0.42	0.24	-0.14
Max drawdown	-6.23%	-5.86%	-55.37%	-3.82%	-33.31%	-67.65%
Skewness	0.42	0.33	-0.55	0.15	-1	-0.79

CHAPTER 20

Hedge Fund of Funds

Funds of hedge funds (FoHFs) are a type of investment company that invests in hedge funds—in a sense, it is both a strategy and a fund structure. FoHFs grew in popularity along with hedge funds; however, they have had to adjust to cope with a changing investment landscape, which has included less investor interest in the FoHF structure.

This chapter addresses both the typical strategies employed by FoHF managers and the challenges that these managers have faced in recent years. Recent history has shown that the FoHFs that are continuing to thrive are the ones that offer a combination of the following: access to new manager talent, wrappers such as the European Union's Undertakings for Collective Investment in Transferable Securities Directives (UCITS) and registered investment companies (RICs), which make these funds more accessible, an ability to offer customized services, and hedge fund advisory relationships.

PORTFOLIOS OF MULTIPLE HEDGE FUNDS

FoHFs are investment companies that pool together the assets of multiple investors and invest these funds in hedge funds. FoHFs are structured similarly to hedge funds with a general partner, limited partners, investment manager, and some of the same service providers. They face similar regulations and restrictions as hedge funds in terms of investor eligibility, marketing, and offering documents. The key difference is that FoHFs typically do not take market positions.

The FoHF structure is comparable to other more familiar vehicles such as mutual funds. Whereas mutual funds invest in stocks or bonds, FoHFs invest in hedge funds. In both cases, they present investors with alternatives to investing directly in stocks, bonds or hedge funds.

FoHFs have historically been marketed as offering diversification through the inclusion of multiple hedge funds, conducting due diligence on underlying managers, providing access to exclusive managers, and possessing expertise in selecting future superstar managers (Figure 20–1). In exchange for these value offerings, fund of funds managers typically charge investors a management fee of 1% and an incentive fee of 10%, which is charged over and above the 2/20 compensation of the underlying managers.

TYPES OF FoHFs

FoHFs come in a wide variety of types and strategies, from globally diversified FoHFs that may have 50 or more hedge funds in their portfolio, to FoHFs that only invest in one hedge fund. FoHFs can be differentiated by a number of criteria, including the number and diversity of hedge funds in their portfolio, the extent to which they have a strategy focus, the geographical concentration, and the level of exposure to market movements. The following is an overview of some of the major types of FoHFs.

Globally Diversified FoHFs

Globally diversified FoHFs are the most common type and account for the largest share of assets under management. As the name implies, their portfolio includes hedge funds from a wide range of strategies. They sometimes have as many as 100 or more hedge funds in their portfolio, although 30–50 hedge funds is more common.

Globally diversified FoHFs have advantages and disadvantages. The main advantage is that their extreme diversification has

FIGURE 20-1

Funds of Hedge Funds: Seek to Assemble the Optimal Mix of Managers and Strategies

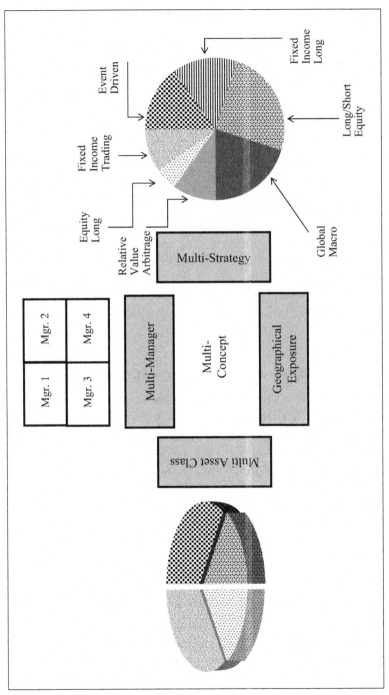

meant that these FoHFs tend to have relatively low volatility and relatively low correlation to the major markets or, indeed, to the hedge fund universe. Globally diversified FoHFs have traditionally been used as a source of stability and diversification in portfolios. Their low volatility has also led to numerous product offerings that add leverage to fund of funds, often using structured products provided by banks and known as "absolute return" or "guaranteed principal" structures.

The advantages of these FoHFs are also potential sources of disadvantage similar to the problem faced by mutual funds that choose a diversified group of stocks. Analysis and experience has shown that as the number of hedge funds in a globally diversified portfolio increases, their performance tends to converge to a mean. For example, a portfolio of 30 or more stocks converges to the performance of the S&P 500 (this explains the high correlation between the Dow Jones Index, which has 30 stocks, and the S&P 500). In a similar manner, globally diversified FoHFs tend to have similar returns and volatilities, making it difficult to differentiate one from another.

Style- and Strategy-Specific FoHFs

FoHFs are often concentrated in one or few hedge fund styles and strategies. Thus, there are FoHFs for virtually every hedge fund strategy, including equity long/short, market neutral, global macro, distressed debt, event-driven, fixed income, etc. The rationale for these funds is that a portfolio of several managers in a strategy offers improved risk management and wider range of potential returns than a single manager. As with globally diversified FoHFs, there is a tendency to revert to a mean as the number of managers increase, diluting the potential benefit of high-performing managers.

Sector FoHFs

Sector FoHFs focus on a specific market or geographical region. Examples of the former are FoHFs that focus on foreign exchange, emerging markets, equity markets, fixed-income markets, mortgage-backed securities, distressed debt, and, more recently, insurance and weather derivatives. Examples of the latter include regional FoHFs (e.g., Asian or European) and country-specific FoHFs (e.g., China or India).

Directional Versus Risk-Controlled FoHFs

FoHFs are often constructed specifically to have a directional market bias, which means that their performance will have a correlation with the relevant market, which may include equities, fixed income, and currencies. These FoHFs will choose hedge funds that have directional market focus such as global macro or long/short equity funds. Risk-controlled FoHFs in contrast, will choose hedge funds that pursue strategies with limited market exposure, such as relative value, equity market neutral, or multistrategy hedge funds.

Emerging Managers

Because of the current popularity of emerging manager and smaller hedge funds, the number of FoHFs that pursue this approach has increased in recent years. These funds by definition are limited in the amount of money they can put to work with any one fund, and thus need to choose between a focus on just a few funds or a more inclusive approach. As early investors, FoHFs pursuing this strategy are often able to gain concessions on issues such as fees, redemption rights, and transparency. These funds are closely related to seeding and incubation funds, which put money into an emerging manager in return for an equity or profit-sharing arrangement.

GROWTH OF FoHF

The growth of FoHFs has mirrored the growth of hedge funds, growing exponentially from just over 1.8 billion in 1990 to 1.2 trillion by 2007, when they accounted for over 50% of assets in hedge funds (Tables 20–1 to 20–3). One of the reasons for this growth was the fact that FoHFs as a group did not have a negative return until the credit crisis (with the exception of a minor drawdown in 1993). This, together with their relatively low volatility and low correlation with the major markets, led to

TABLE 20-1

FoHF Performance 1990–2011

	HFRI FOF: Conservative Index	HFRI FOF: Diversified Index	HFRI FOF: Market Defensive Index	HFRI FOF: Strategic Index	HFRI FOF: Composite Index	MSCI World (MXWO Index)	Barclays Aggregate Bond Index	Barclays High-Yield Credit Bond Index
Yearly average return	6.73%	7.46%	8.45%	10.85%	7.95%	5.23%	7.13%	10.13%
Annualized standard deviation	4.02%	6.09%	5.93%	8.79%	5.91%	15.67%	3.76%	9.45%
Sharpe ratio	0.35	0.33	0.54	0.54	0.41	−0.02	0.53	0.43
Max drawdown	−20.36%	−21.75%	−8.97%	−26.80%	−22.20%	−55.37%	−5.15%	−33.31%
Skewness	−1.7	−0.45	0.17	−0.47	−0.67	−0.61	−0.3	−0.92
Kurtosis	7.4	3.85	0.87	3.28	3.8	1.22	0.75	7.75

TABLE 20–2

FoHF Performance 1998–2011

	HFRI FOF: Conservative Index	HFRI FOF: Diversified Index	HFRI FOF: Market Defensive Index	HFRI FOF: Strategic Index	HFRI FOF: Composite Index	MSCI World (MXWO Index)	Barclays Aggregate Bond Index	Barclays High-Yield Credit Bond Index
Yearly average return	4.14%	4.75%	6.12%	5.09%	4.71%	4.04%	6.14%	7.93%
Annualized standard deviation	4.40%	6.50%	5.58%	8.90%	6.29%	16.85%	3.56%	10.42%
Sharpe ratio	–0.25	–0.09	0.19	–0.05	–0.1	–0.11	0.31	0.19
Max drawdown	–20.36%	–21.75%	–8.97%	–26.80%	–22.20%	–55.37%	–3.82%	–33.31%
Skewness	–1.72	–0.49	–0.1	–0.63	–0.74	–0.67	–0.4	–0.96
Kurtosis	6.74	4.22	0.73	4.49	4.04	1.17	1.4	6.84

TABLE 20-3

FoHF Performance 2007-2011

	HFRI FOF: Conservative Index	HFRI FOF: Diversified Index	HFRI FOF: Market Defensive Index	HFRI FOF: Strategic Index	HFRI FOF: Composite Index	MSCI World (MXWO Index)	Barclays Aggregate Bond Index	Barclays High-Yield Credit Bond Index
Yearly average return	−0.20%	0.16%	3.69%	−0.02%	0.07%	−1.22%	6.51%	10.81%
Annualized standard deviation	5.62%	6.42%	6.10%	8.26%	6.72%	20.42%	3.60%	14.22%
Sharpe ratio	−0.99	−0.82	−0.2	−0.7	−0.81	−0.36	0.42	0.24
Max drawdown	−20.36%	−21.75%	−8.07%	−26.80%	−22.20%	−55.37%	−3.82%	−33.31%
Skewness	−1.76	−1.26	0.21	−1.09	−1.21	−0.55	0.15	−1
Kurtosis	4.06	2.32	−0.13	1.72	2.16	0.74	1.58	4.62

their inclusion in the portfolios of many investors, both institutional and individual.

However, the assets managed by FoHFs as a share of total hedge fund assets have declined sharply—from 50% in 2007 to 35% in 2011—in the wake of the credit crisis. The reasons for this reversal of fortune include the following:

- FoHFs, which were long seen as the ultimate "absolute return" vehicle lost money during the credit crisis and turned out to be correlated with hedge funds and other markets.
- Many FoHFs were investors in Madoff (and other hedge funds that imploded or lost money), raising questions about their effectiveness in conducting due diligence on hedge funds.
- FoHFs, faced with redemption requests by their investors, in turn flooded hedge funds with redemptions, causing many to put up gates, which in turn meant that FoHF investors were faced with restrictions on redemption.

However, the more important reason is structural: many FoHF investors, such as pension funds, initially allocated to them because of a lack of experience in selecting managers, lack of experience performing due diligence, and difficulty accessing the best in class managers. Increasingly, large investors have shifted to direct investment in hedge funds—especially the larger, better known "brand" hedge funds—bypassing FoHFs (Figure 20–2).

THE CASE FOR INVESTING IN FoHFs

A popular article cuts to the chase when it asks: "Do Fund of Funds Deserve Their Fees on Fees?" FoHFs have been marketed and utilized on the basis of their benefits to investors, especially in manager selection, due diligence, risk management, access, and portfolio construction services.

Because they pool together the assets of multiple investors, FoHFs are able to gain the benefits of size in their relationship to hedge funds. This translates into some specific benefits for investors, including the following:

FIGURE 20–2

Estimated Number of Funds: Hedge Funds vs. Fund of Funds 1990 – 2011

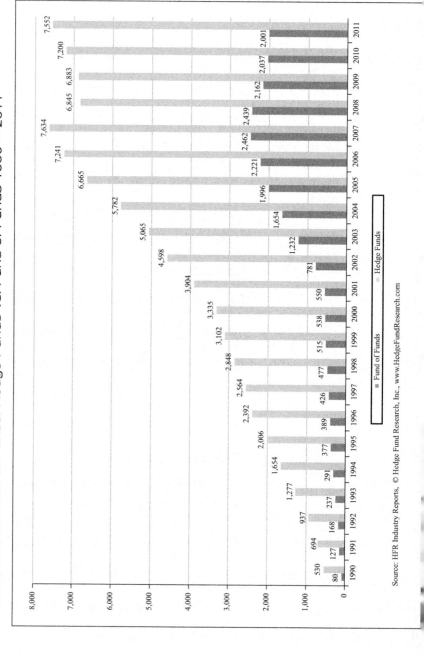

Source: HFR Industry Reports, © Hedge Fund Research, Inc., www.HedgeFundResearch.com

Access to closed funds: FoHFs are able to invest in many funds that are closed to other investors. The larger FoHFs have substantial assets to invest, making them attractive to hedge funds. In addition, many FoHFs have had a long history of investing with popular hedge funds, and are often able to invest additional funds.

Allows small investments to multiple funds: Hedge funds often have minimum investment amounts that effectively limit the ability of smaller investors to invest in multiple managers. FoHFs pool investors' funds and are therefore able to meet these minimum requirements and diversify their holdings.

Negotiate favorable fees and conditions: The scale of FoHF assets and their relationship with individual hedge funds often allow them to gain preferential treatment from hedge funds, for example, preferential redemption provisions, lower fees, greater transparency, and access to future capacity for investment. These benefits are often formalized in "side letters."

Access to leverage and structured products: FoHFs at times offer leverage and "principal protection" programs to investors. Leverage is provided by banks who use the underlying portfolio of hedge funds as collateral on their lending.

Liquidity management: FoHFs have the potential to offer investors greater liquidity than would be available through direct investing, although there are limitations since liquidity is ultimately constrained by the liquidity of the underlying hedge funds.

One tactic is for FoHFs to invest in hedge funds that offer liquidity, for example, CTA and equity long/short and fixed-income arbitrage. This, however, has a problem: it limits the FoHFs to a narrow range of hedge fund styles and may limit their investment in more illiquid funds that may offer the best returns. Another potential drawback is that large-scale investor redemptions are met by liquidating the more liquid hedge funds, leaving behind a portfolio with a different composition than initially contemplated or established.

Another strategy used by FoHFs is to establish a redemption "buffer" either in the form of keeping a portion of their assets in liquid form or establishing credit lines with banks. A more onerous option is for FoHFs to impose liquidity restrictions such as gates and lockups, an option that many FoHFs used in the credit crisis.

TRENDS IN FoHFs

FoHFs are undergoing a fundamental transformation that has led some observers to question their future role in the hedge fund industry. The *Economist* magazine, for example, ran a recent story about FoHF named "Going, Going, Gone?" However, FoHFs still control $600 billion in assets and are adopting strategies to deal with a changed environment. This section addresses the pressures besetting FoHFs as well as their responses

Growth of Direct Investing in Hedge Funds

Three trends intersected to undermine the intermediary role of FoHFs between hedge funds and investors. First, the entry of extremely large institutional investors into hedge fund investing has given them the expertise and clout to deal directly with hedge funds. Hedge funds, on their side, are eager to tap into this source of future growth and long-term investing approach and are specifically gearing up to manage direct investments by these institutions. They are following an explicit strategy to become "institution ready" by sinking resources into risk management, compliance, operational infrastructure, and regulatory registration.

Third, institutional investors have begun to ask hedge funds for managed accounts, which segregate an institution's funds into an account that they control and can monitor on an ongoing basis. Managed accounts bypass FoHFs and are managed directly by hedge funds (Figure 20–3).

Concentration of the FoHF Assets

There is a clear trend to a concentration of assets with the largest FoHFs. In the past several years, for example, the new money flowing into the FoHFs sector is disproportionately aimed at larger FoHFs. Figure 20-4 shows the largest 25 FoHFs as of the end of 2011. In addition to the size of the firms, it is worth noting that a large number, especially in the top 10, are managed by banks (UBS, Goldman Sachs, Credit Suisse, etc.) and traditional money management companies (for example, Blackstone, the world's largest FoHF management company and BlackRock).

FIGURE 20-3

Direct Allocations vs. FOHFs

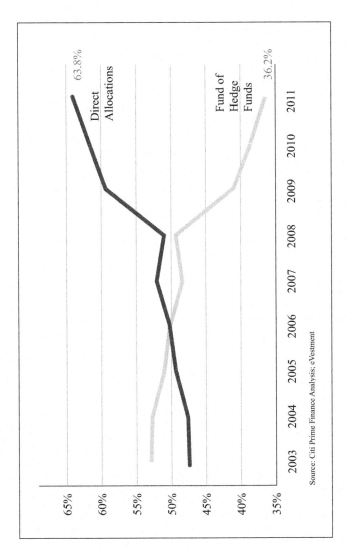

Source: Citi Prime Finance Analysis; eVestment

FIGURE 20-4

FoHF Managers Ranked by Assets 2011

FoHF Managers	FoHF Assets under Management (in $ Bln)
Blackstone Alternative Asset Management	$37
UBS	30
Grosvenor Capital	24
Permal Group	21
Goldman Sachs	20
BlackRock	18
Lyxor Asset Mgmt.	16
Union Bancaire Privee	15
Mesirow Advanced Strategies	14
Man Group	14
Credit Suisse Asset Management	12
Aurora Investment Mgmt.	11
K2 Advisors	10
J.P. Morgan	10
Pacific Alternative Asset Mgmt. Co.	9
Morgan Creek Capital Mgmt.	9
Financial Risk Mgmt.	9
Morgan Stanley Investment Mgmt.	9
Gottex Fund Mgmt.	8
GAM	8
Fauchier Partners	8
Rock Creek Group	7
EIM Group	7
Arden Asset Mgmt.	6
Prisma Capital Partners	6

Where does this leave the smaller FoHFs?

Economics is one factor at work here. To compete for the institutional funds, a FoHF will need significant investment in resources, which will only reinforce the trend to concentration. Thus, smaller FoHFs will need to focus on strategies that require fewer resources.

One approach taken by FoHFs is to pursue niche areas—such as emerging managers—that do not call for scale and may be overlooked by the larger FoHFs. They will be able to operate on a smaller scale—and may be able to underprice larger FoHFs—and by focusing on niches may be able to show that they can provide performance and/or diversification benefits that are not available from the larger funds.

Another approach is to become more like consulting firms (who are already making inroads in this area) and provide an advisory relationship with clients that may include the development of customized portfolios, risk management, and due diligence. These advisory relationships will not need significant investments in infrastructure and can therefore be offered at a lower cost to investors.

Possible Drawbacks of Concentration

The concentration of assets with the larger FoHFs, combined with a similar concentration among hedge funds, may present some drawbacks for investors. First, concentration has a feedback loop that leads to more concentration. The mutual fund industry is an example of this. The concentration may also cause a convergence of results as larger and larger firms are forced to invest with the same hedge funds. Finally, there is the danger of massive redemptions as large institutions redeem from large FoHFs who in turn redeem from large hedge funds. We saw this problem during the credit crisis.

Consolidation of the FoHF Industry

The last few years have seen an accelerating trend for the consolidation of the FoHF segment with larger firms purchasing smaller firms. In the years leading up to 2007, FoHF managers invested heavily in staff, infrastructure, and operational support services in order to serve a booming investor base. As the FoFH industry shrinks, these expenses have made many FoHFs economically unviable unless they have significant assets under management. However, industry consolidation has led instead to a decline in assets for many FoHFs. The likely result is further consolidation within the industry.

There have been some notable cases of consolidation, such as the purchase of FRM by the Man Group, one of the largest FoHF groups. However, the fact that FRM did not receive any upfront payment speaks to the difficulties in this consolidation. As with any merger or acquisition, there are the attendant issues in combining cultures, personnel, inherited exposures, and investment philosophies. In addition, the redundancy in funds, strategies, clients, and hedge fund due diligence is often an example of 2 plus 2 equal 3. The successful acquisitions will be ones where the firms have clear synergies in terms of expertise (e.g., a regional or country focus), client base (e.g., an institutional, high-net-worth, or regional base), and personnel.

PART SIX

Hedge Funds and Investment Portfolios

CHAPTER 21

Modern Portfolio Theory and Efficient Market Hypothesis

This chapter covers some complicated technical subjects in modern portfolio theory and investment management. However, an understanding of these subjects is necessary to understand how investments are managed in a portfolio context. Investors need to consider how hedge funds work with their other investments; to take a portfolio approach to their investments. The central question in this chapter is whether the prevalent methods used in the investment industry for managing investment portfolios lead to portfolios that provide investors with "optimal" or even favorable risk adjusted returns. To anticipate the answer, the evidence is mixed and complicated by the fact that traditional portfolio management methods have been questioned and undermined by competing theories, notably those that emerged from the field of behavioral finance.

The dominant methods used by the investment management industry for analyzing and constructing investment portfolios are based on modern portfolio theory (MPT), which emerged in the 1950s and 1960s and has become dominant in academia and in traditional investment management. It is also widely influential in the hedge fund and alternative investment arena.

MPT owes its genesis to Harry Markowitz, whose famous 1952 paper stated that "investing is a bet on an unknown future . . . You have to think about risk as well as return." (Markowitz, 1952) While this seems uncontroversial, it has spawned a multitrillion dollar asset management industry around the central idea that there is a trade-off between risk and return: to gain additional returns, investors must accept additional risk.

Another basic tenet of MPT, especially relevant for hedge fund investors, is that the appropriate benchmark for evaluating an investment is at the portfolio level, not the individual security or even asset class. In other words, no investment stands alone; it needs to be evaluated in the context of an investor's total investment portfolio. In what has been described as the only "free lunch" in finance, MPT states that the addition of an investment to a portfolio with a low correlation with the other portfolio investments leads to a reduction in the risk of the overall portfolio. This can be true even if the added investment has a higher risk (as measured by standard deviation) than any of the other portfolio investments.

MPT has evolved into two main models: the Capital Asset Pricing Model CAPM and the efficient markets hypothesis, which are addressed below in turn.

CAPITAL ASSET PRICING MODEL AND MEAN–VARIANCE OPTIMIZATION

CAPM was developed in the 1960s by William Sharpe and John Lintner drawing on the work of Harry Markowitz. They advanced the idea that each investment contains two distinct risks: systematic risk, which affects the price of all securities and cannot be diversified away; for example, inflation, stock market movements or interest rates; and unsystematic risk, which is specific to individual investments and can be diversified away by increasing the number of uncorrelated investments in a portfolio.

CAPM puts forth the concept that by having a large number of assets in their portfolio, investors can average out unsystematic risk and create a sufficiently diversified portfolio so that the only remaining risks are systematic risks. When this is done successfully, investors can then gauge the required return on an asset on the basis of its riskiness in the portfolio context as opposed to its stand-alone risk of each asset.

CAPM also assumes that investors are risk averse and only care about the mean return and the variance (a measure of risk) of that return for their portfolio. The model is thus called mean–variance optimization (MVO) since investors seek to minimize the variance of portfolio return given the expected return and maximize the expected return given the variance.

PORTFOLIO CONSTRUCTION USING MVO

MVO is the cornerstone of MPT and the CAPM. While intellectually elegant, it has one drawback: it is rarely used by investors in its "pure form" for portfolio construction without adding qualitative overlays or constraints that, for all intents and purposes, weaken the results of the optimization.

MVO calculates the allocation of assets in a portfolio to achieve an "efficient portfolio"—the portfolio with the highest expected return for a given level of risk. Efficient portfolios are those that minimize risk associated with getting a specific return. By calculating an efficient portfolio at every possible risk level, MVO yields an "efficient frontier," which is the possible combination of assets that would form efficient portfolios.

Figure 21–1 is typical of the output of an MVO, in this case the optimization of a portfolio composed entirely of stocks and bonds.

FIGURE 21–1

Illustration of Modern Portfolio Theory (MPT) and Capital Asset Pricing Model (CAPM)

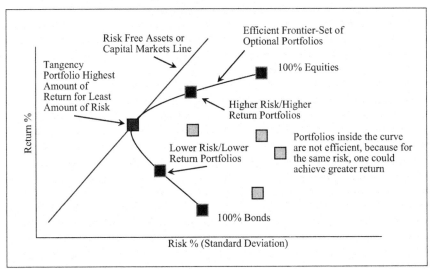

The two axes are the portfolio's return and risk (standard deviation) measured in percent. The black line is the efficient frontier. Various points along the line represent portfolios with different mixes of stocks and bonds. The point at which the straight line is tangent to the curve represents the amount of least risk that is achievable with this asset mix. Other asset mixes are possible and the ultimate one selected depends on the level of risk the investor is willing to accept; however, the mix must be on the efficient frontier line if it is to maximize the return for a given level of risk.

One of the reasons for the popularity of MVO is the minimal amount of information needed for each asset in the portfolio to derive this efficient frontier: these include historical return, historical volatility (as measured by standard deviation), historical correlation between assets, and the investor's tolerance for risk. The MVO investment process is shown in Figure 21–2. There are any number of commercially available software programs that will calculate an efficient frontier distribution, including Barra and PerTrac, both of which also provide easy access to hedge fund databases such as HFR.

FIGURE 21–2

Mean Variance Optimization Investment Process

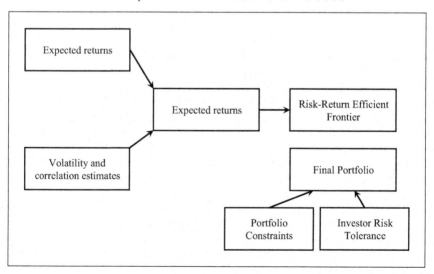

THE PROBLEM WITH MVO

The reasons that MVO is seldom used in its theoretical formulation are relatively well known. Aside from issues of the accuracy of the data used in hedge fund analysis, a number of assumptions underlie the MVO method: assumptions that often prove to be wrong. The main assumptions are:

- All the inputs for the analysis are 100% accurate; there is no uncertainty.
- The data used to calculate the returns for each asset are:
  - Normally distributed
  - Constant over time
  - Set to the appropriate time frame
- The standard deviation and correlations are constant over time.
- Markets are liquid, efficient, and frictionless.

Each of these assumptions contains major problems. For example, the returns of hedge funds are not normally distributed and have a pronounced fat tail. Further, hedge fund returns, standard deviations, and correlations are not stable over time. These violations of the MVO assumptions are important since the assumption implicit in MVO is that the historical returns are representative of future returns. Finally, markets are not liquid or frictionless and not as efficient as the theory would require.

One of the major problems with the MVO method is that it generates portfolios that are dominated by a small number of assets. The mathematics of the MVO is such that assets that have higher risk-adjusted returns squeeze out those that are even marginally lower. As a result, the recommendations of MVO are unstable and very often overweight some assets and underweight others that have only slight differences in their risk and return. (See Figure 21-3.)

ATTEMPTS TO "FIX" MVO

Constrained Optimization

One commonly used approach to modify the MVO process is to place minimum and/or maximum constraints on the amount that may be allocated to any given hedge fund and/or hedge fund strategy. The problem with this approach is that it tends to drive the allocation to the maximum and minimum constraints, as illustrated below. An unconstrained MVO leads to a portfolio that allocates 45.57% of the portfolio to event-driven hedge funds and 46.2% to global macro hedge funds. If the MVO is constrained so that no single hedge fund can have an allocation of less than 5% or greater than 20%, the result, as shown in Table 21–1, drives each hedge fund allocation toward either 5% or 20%.

As should be clear by comparing the radical differences between allocations in the unconstrained MVO portfolio and the portfolio with minimum and maximum constraints, constraints effectively override the results of the MVO analysis with the subjective assumptions of the manager. Constraints are effective recognition of incomplete information and lack of trust in the results of MVO. No investment manager will take the risk of actually allocating the majority of their portfolio to two instruments.

TABLE 21–1

Unconstrained Versus Constrained MVO

	Unconstrained MVO Portfolio	5% Minimum 20% Maximum Constraint
Convertible arbitrage index	0.00	9.09%
Dedicated short bias index	0.00	5.00
Emerging markets index	0.00	5.00
Equity market neutral index	8.23%	20.00
Event driven index	45.57%	20.00
Fixed income arbitrage index	0.00	5.00
Global macro index	46.20%	15.17
Long/short equity index	0.00	5.74
Managed futures index	0.00	5.00
Fund of funds index	0.00	5.00

Black–Litterman Solution

A more theoretically satisfying approach and one that has gained in popularity among investment managers is the Black–Litterman (B–L) model, which is a variant of MVO but begins with the assumption that historical returns are not the correct measure of future returns. The approach is also wary of forecasted returns, which vary widely from one forecaster to another. The B–L approach posits that the starting place for asset allocation is the implied returns of the existing asset allocation in the marketplace. In the case of hedge funds, the starting point is the actual allocation of assets among the various strategies. B–L then calculates the returns implied by this allocation, and uses these as inputs into an optimization program.

While the details of the B–L method are complex and beyond the scope of this book, the advantage to B–L is that it produces portfolio results that are realistic and can be used to actually construct portfolios.

INDUSTRY PRACTICE FOR DERIVING OPTIMAL PORTFOLIOS

The shortcomings of MVO have left hedge fund investors to develop other methods for determining "optimal" portfolios. These methods apply to both portfolios of hedge funds and portfolios that include hedge funds and other investments. The approach most commonly used is to construct and compare hypothetical portfolios that include different mixes of assets, including hedge funds, and then see how they would have behaved in the past, assuming that this is an indication of how they will perform in the future.

The AIMA/KPMG Study on the Value of the Hedge Fund Industry, for example, is typical of this type of portfolio construction. The study constructs a portfolio composed of one-third each of stocks, bonds, and hedge funds, and compares it with a "traditional" portfolio of 60% stocks and 40% bonds. On the basis of these results, the study concludes: "Hedge funds provide economically important, risk-adjusted performance that provides investor with diversification benefits, even during the most difficult macroeconomic environment." The equal-weighted portfolio policy in

TABLE 21—2

Hedge Funds' Diversification Benefits

	1/3 in Hedge Funds, Stocks, and Bonds	60/40 in Stocks and Bonds	Difference	p-Value
Mean	7.52	6.80	0.72	
Std	7.36	9.52	−2.16	
Skewness	−0.83	−0.72	−0.11	
Kurtosis	1.94	1.73	0.21	
Sharpe	0.53	0.34	0.19	0.001
Max drawdown (%)	−0.28	−0.36	0.08	
Value at risk at 5%	3.55	4.67	−1.12	

Source: Centre for Hedge Fund Research

hedge funds, global stocks, and bonds outperforms the conventional 60/40 allocation to stocks and bonds with significantly higher Sharpe ratio and lower tail risk. Specifically, the analysis concludes that an institutional investor, who adds hedge funds to the conventional 60/40 portfolio policy, can gain economically important benefits of diversification (Table 21–2).

CHAPTER 22

Behavioral Critique of Efficient Market Hypothesis

The efficient market hypothesis (EMH) is another aspect of modern portfolio theory that states that an investor cannot consistently earn returns above the average returns of the market. A corollary of the hypothesis is that markets follow a "random walk" that precludes the possibility of predicting or gaining from market trends. According to the hypothesis, any deviation from efficient market prices will be exploited by arbitrage until the deviation is eliminated. Clearly, the EMH presents a challenge for hedge funds. If it is true, then hedge funds would be unable to generate risk-adjusted returns that are better than the average returns available in the marketplace, for example by investing in an S&P 500 Index mutual fund. It is no coincidence that Burton Malkiel, author of *A Random Walk Down Wall Street* and a leading advocate of EMH, is also one of the most vocal critics of hedge funds.

EMH rests on a number of assumptions that were laid out largely by Nobel Laureate Paul Samuelson. These assumptions included the following:

- Individual investors form investment expectations rationally.

- Expectations are based on all available information.

- Markets aggregate information efficiently.

- Equilibrium (i.e., market) prices incorporate all information.

From these assumptions, EMH derived the theory that in an efficient market (i.e., a competitive, large, liquid market where information is complete and widely disseminated and the cost of trading is minimal), future price changes cannot be predicted since market prices already incorporate all the information and expectations of all market participants.

"ANIMAL SPIRITS": BEHAVIORAL FINANCE AND THE CHALLENGES TO EMH

One of the criticisms of EMH is that these assumptions do not exist in the real world. There have been a number of challenges to EMH, but the most trenchant comes from behavioral finance, which points out that humans do not always act rationally and that investment decisions are tainted by emotions that cast doubt on the EMH. The two leaders of behavioral finance, Kahneman and Tversky, laid out their theory in 1979 in an article called "Prospect Theory: An Analysis of Decision Under Risk." Behavioral finance theory has identified a number of biases endemic to all people and that these biases influence investment decisions. These include the following:

- *Anchoring:* Decisions are based on information that seems to support the correct answer.

- *Magical thinking:* We attribute causes to a desired outcome even if the outcome is random.

- *Mental accounting:* We divide information into different compartments and try to optimize each compartment rather than the whole.

- *Overconfident behavior:* We overestimate our ability to make correct decisions, discounting past experience and contrary information.

- *Persuasion effect:* We rely more on the source of information than on the content.

- *Prospect theory:* We are more averse to taking losses than we are to keeping profits.

- *Biased expectations:* People tend to be overconfident in their predictions of the future.

- *Reference dependence:* Investment decisions are affected by an investor's reference point (i.e., existing prices of securities), which may be arbitrary.

- *Representativeness bias:* We tend to think that existing trends are likely to continue.

The implication of these behavioral biases is that markets are not efficient and it is therefore possible to profit from market inefficiencies if an investor can predict how these biases distort market prices.

Two modifications to EMH, based largely on behavioral finance, were developed by Andrew Lo in "The Adaptive Market Hypothesis" (Lo, 2004) and by Robert Schiller in *Irrational Exuberance* (Schiller, 2007).

Lo's theory is that investors do not have the time or ability to perform the "utility optimization" demanded by EMH. Instead, they engage in "satisficing," making choices that are satisfactory, even if not optimal. Through trial and error, investors form a set of rules, known as "heuristics," that guide their decisions. The problem arises when, as environmental conditions change, the heuristics turn out to be inappropriate or even self-defeating.

Schiller's theory is that investors are prone to behavior that causes "irrational exuberance," a strong belief that a trend in the market will continue. This behavior leads investors to ignore contradictory information and leads to the "bandwagon effect" and "market contagion" that are the hallmarks of a "bubble." Schiller explains both the technology bubble of the 1990s and the real estate bubble of the 2000s as manifestations of investors' irrational exuberance.

Lo and Schiller's theories are clearly relevant in explaining the credit crisis as well as the problems in investment analysis. The wild card in both theories is that these biases can exist for long periods of time, and it is therefore impossible to predict when the markets will correct. This is clearly evident by the long duration of the rise in housing prices between 2003 and 2007.

IMPLICATIONS OF BEHAVIORAL FINANCE

The behavioral finance criticisms of mean–variance optimization (MVO) imply that it is possible to derive returns that are higher than average market returns. The problem, however, has been to develop approaches that take advantage of the findings of behavioral finance.

The exception is in trend following or momentum of securities' prices. Andrew Lo has done extensive research in this area and found that markets do have trends and momentum that can be used to generate profits. These trends are derived from the behavior of market participants and essentially mean that there is information stored in past performance that will predict future performance.

CHAPTER 23

Institutionalization of Hedge Funds

While institutional investment in hedge funds has risen steadily over the past 20 years, the great majority of this increase has occurred in a spurt of growth between 2001 (the bursting of the Internet bubble) and 2007 (the onset of the credit crisis). This rapid growth was a result of a shift in the perception of hedge funds by institutions from a source of outsized returns (and possible outsized risk) to possessing the potential to provide diversification benefits, low volatility, and a potential source of alpha in investment portfolios. The transition was aided by the growth of the fund of hedge fund (FoHF) industry and the acceptance of hedge funds by some of the larger pension fund and endowment-and consulting firms such as Cambridge Associates and Russell Investments, who developed separate groups devoted to alternative investments.

The hedge fund industry reached a milestone in the past few years as institutional investors overtook wealthy individuals as the largest group of hedge fund investors, accounting for nearly 60% of their total assets. The trend points to institutions playing more and more of a role in the hedge fund universe; more than for mutual funds, where there are no restrictions on individual investments (Figure 23–1).

As Figure 23–2 shows, endowments and foundations, which had been the trailblazers in terms of institutional investments in

FIGURE 23-1

Hedge Fund Asset Evolution over Time

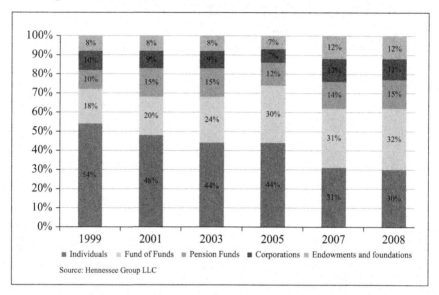

Source: Hennessee Group LLC

hedge funds, increased the share of their portfolios that were placed in hedge funds from 12% in 2002 to nearly 23% in 2007. Despite the disappointing performance of hedge funds during the credit crisis, institutions maintain nearly 20% of their funds in hedge funds. This has much to do with the influence of the "Yale endowment model," which is described below.

Sovereign wealth funds were later entrants into hedge funds, but showed a marked increase in the 2000s. A number of sovereign wealth funds, notably those of Abu Dhabi, Saudi Arabia, and Singapore, had been early and significant investors in hedge funds. However, this trend became more generalized and hedge funds now account for nearly 7.6% of their assets.

Pension funds were late entrants into hedge fund investments primarily because of the institutional and regulatory hurdles that had to be overcome before a new asset class was allowed into their portfolios. Indeed, the first significant investors were the largest public pension plans that had the resources to analyze and vet hedge funds as investments, including CalPERS, the largest pension fund in the United States, Stichting Pensioenfonds ABP, the

FIGURE 23-2

Growth of Institutional Investor Interest in Hedge Funds by Segment

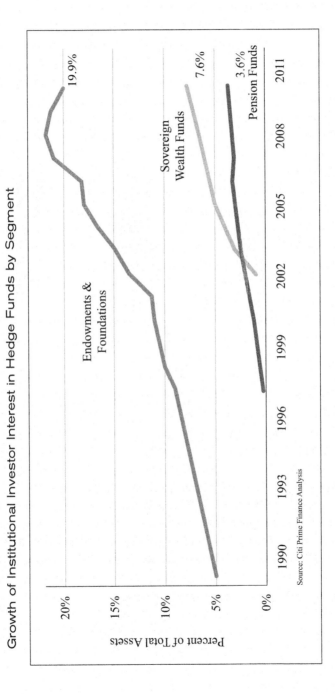

Source: Citi Prime Finance Analysis

FIGURE 23-3

Breakdown of Institutional Assets by 2016

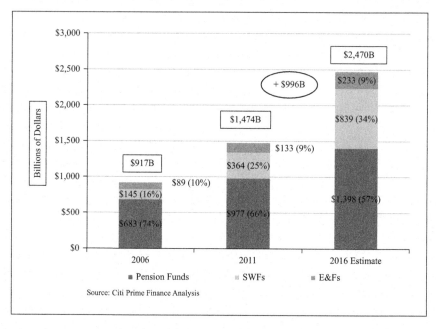

massive Dutch pension fund (with over $300 billion in assets under management), and several U.K. pension funds.

The picture looks very different from the viewpoint of the hedge fund industry. As shown in Figure 23–3, while endowments have a larger portion of their assets in hedge funds, it is pension funds and, increasingly, sovereign wealth funds that dominate the amount of assets managed by hedge funds. This is because of the massive size of both these segments. Sovereign wealth funds control around $5 trillion in assets as of 2012, while pension funds, as the largest pool of assets in the world, control over $27 trillion (Table 23–1).

INSTITUTIONAL INVESTORS

Institutional investors include foundations and endowments, pension funds, insurance companies, and sovereign wealth funds. These institutions share a number of common features:

TABLE 23–1

Largest Sovereign Wealth Funds

Country	Sovereign Wealth Fund Name	Assets $Billion	Inception	Origin
Norway	Government Pension Fund – Global	$656.2	1990	Oil
UAE – Abu Dhabi	Abu Dhabi Investment Authority	$627	1976	Oil
China	SAFE Investment Company	$567.9**	1997	Non-Commodity
Saudi Arabia	SAMA Foreign Holdings	$532.8	n/a	Oil
China	China Investment Corporation	$482	2007	Non-Commodity
Kuwait	Kuwait Investment Authority	$296	1953	Oil
China – Hong Kong	Hong Kong Monetary Authority Investment Portfolio	$293.3	1993	Non-Commodity
Singapore	Government of Singapore Investment Corporation	$247.5	1981	Non-Commodity
Singapore	Temasek Holdings	$157.5	1974	Non-Commodity
Russia	National Welfare Fund	$149.7*	2008	Oil
China	National Social Security Fund	$134.5	2000	Non-Commodity
Qatar	Qatar Investment Authority	$115	2005	Oil

Source: SWF Institute

- Institutions operate in a highly regulated environment and must comply with a number of federal and state laws governing the rights, responsibilities, and liabilities of their positions.

- Institutional investors are responsible for generating sufficient income to cover the expenses of their plan (i.e., pension benefits, insurance payments, university expenses) while maintaining their principal assets, which are the foundation for all future revenues.

- Institutional investors are striving to meet their short- and long-term commitments in the present economic environment of low single-digit interest rates, stock markets that have not risen in a decade, and increased correlation among formerly diverse investments.

- Institutions, often working with consultants, attempt to follow a well-defined, structured investment process that has some theoretical underpinning.

Institutional investors have traditionally been interested in the theoretical underpinnings of their investment management as a result of their close academic affiliations, their reliance on the mainstream products of the investment industry (notably mutual funds), and their extensive use of consultants, many of whom have academic affiliations. Indeed, the main industry associations, such as the CFA Institute, which administers the Chartered Financial Analyst designation, an important accreditation for those in the industry, is a fount of theoretical discussion and analysis of investment theories.

The issue of how hedge funds fit into an overall portfolio is especially important for institutional investors who have long approached investment from an asset allocation and portfolio management perspective. For these investors, hedge funds are seen as one more investment that needs to fit into a crowded portfolio of investments that are placed into an asset class and compared with other investments in that asset class. Their correlation with other assets is calculated, as is their "alpha" contribution to the portfolio. As a result, the question of where hedge funds fit into this landscape has become central for hedge funds and for institutional investors.

HOW DO HEDGE FUNDS FIT INTO AN INSTITUTIONAL PORTFOLIO

Because of their massive assets, institutional investors have become one of the most intensively studied and analyzed group in the financial industry. In-depth studies, surveys, and industry publications seem to take measure of every nuance of their investment strategies and philosophies. A short list of purveyors of this type of information includes Preqin, Pensions and Investments, Russell Wyatt, Citigroup, and KPMG.

Figure 23–4 reports the results of a large-scale study of institutional investors conducted by Casey Quark and BNY Mellon. According to this survey, institutional investors by a margin of two to one are more interested in the "diversified uncorrelated returns" available from hedge funds than from absolute returns.

This emphasis has led many institutions to consider hedge funds as a part of their core, long-term portfolios rather than a "satellite" investment. It has also led to a change from a monolithic view of hedge funds as a group to a more granular view where different types of hedge funds may play different roles in their investment portfolios. One representative pension fund views hedge funds as comprising the following groupings, with each grouping having a different role in its investment portfolio:

- *Directional long/short hedge funds*, defined as those with at least 50% net long or short exposure, are used to reduce the volatility of their portfolio's equity exposure and protect the portfolio against downside risk. The financial crisis proved the usefulness of this strategy: these hedge funds lost "only" 20% while major equity indices were down 40%, in the same period.

- *Global macro and CTAs* can reduce volatility and protect downside risk against the effects of macro risks, such as inflation, interest rates, commodity, and currency movements, as well as provide some "tail risk" protection during regular periods of market turmoil.

- *Absolute return strategies*, including market neutral, some fixed-income arbitrage, and statistical arbitrage, that have

FIGURE 23-4

What Is Your Investment Rationale for Hedge Funds?

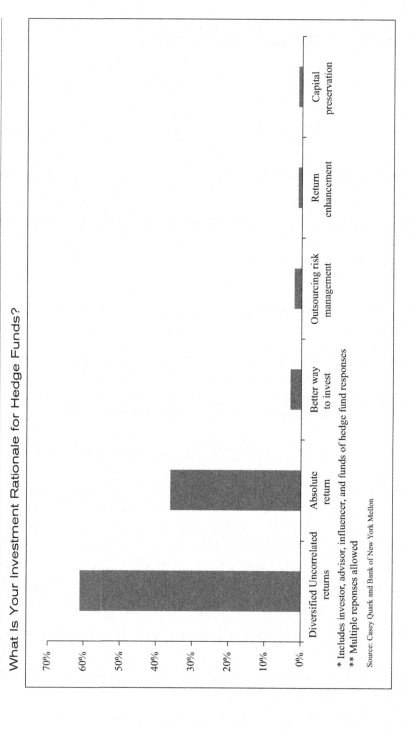

* Includes investor, advisor, influencer, and funds of hedge fund responses
** Multiple reponses allowed

Source: Casey Quark and Bank of New York Mellon

very low net long or short exposure to major markets. These funds are selected to provide uncorrelated returns In a portfolio. They have low betas and are seen as possible providers of portfolio alpha.

HOW INSTITUTIONS INVEST

The manner in which institutions invest in hedge funds has also changed over the past decade. There has been a trend away from reliance on FoHFs toward direct investment in multiple, individual hedge funds either using the institutions' own expertise or with the assistance of fund of funds, specialized consultants, and via "platforms" developed by some large banks. In the discussion that follows, I will discuss three aspects of how institutions invest: their reliance on direct investment in "brand names," the role of "intermediaries," and the convergence of hedge funds and long-only managers.

Investment in Brand Names

There has been a distinct move by institutions to invest in "institutional-ready" hedge funds whose size, scale, infrastructure, and institutional client base has made them a "safe" bet to institutional boards. In choosing hedge funds, U.S. and European pension managers have tended to buy into a select group of established names such as Brevan Howard, Renaissance, Lansdowne, Millennium, Winton Capital, Pershing Square Capital Management, Och-Ziff Capital Management, and Viking Global Investors.

This trend is documented in Figure 23–5, which shows the very different investor profile of larger hedge funds (those with $1 billion and more in AUM) and smaller hedge funds, defined as those with an AUM under $100 million. The larger hedge funds receive a much greater share of their assets from institutions and from fund of funds, who also invest institutional assets.

Evolving Role of Investment Intermediaries

Institutional investors, particularly pension funds, have always been heavily reliant on consultants in determining their long-only

FIGURE 23-5

Source of Hedge Funds Assets by Type of Investor

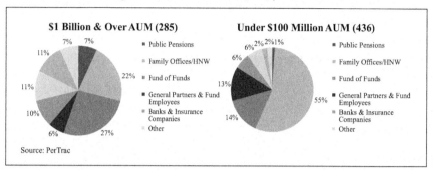

Source: PerTrac

allocations. With direct investment in hedge funds, institutional investors have become increasingly reliant on these consultants who are often seen as a critical "seal of approval" in terms of manager selection, portfolio construction, and operational due diligence. These consultants effectively maintain "lists" of approved hedge funds. These lists determine where the bulk of institutional assets will be allocated.

The decline in the use of fund of funds by institutions has led to a competition and some convergence of fund of funds and consultants. Before 2008, there was a clear separation between FoHFs and consultants. FoHFs were primarily used to obtain access to hedge fund managers. The quality of their access was based on their ability to perform due diligence and evaluate managers, and they required that investors turn over trading authority of their capital by investing in a commingled fund.

An evolving model has institutions investing directly in hedge funds and utilizing consultants (including fund of funds that have adopted consulting businesses) and their own in-house capabilities to conduct the traditional fund of fund functions of manager selection, due diligence, and portfolio construction.

THE BATTLE FOR INSTITUTIONAL ASSETS: HEDGE FUNDS AND LONG-ONLY CONVERGE

There is widespread consensus that institutional assets will dominate the hedge fund industry in the future. It is therefore natural that hedge funds and long-only firms would gird themselves for the battle for these lucrative assets. A number of trends can be discerned from this fast-changing arena.

First, the number of large hedge fund managers with $5 billion or more in AUM is growing, and as these organizations mature they are exploring expanded product opportunities. The ability of some managers to continue raising assets in their core hedge fund offerings becomes constrained above a certain level because of short-side capacity concerns and the problem of generating alpha and high returns when they become too large. Other managers have extensive sunk infrastructure costs and are looking to enhance their margins and leverage their trading expertise by creating new products for existing investors or that target new audiences. Having proven their ability to generate alpha in the long side of the long/short product, they see no reason not to pursue the long-only sector.

Former long-only behemoths looked with envy for years as hedge funds garnered assets from their clients at higher fees and with considerably less administrative, marketing, and operational expenses. They have a number of advantages that will undoubtedly make them strong competitors in this space. For one, they are massive. BlackRock, the largest, manages $3.7 trillion, larger than the U.K. GNP, and has global marketing groups with access to every large institutional investor in the world. Large, long-only firms are also registered with regulatory and enforcement agencies, and thus subject to full disclosure and transparency requirement. They are willing to provide products and services at costs that are well below hedge fund industry levels. Finally, and perhaps most important, they are able to offer products that will undoubtedly compete with some of the hedge fund products.

YALE ENDOWMENT MODEL

The Yale Endowment Model, based on the investment experience of the Yale University endowment under the management of David Swensen, has been instrumental in the growth of institutional investments in hedge funds and other alternative investments. As one of the most successful endowments over a 20-year period, the model has become widely used by institutional and high-net-worth investors, especially after 2000, when Swensen wrote *Pioneering Portfolio Management:*

An Unconventional Approach to Institutional Investment. The key point of the book, from our perspective, is his advocacy for the role of hedge funds (along with private equity and real estate) in institutional investment portfolios. The key principles of the Yale model are as follows:

- Invest in equities rather than fixed income because it is better to be an owner rather than a lender.

- Hold a diversified portfolio; avoid market timing.

- Invest in private markets that have incomplete information and are relatively illiquid to increase long-term incremental returns.

- Allocate capital to investment firms owned and managed by the people actually doing the investing to reduce conflicts of interest.

Yale's portfolio is structured using a combination of academic theory and informed market judgment. The theoretical framework relies on mean–variance analysis, which was described above. Using statistical techniques to combine expected returns, variances, and covariances of investment assets, Yale employs mean–variance analysis to estimate expected risk and return profiles of various asset allocation alternatives and to test sensitivity of results to changes in input assumptions.

Yale's seven asset classes are defined by differences in their expected response to economic conditions, such as price inflation or changes in interest rates, and are weighted in the portfolio by considering risk-adjusted returns and correlations. The university combines the asset classes in such a way as to provide the highest expected return for a given level of risk.

Approximately half of the portfolio is dedicated to event-driven strategies, which rely on very specific corporate events, such as mergers, spin-offs, or bankruptcy restructuring to achieve a target price. The other half of the portfolio contains value-driven strategies, which involve hedged positions in assets or securities that diverge from underlying economic value. Unlike traditional marketable securities, absolute return investments have historically provided returns largely independent of overall market moves.

Two other important aspects of his investment philosophy include:

Alignment of Interests

An important attribute of Yale's investment strategy concerns the *alignment of interests* between investors and investment managers. To that end, absolute return accounts are structured with performance-related incentive fees, hurdle rates, and clawback provisions, which allow the endowment to recoup fees in case of negative returns. In addition, managers invest significant sums alongside Yale, enabling the university to avoid many of the pitfalls of the principal–agent relationship.

Long-Term Investing

Yale's large allocation to nontraditional asset classes stems from their return potential and diversifying power. Alternative investments, by their very nature, tend to be less efficiently priced than traditional marketable securities, providing an opportunity to exploit market inefficiencies. The endowment's long-time horizon is well suited to exploit illiquid, less efficient markets such as venture capital, leveraged buyouts, oil and gas, timber, and real estate.

The Yale model is meant to be a long-term investment model and its results can only be judged on that basis. For example, endowments that adopted the approach a decade ago and made double-digit returns for seven years before suffering two horrendous years (before 2010) would have done well. However, those that only implemented the strategy four years ago probably had two good years and two horrendous years.

A final aspect of the Yale model worth noting is that its success relies on choosing top-performing managers within the hedge fund (and other alternative investment) industry. As noted above, the dispersion of hedge fund returns are such that the returns experienced by investors are highly dependent on the selection of managers.

PENSION FUNDS: CALPERS CASE STUDY

As of 2012, public pension funds in the United States as a whole only had 76% of the assets they needed to meet their projected future obligations, according to a survey released in June 2012 by the National Conference on Public Employee Retirement Systems in Washington. The industry's 23% loss in the fiscal year ended June 2009, the biggest in its history, reduced returns to 5.4% in the 10 years ending in 2009. Public pension funds have been under pressure to meet their projected obligations amid low interest rates, an economic slowdown, and Europe's debt crisis.

California Public Employees' Retirement System (CalPERS), the largest U.S. public pension fund with $228.5 billion in assets, has long turned to hedge funds to increase their returns. In line with the industry, CalPERS' assets dropped by 28% from December 2007 to June 2009. The portfolio has bounced back considerably having gained 13.3% in fiscal 2010 and 21.7% in 2011. The fund, which had been fully funded when the recession began in December 2007, said in January 2012 that it had only about 70% of the money it needs to cover benefits promised to government workers upon their retirement.

CalPERS invested $5.2 billion in hedge funds by the end of 2011, about 2% of its total investment portfolio, which, as it points out, makes it a substantial fund of funds business in its own right. The fund's present existing investment policy allows it to invest up to 5% of its assets in hedge funds, adding potential room for more hedge fund investments.

Mechanics of Investing

CalPERS has a three-pillar investment policy consisting of alignment, transparency, and liquidity. It makes 60% of its hedge fund investments directly by allocating to large managers and relies on fund of funds for regionally focused investments and those in smaller and newer managers. CalPERS has been in the forefront of insisting on scaling fees to performance and has used strategies such as clawbacks and extensions of high-water marks, as well as reduction in fees. The fund is also insistent on maintaining crucial functions—including manager selection, due diligence, and oversight—inside the organization, and has increased staff size accordingly.

Objectives of Investing

In 2002, CalPERS' CIO Mark Anson decided that the main point of investing in hedge funds was to reduce volatility in the plan's overall portfolio, rather than trying to achieve outperformance.

Anson wanted to protect the portfolio from market shocks such as the bursting of the dot-com bubble. However Joseph Dear, the present CIO, has set a performance benchmark for the hedge fund program of U.S. Treasury bills plus 5%. Its goal is to gain equity-like return at a lower level of risk. However, their hedge fund program has underperformed this benchmark.

Separating Alpha and Beta

This is an important issue for CalPERS whose philosophy is that paying hedge fund fees for a beta exposure to stocks or bonds that can be gained from index mutual funds does not make sense. However, CalPERS admits that separating alpha from beta in practice is a nontrivial problem that requires extensive analysis and time commitment.

Asset Class Versus Risk-Based Allocation

The institutional sector, along with CalPERS, has been focused on the use of "risk-based" versus "asset-based" approaches to portfolio construction. Traditionally, portfolios have been constructed on the basis of the inclusion of various asset classes as defined by traditional asset management: stocks, bond, real estate, etc. The change to a focus on risk-based investment is driven by the fact that different asset classes have exposure to common risks. For example, CalPERS finds that its overall portfolio has a 63% exposure to equities, despite the fact that equities as an asset class are a much smaller component of the portfolio.

CHAPTER 24

Hedge Funds and Retail Investors

Many high-net-worth individuals and family offices have been investing in hedge funds for decades. In the past several years, this interest had become more widespread and reached down to individuals that do not meet the criteria of qualified investors needed to invest in the traditional hedge fund (and fund of funds) limited partnership structure. The economics of these efforts to provide hedge fund programs to individuals is simple; with over $60 trillion invested in long-only investment vehicles (compared to $2 trillion in hedge funds), attempting to tap the long only market is a natural strategy for both hedge funds and mutual fund companies.

Alternative products in the mutual fund and ETF space include a wide diversity of products and strategies such as commodities, Treasury Inflation-Protected Securities, REITS, emerging-markets equities and bonds, listed private equity, infrastructure securities, equity volatility, and active strategies used by hedge funds (see Figure 24-1).

There has been a proliferation of vehicles that have some of the characteristics of hedge funds, but allow non-qualified investors to participate. According to a survey by Morningstar, a well-known investment information company, there are currently around 644 alternative-style funds—251 mutual funds and 393 exchange-traded funds, which are mutual funds that trade like stocks. The majority of these were formed in 2011. Interestingly, while the assets of these "alternatives" funds has grown to over $100 billion by 2012 following five years of cash inflows, those of traditional equity funds have declined.

While broad generalizations are always oversimplifications, it is fair to say that retail investors (or more correctly, their advisers) are interested in alternatives because of their potential diversification benefits and risk control, as well as the potential for higher returns than are available from fixed income and equity investments.

FIGURE 24-1

Total Assets in Alternative Mutual Funds & Alternative ETFs

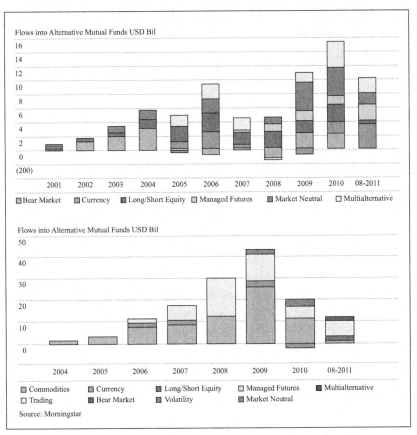

Source: Morningstar

130/30 FUNDS

The Investment Company Act of 1940 allows mutual funds a limited amount of shorting, leverage, and investment in illiquid securities. There are some constraints: shorts or other future obligations to pay must be covered; shorts and leverage are governed under "senior securities" rules, which require minimum asset coverage (after including short proceeds) of 300% of the amount borrowed; liquidity rules call for at least 85% of a fund's assets to be invested in liquid securities—those that can be sold within seven days at approximately the last valuation. However, despite these limitations, many alternative strategies have been packaged in 1940 Investment Advisers Act structures, including mutual funds, ETFs, and closed-end funds.

So-called 130/30 mutual funds were introduced with great fanfare in the mid-2000s as the answer to bringing hedge funds to the masses of investors. They have certainly been the most successful at entering the retail and institutional space, undoubtedly because their mutual fund structures are already familiar to investors and its strategy of long/short equity is a variant of the long only equity funds that dominate the mutual fund industry. Indeed, the major critique of these funds is that they too closely resemble traditional long-only funds and only faintly resemble hedge funds. Their poor performance in preventing losses during 2007–2008 slowed their growth, but it seems likely that it will resume.

The mechanics of a 130-30 fund are diagrammed in Figure 24-2. These funds start with investments in stocks, as in a traditional equity fund. If we assume a $100 million fund, then the manager will purchase a mix of equities with a value of $100 million. Next, the fund will take equity short positions in the amount of $30 million (30% of the fund's assets) using either short sales of individual stocks or of equity indices (i.e., S&P 500). The proceeds of the short sale are then used to purchase $30 million of additional equities. The result is a vehicle that has long bets equal to 130% of the fund's assets; offset by 30% in short positions. (Note, in practice, the fund can be anywhere from 120/20 to 140/40.)

Thus, 130/30 funds utilize two of the characteristics of hedge funds; short positions and leverage. However, the mutual fund structure provides the advantages of liquidity, transparency, lower fees than hedge funds, and no incentive compensation.

FIGURE 24-2

130/30 Mechanics

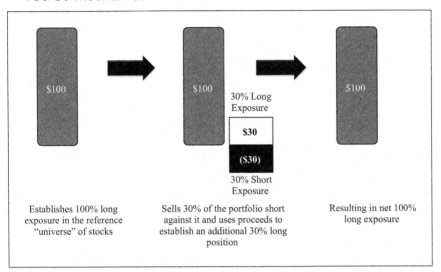

Establishes 100% long exposure in the reference "universe" of stocks	Sells 30% of the portfolio short against it and uses proceeds to establish an additional 30% long position	Resulting in net 100% long exposure

The theoretical benefits of these vehicles include the following:

- they provide some downside protection during bear markets because of the short position

- they allow managers to invest in more long positions, which may lead to additional profits, especially during bull markets

- if properly done, the short component can add value if the stocks selected for shorting do worse than the general market

The key question for investors is whether 130/30 funds actually work in providing portfolio diversification and returns that are at least comparable to (if not higher than) either long/short hedge funds or long only equity funds. The results thus far have been relatively disappointing, although the products have only been around for a few years. Three key problems are noteworthy:

- With only 30% in short position (largely offset by an additional 30% in long positions) it is difficult to provide enough diversification from long only equity positions (i.e., do these vehicles have a low beta with the stock market?) to justify their high fees (relative to long only mutual funds).

- Since many long only managers are inexperienced in short selling, they may not be able to add value to this side of the portfolio.

- Although managers have a total of 160% of assets to take positions, the benefit of the additional 60% depends on their ability to produce returns that outperform the long-only strategy. The mutual fund industry's overall inability to accomplish this task in their long-only funds gives one pause as to whether they can do this in the 130/30 vehicles.

EXCHANGE-TRADED FUNDS

Exchange-traded funds (ETFs) control almost $1.5 trillion of assets. Unlike units in a conventional mutual fund, ETFs can be traded all day long; they have become a means for hedge funds to speculate

TABLE 24–1

Hedge Fund Characteristics Across Domiciles

Investment Trait	Feature of Hedge Funds Across Domiciles	Feature of Open-End, Closed-End, or ETFs Across Domiciles
Public access	Uncommon	Required
Marketing	Very limited, permitted in certain domiciles and structures	Fully permitted with regulated content for public dissemination
Hedges/shorts	Common	Some
Use of leverage	Common	Some, with limitations
Performance fee	Common	Some
High minimum investment	Common	Some
Infrequent redemptions	Common—monthly or quarterly	Uncommon
Pricing requirements	Uncommon	Daily with some exceptions
Redemption gates	Few regulations, but limited in certain structures	Rarely permitted

on the market throughout the trading day, allowing them to make complex bets on illiquid asset classes. See Table 24-1 for a comparison of different types of hedge fund-type products.

Some ETFs are based on commodity indices and property markets; there are leveraged ETFs that offer a geared return on a given index, inverse ETFs that aim to go down when a benchmark goes up (and vice versa) and, inevitably, leveraged inverse ETFs.

EXAMPLES OF ETF ABSOLUTE RETURN FUNDS

Credit Suisse Merger Arbitrage Liquid Index (CSMA): tracks hedge funds using merger-arbitrage strategies. On average, the portfolio will cover 30 to 50 different deals. When it's a cash deal, the fund will buy the target, playing the averages that its price will move closer to the premium paid by the acquirer as the date of the transaction nears. When a deal is primarily made through stock, the exchange traded note will buy the target and short the acquirer.

WisdomTree Managed Futures Strategy (WDTI) tracks 24 futures contracts, ranging from gold and crude oil to the euro as well as corn. The mix is broken into more than a dozen sectors. WDTI's benchmark goes long on sectors when their price is trading above the exponential seven-month moving average. Sectors whose prices show the least momentum are generally shorted.

Dreyfus Emerging Currency Fund (CEW) invests in some dozen currencies, with about 42% in Asia and another 25% in Latin America.

ETF RISKS

Many ETFs do not hold the underlying assets upon which their value is calculated. The portfolio of an S&P 500 ETF, for example, may not consist of a broad range of stocks but of a derivative position with an investment bank as counterparty.

These "synthetic" ETFs are especially common with relatively illiquid asset classes. It may be too costly or impractical to replicate a targeted index of, for example, emerging market stocks. To synthesize this index, the ETF provider usually enters into a transaction known as a total return swap with a bank. The bank agrees to pay the provider an amount equal to the return on the emerging-markets index and the ETF provider hands over cash in return. The bank now has to manage the risk of replicating the index; the provider faces the risk that the bank might go bust. So the ETF provider requires the bank to provide collateral.

However, the collateral is usually unconnected with the index. For example, emerging-markets ETF may have collateral in the form of U.S. and European equities and bonds. Most of it had nothing to do with emerging markets. Were the bank counterparty to fail, the index provider would be left with assets that were unrelated to the target portfolio. In the United States, products labeled as ETFs must hold at least 80% of the portfolio in securities matching the fund's name.

One implication of synthetic ETFs is that they may not provide the liquidity desired by investors. Thus, in principle ETFs offer on-demand liquidity to investors while they are in some cases based on much less liquid underlying assets. However, in the event of a market sell-off or in the underlying markets in any particular ETF, there is a risk of liquidity problems.

HF REPLICATION: PASSIVELY INVESTING IN HEDGE FUNDS

Hedge fund replication refers to programs that attempt to replicate the performance characteristics of hedge funds utilizing liquid traded instruments such as ETFs and futures contracts and other derivative instruments. These programs are based on research that suggests that the returns of many hedge fund strategies are largely driven by common factors that can be replicated through investments in liquid index investment products. The research is based on statistical tools such as regression or factor analysis that determine the factors and weights that will most closely replicate the hedge fund strategy.

Hedge fund replication is a natural outgrowth of the many studies that attempted to find the factors or 'drivers' that account for hedge fund returns and volatility. William Fung and David Hsieh, for example, utilized William Sharpe's return-based style analysis and found that a number of factors can explain a significant percentage of the returns of overall hedge fund indices as well as those of some strategies. Fung and Hsieh's model identified the following seven factors as having a role in determining hedge fund returns:

- S&P 500

- Small cap and large cap

- 10 year bond yield

- Credit spread between corporate bonds and U.S. Treasury bonds

- Trend following in bond price movement

- Trend following in FX prices

- Trend following in commodities prices

Replication products offer the possibility of providing investors with greater transparency and liquidity and to provide access to a wider group of investors than hedge funds. Because these products are relatively new, it is difficult to evaluate their performance compared to hedge funds. It is already clear that the quality of replication (or the extent to which they mirror the hedge fund index) vary considerably among different hedge fund styles, and that it may be difficult to replicate the returns of hedge funds that invest in less liquid products.

Examples of HF Replication Products

A growing number of products were developed to implement the findings of hedge fund replication including the Merrill Lynch Factor Index and Goldman Sachs Absolute Return Tracker (GSART) Index. Morningstar® Nexus Hedge Fund Replication Index is an attempt to replicate the Morningstar Broad Hedge Fund Index. This index is a daily-return index currently composed of approximately 20 liquid financial instruments, including equity index futures, sovereign debt futures, currency contracts, and commodity futures. The commodity futures include positions in precious metals, energy, agricultural commodities, and industrial metals.

IndexIQ had been particularly active in this space, introducing products that not only attempt to replicate overall hedge fund returns, but also those of individual hedge fund strategies. The IQ Hedge Multi-Strategy Tracker ETF attempts to replicate the risk-adjusted return characteristics of hedge funds using various hedge fund investment styles, including long/short equity, global macro, market neutral, event-driven, fixed-income arbitrage and emerging markets. The IQ Hedge Macro Tracker ETF tracks the IQ Hedge Macro Index, which seeks to replicate the risk-adjusted return characteristics of a combination of hedge funds pursuing a macro strategy and hedge funds pursuing an emerging markets strategy. The ProShares Hedge Fund Replication ETF seeks to track the Merrill Lynch Factor Model-Exchange Series, which in turn is based on the HFRI index. An expanded list is presented in appendix B.

SEC REGISTERED FoHF

An increasing number of fund-of-funds operators are seeking to register vehicles with the SEC in a bid to expand their target audiences to retail investors. These registered investment companies, commonly called RICs, include firms such as AllianceBernstein, Arden Asset Management, BlackRock and Fund Evaluation Group.

Designation as a registered investment company means a vehicle can admit an unlimited number of investors, and therefore set a relatively low minimum-investment requirement. The larger capacity makes registered investment companies attractive to big brokerage houses, which can offer them to wealthy clients that want exposure to hedge funds but can't meet by the minimum investment thresholds. AllianceBernstein, for example, is seeking to register a vehicle with a $20,000 investment minimum.

Registered investment companies must comply with most mutual fund regulations, including tougher reporting and liquidity requirements. For investors, there's also a distinct tax advantage—namely, that clients of registered investment companies receive the standard IRS Form 1099, rather than the more burdensome Schedule K-1 that goes to private-fund investors.

PART SEVEN

Managing Hedge Fund Portfolios

CHAPTER 25

Manager Selection and Due Diligence

The construction of portfolios of multiple hedge funds, whether by a fund of hedge funds (FoHF) or an investor investing directly in hedge funds, typically follows a series of steps, as shown in Figure 25–1.

MANAGER SELECTION

A core function of FoHFs is to select managers from the thousands available for inclusion in their portfolio. The goal of this process is to identify managers with superior performance and risk management relative to their peers, as well as to identify any potential problems through the due diligence process. Investors identify hedge funds in a number of ways including by reputation, personal relationships, conferences, and so on. One common method is to use commercial databases, such as Hedge Fund Research, to screen managers along various quantitative criteria (i.e., risk, return, Sharpe, peer group and index ranking, etc.) and qualitative criteria (strategy, redemption restrictions, investment minimums, etc.) and thus narrowing the hedge fund universe to a manageable number, who are then subjected to more intensive research.

Peer group analysis involves comparing hedge funds that pursue similar strategies. Normally, hedge funds are also compared with the relevant strategy benchmark with the goal of selecting

FIGURE 25–1

The Portfolio Construction Process

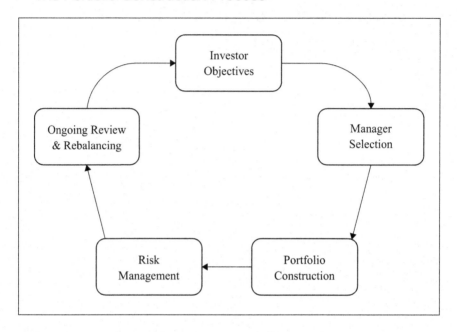

hedge funds that are in the upper tier among their peers. The comparisons are conducted using a range of statistics including return, standard deviation, correlations with relevant benchmarks, and maximum drawdowns. In recent years, the alpha of each hedge fund has been measured as a measure of the extent to which the fund outperforms its peers and the strategy benchmarks.

Once a universe of potential hedge funds have been selected, the FoHFs typically begin a due diligence process that becomes more detailed and intensive as the pool of potential hedge funds becomes smaller.

HEDGE FUND DUE DILIGENCE

Conducting due diligence on hedge funds presents a host of problems not found in a similar exercise for, say, mutual funds. Because of their exemption from many regulations, hedge funds are not required to provide the type of minute information required of mutual funds, although that is beginning to change as a result of the Dodd-Frank Act. Thus, hedge fund investors are left on their own in how to vet hedge funds.

While there is no one due diligence standard in the industry, there are a several recommended best practices and due diligence questionnaires that are widely used, at least as a starting point, in conducting due diligence. The Managed Funds Association, the hedge fund industry association, has a published a "Model Due Diligence Questionnaire for Hedge Fund Investors," and the Alternative Investment Management Association, a U.K.-based industry association, has published "Due Diligence Review of Hedge Fund Managers." A model due diligence questionnaire is presented in appendix A.

It should be noted, however, that due diligence is more than filling out a questionnaire. It requires a thorough understanding of the hedge fund's strategy, the risks inherent in the strategy and how they are controlled; the background and experience of the key personnel; the operations and administration of the fund; the independent service providers; and the fund's performance. This information is gained through a combination of discussions with the hedge fund key personnel, review of the fund's operations, quantitative analysis of the fund's risk and returns, comparison to peer groups and indices, review of all marketing and offering documents, among other factors.

In broad terms, hedge fund due diligence consists of two parts: initial due diligence, which is conducted before investing in a fund; and ongoing due diligence, which occurs throughout the tenure of the investment. Typically, much of the information gleaned from initial due diligence (i.e., the educational background of the fund manager) does not change much over time. The ongoing due diligence is therefore focused on monitoring any changes in the fund's personnel, strategy, operations, or service providers that could lead the investor to reconsider their investment.

The following is a broad overview of the areas that are typically covered in a due diligence process. It is not meant to be comprehensive or to be a substitute for understanding the particular features of any individual hedge fund or an in-depth understanding of the fund's strategies, risks, and personnel.

Background of Key Personnel

This calls for checks on the educational and professional background of the key personnel, including any regulatory or legal problems. References from previous employees and work partners may also be included in this process. There are a number of firms that offer to conduct background checks on hedge fund managers; a labor-intensive and specialized product that many larger investors outsource. While clearly subjective, in-depth discussions with managers and key personnel can also be revealing.

Fund Offering Documents

As described above, hedge funds are required to provide investors with several offering documents, including a private placement memorandum, partnership agreement, and fund subscription agreement. These should be carefully reviewed (possibly with an attorney) and the key information understood. The documents together with any marketing material should provide information on the fund's strategy, risks, service providers, personnel background, redemption limits, and other critical information.

Fund Strategy and Strategy Risks

The fund's trading and investment strategy is clearly the mainspring for its performance and performance risks, and needs to be thoroughly understood. The information collected should include the markets traded, the types of instruments used, the leverage involved, and the decision process for making investment decisions. Any quantitative models or factors should be reviewed.

Equally important is to understand the risks that are part of the hedge fund's strategy and the risk management system in place at the fund, including any quantitative and/or qualitative risk management measures, limitations on leverage, diversification requirements, position limits, etc. It is important to understand if the risk management practice is written and formalized, and the structure and personnel in place, to monitor and enforce the risk limits. One important feature here, and an ongoing issue in managing any trading operation, is how to maintain the independence of the risk management function from interference by traders, who may also be the owners or bosses.

Operational Due Diligence

Operational due diligence has received increased emphasis following the Madoff fiasco because several aspects of his operation have been cited as "red flags" that could have warned investors that something was amiss. The fact that Madoff was only exposed when his sons turned him in to the FBI and not based on the due diligence of thousands of investors over nearly two decades has led to an industry-wide focus on this aspect of due diligence.

The following list includes some of the areas considered important in this process:

- Verify that the business location is as stated in the legal documents.
- Review key internal operations groups.
- Review the trade process.
- Verify that the disaster recovery site is operational and working.
- Review the working relationships with service providers.
- Review the compliance function.
- Review the fund's process for NAV accounting, valuation, and pricing.
- Review the manager's procedures and operational and risk management.

CHAPTER 26

Risk Management

RISK MANAGEMENT

By their very nature, hedge funds often take leveraged positions using derivatives in often illiquid markets, all of which make hedge funds prone to a wider variety of risks than one would find in other investment vehicles.

Following the losses that resulted from the credit crisis and exposure of the Madoff Ponzi scheme, risk management has become a pressing priority for hedge funds. It should be pointed out that the issues dealing with risk management are not unique to hedge funds; many of the issues discussed below also apply to banks, investment banks, and other investment managers.

A partial list of hedge fund risks includes the following:

- *Market risk:* Because of their leveraged positions, hedge funds often have large exposures to a wide variety of markets. The amount of market risk varies for different strategies and the extent to which they are vulnerable to risk factors, including leverage, market exposure, use of derivatives, and investment in illiquid markets and securities.

- *Concentration of positions:* Although many hedge funds have limitations on the concentration of their portfolio to specific markets or instruments (e.g., that no one position can be more than 5% of the portfolio), they still have wide latitude, which at times can cause overcon-centration. The most prominent examples are Amaranth Advisors, which essentially lost all its assets because its trader took a leveraged position on natural gas with 90% of the fund's assets, and, on the other side, Paulson & Co. whose concentrated bet against the subprime mortgage market resulted in a gain of $15 billion on $12.5 billion in assets in 2007, earning John Paulson, the fund manager, $3.5 billion.

- *Unhedged positions:* Despite their name, many hedge funds do take "directional" bets or one-way positions in various markets and strategies. If the market goes against them, they will incur losses. The larger the position and the more highly leveraged, the larger the losses. Also important is the liquidity of the markets, which affects their ability to cut losses or even reverse their position. Long-Term Capital Management (LTCM) will serve as the poster child for this risk for a long time.

- *Illiquid markets:* Hedge funds are prominent in a number of relatively illiquid markets, including emerging markets, distressed debt, structured products, and PIPES. If hedge funds are forced to sell their positions during times of market stress, the price they receive for their assets may be extremely low. In extreme cases, as during the Russian debt default and the credit crisis, there is no market at all.

- *Operational risk:* Hedge funds operate in complex markets using derivatives and leverage. Some also trade frequently. They are thus prone to operational risks that arise from flaws in policies, procedures, and safety checks designed to ensure that risk limits are enforced; accounts and payments are monitored; trades are properly settled and valued; and compliance to regulatory and market policies and practices are enforced. There is an oft-reported survey that claims 90% of hedge fund "disasters" are caused by operational risk, but this strikes the author as dubious given the ability of the market to inflict severe losses on numerous hedge funds on a regular basis. One type of risk, fraud risk, is especially pernicious as shown by recent cases, including Bayou, Madoff, and Manhattan Investment Fund.

Broadly, we can classify risk management as quantitative (or statistical) and qualitative. In the past decade, the most oft-used statistical measure is value at risk (VaR). One of the reasons (perhaps the main reason) for the widespread adoption of VaR is that it is one of the few quantitative tools that can be used with easily available data and widely used software.

Value at Risk

Value at risk (Figure 26-1) is a statistical measure of the "maximum" loss that a portfolio might sustain over a period of time, given a certain probability level. It may be expressed as dollar amount or as a percentage of fund assets. A typical VaR analysis

FIGURE 26−1

Value at Risk (VaR)

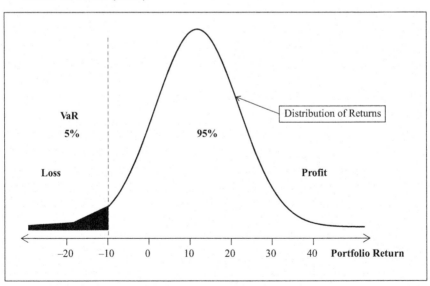

would conclude that "this portfolio has a VaR of $1 million or 10% of fund assets (assuming a $10 million fund) over the coming month at a 95% confidence level." This statement is interpreted as follows:

- There is a 95% probability that the losses to the portfolio will be less than $1 million in the coming month.

- There is a 5% probability that the fund could lose more than $1 million in the next month. However, importantly, VaR does not estimate how much that loss would be. This portfolio can result in a loss of $2 million or $5 million. There is no way to tell from the VaR analysis.

Key assumptions behind VaR

The two key assumptions behind VaR are that 1) historical and future prices of an asset are normally distributed, in which case VaR is a measure of standard deviation; and 2) historical data can be used to project future risks. By definition, we know that a normal distribution is constructed so that 68.2% of the likely outcomes are within 1 standard deviation of the average. Similarly, 2 standard deviations capture 95.4% of outcomes and 3 standard deviations incorporate 99.8% of likely outcomes.

These problems result in a phenomena known as "fat tails." Fat tails refer to the fact that prices in the real world do not follow a normal distribution. In fact, there is a higher probability that prices will fall outside the standard deviation measures much more frequently (and at greater severity) than predicted by a normal distribution.[*]

To highlight this concept, consider LTCM, which relied on VaR to measure its risk. On October 13, 1989, the S&P 500 dropped about 6% causing large losses for LTCM. By the normal distribution assumptions of VaR, using standard deviation to measure risk, this large a market decline is a 6 standard deviation move, which should only occur once in every 14,756 years. To take a more extreme example, when the S&P fell by 29% in October, 1987,

---

[*] One of the well-known shortcomings of VaR is its assumption of a normal distribution of returns and failure to incorporate fat tails into the measure. A variant of VaR, known as conditional VaR (CVaR) or "expected shortfall," incorporates some of the possible losses from fat tails. This is performed by assessing the likelihood (at a specific confidence level) that a specific loss will exceed the value at risk.

it experienced a 27 standard deviation event; one that should only occur once in 10 to the 160th power, or greater than the age of the universe.

Loss distribution during time of crisis

Unfortunately for the usefulness of VaR as a risk measurement, financial crises occur regularly and with more severity than implied by the normal distribution model. In fact, crises seem to occur every five years or so. In broad terms, there are four types of crises that move markets into the "fat tails" area of risk:

- Relative value hedge fund crises in which closely linked or correlated instruments diverge. Examples here are currency carry trades and high-yield or distressed debt arbitrage.

- Macroeconomic crises marked by large changes in interest rates, currencies, commodities, inflation, and economic growth. These crises typically result in large movements in the stock and bond markets.

- Equity market declines such as the bursting of the Internet bubble, the 1987 crash, and the credit crisis decline in 2008.

- Emerging-market debt crises such as the Russian debt default of 1998. These crises tend to occur in conjunction with problems in the developed nations, especially increases in interest rates and declines in economic growth.

When a financial crisis does occur, it is typically accompanied by a number of characteristics, all of which tend to harm most hedge fund strategies:

- A decline (or outright losses) in the return of many if not most hedge fund strategies.

- Increased correlation between asset classes, which results in an increase correlation both between hedge fund strategies and between these strategies and the marketplace.

- A pronounced increase in volatility

- Reduced liquidity in some markets

The performance of hedge funds during economic and financial crises has not been in line with their claim of providing positive returns in all markets and a low correlation with the marketplace.

Proposed palliatives to limitations of VaR

In recognition of the limitations of VaR, industry practitioners, academics, and regulatory agencies (including the Federal Reserve Bank) have proposed that VaR should be accompanied by other risk management tools, notably stress testing, scenario analysis, and conditional VaR.

Stress testing and scenario analysis are similar. They both entail constructing various economic scenarios and calculating the effect of these scenarios on the performance of a hedge fund or FoHF. The distinction is this: stress testing assumes a range of changes in specific economic or market factors such a 10% decline in the stock market or a 1% increase in interest rates. Scenario analysis takes an actual historical scenario (e.g., the 2007–2008 credit crisis) and tests how a portfolio would have performed under that scenario. The difference between the two approaches is that stress testing uses hypothetical changes in variables, while scenario analysis uses those that actually existed during a particular crisis.

Both scenario analysis and stress testing use the factor-based analysis we met before in discussing the "drivers" of hedge fund return and replication. The factors that are stressed are the ones that are found to influence the risks and returns of the fund or portfolio being analyzed. One example of a set of "drivers" is the seven factors identified by Fung and Hsieh as the drivers for the aggregate hedge fund index.

Both stress testing and scenario analysis use historical data to project into the future. While they are relatively easy to perform using standard spreadsheets, they are more difficult to interpret and more difficult yet to put into practical use. One approach used by hedge funds to mitigate these problems has been to hire risk managers that have extensive experience in a variety of market settings, and can therefore add a qualitative perspective to the numbers.

Risk Analysis of Individual Hedge Funds

Performing a quantitative analysis on an individual hedge fund, an index or a strategy are similar. For example, a regression analysis of the returns of a high technology–focused fund used the following factors in a regression analysis: S&P 500, NASDAQ, and the HFRI Technology Index. Regression analysis identifies the following sources of market risk and fund behavior:

Adjusted beta to S&P: 0.21

Adjusted beta to NASDAQ: 0.54

Adjusted beta to HFRI Technology Index: 1.31

Maximum drawdown: 6.69%

Some of the analysis and conclusions that could be based on this analysis include the following:

The fund is vulnerable to large drawdowns during market stress.

The fund has relatively little exposure to S&P and NASDAQ equity indices.

The fund uses higher leverage than its peers.

The risk factors in hedge fund strategies described in the accompanying exhibit include the type of factors that can be used to conduct similar quantitative analysis of various strategy hedge funds.

RISK FACTORS IN HEDGE FUND STRATEGIES (WILLIAM K.H. FUNG AND DAVID A. HSIEH, "THE RISK IN HEDGE FUND STRATEGIES", WORKING PAPER)

1. *Trend followers* who seek to profit from large market movements are sensitive to market volatility.

2. *Merger arbitrage* returns are a function of the level of M&A activity in the market, which is in turn dependent on the direction of the market.

3. *Fixed-income* strategies are correlated to changes in default (credit) spread; that is, Moody's Baa yields over the 10-year Treasury constant maturity yield. In addition, specific strategies have unique drivers:

   a. *Convertible bonds (CBs)* correlated to the CSFB Convertible Bond index.

   b. *High-yield funds* correlated to the CSFB High-Yield Bond index.

   c. *Swap spread trades* bet that the fixed side of the spread (difference between the swap rate and yield on Treasury of same duration) will remain higher than the floating side (difference between LIBOR and repo rate).

   d. *Yield-curve spread* trades are "butterflies" betting that bond prices deviate from the overall yield curve for short-run reasons that dissipate over time.

   e. *Mortgage spread* trades are bets on prepayment rates; long position on a pool of GNMA mortgages using a "dollar roll," delta hedged with a five-year IR swap.

   f. *Fixed-income volatility trades* are bets that the implied volatility of interest rate caps tends to be higher than the realized volatility of the eurodollar futures contract.

   g. *Capital-structure (or credit) arbitrage* spreads on mispricing among different securities (i.e., debt and equity) issued by the same company.

4. *Long/short equity* funds have positive exposure to the stock market as well as exposure to long small-cap/large-cap positions, similar to the Fama-French three-factor model:

   a. "Underpriced stocks" are likely to be found among smaller, underresearched stocks.

b. Small stocks are poor candidates for short trades.

c. Do long/short managers exhibit market timing ability?

5. *Convertible arbitrage* return stems from liquidity premium paid by issuers of CBs to the hedge fund community for providing liquidity by buying CBs and hedging the risk:

   a. Volatility arbitrage bet that the embedded option in CB is mispriced

   b. Credit arbitrage bet that the credit risk of the CB is mispriced

6. *Emerging-market hedge funds* have returns that correlated with the IFC Emerging Market Stock Index.

7. *Distressed securities* hedge fund returns are strongly correlated with the CSFB High-Yield Bond index.

CHAPTER 27

Recent Hedge Fund Controversies

Hedge funds have seen fraud, excessive losses due to concentrated bets or leverage, and losses that were belatedly exposed because of lax operational controls and mark-to-market problems. While these are the rare exception, they have drawn widespread attention. The following is a partial list of hedge fund lapses.*

- David Askin, Granite Funds: Lost hundreds of millions in 1994 on mortgage-backed securities, which lost value as interest rates increased; investors did not know about the losses for a period of time because the portfolio was improperly marked to market.

- John Meriwether, Long-Term Capital Management: Lost billions in 1998 on extremely highly leveraged positions in "relative value" strategies.

- Martin Arthur Armstrong, Princeton Economics International Ltd.: Lost hundreds of millions in 1999 owing to poor trading and personal use of funds; solicited Japanese investors to hide losses from original investors.

---

* A website called Hedge Fund Implode-o-Meter (www.hf-implode.com) lists hedge fund problems.

- Michael Lauer, Lancer Management Group: Lost $1 billion over 2003–2007 by taking positions in penny stocks that were improperly valued.

- Brian Hunter, Amaranth Advisors: Hunter, Amaranth's head energy trader, lost $6 billion (out of the fund's $9 billion) in 2006 taking massive, highly leveraged positions in natural gas.

- Samuel Israel, Bayou Group LLC: Israel operated a Ponzi scheme of reporting false returns both to satisfy existing investors as well as attract new investors. Fund losses were hidden by a conspiring accounting firm. Hundreds of millions were lost between 1998 and 2005.

- Thane Ritchie, Ritchie Capital Management: Lost hundreds of millions in 2007 as a result of investments in life insurance settlements.

- Thomas Hudson, Pirate Capital LLC: Suspended redemptions on 80% of the fund's assets in two Jolly Roger Activist funds.

- Victor Niederhoffer (Niederhoffer Matador Fund): Closed after losing 70% of its assets in trading losses in 2007.

- Deephaven Capital Management's "Deephaven Event Fund," which tried "to profit from takeovers," froze redemptions on hundreds of millions, 70% of redemption requested in 2008.

- Peloton ABS Master Fund; Cheyne Finance LLC (Cheyne Capital Management); Caliber Global Investments; Basis Capital Fund Management, Ltd.–Basis Yield Alpha; Oddo & Cie; Mariner Bridge; Bear Stearns High Grade Credit Funds: Hedge funds that lost most or all of their assets when the value of mortgage-backed securities collapsed in 2007–2008.

- Bernard L. Madoff, Bernard L. Madoff Investment Securities (BLMIS): The largest Ponzi scheme in history was exposed in 2008 with an estimated $65 billion in losses incurred over two decades. Madoff claimed to have made consistent returns using an options strategy, "split-strike conversion," and had thousands of investors worldwide, including many banks, funds of funds, governments, and wealthy individuals. Although not a hedge fund (BLMIS was an SEC-registered broker dealer), many hedge funds and FoHFs were investors in his scheme.

- Ospraie Fund lost one-third of its $2.8 billion assets on trading in commodity stocks.

- Turnberry Capital Management lost nearly 50% of its assets in 2007–2008 in distressed debt and credit derivatives positions.

- Perot family Bermuda-chartered fund, Park Central Global Hub Ltd., apparently went into a virtual free fall in November 2008, losing as much as $300 million in one day, with final losses of over $1 billion in various instruments.

- Okumus Capital lost 80% of its assets selling out-of-the-money puts on company stock in 2008.

- Lancelot Investment Management lost over $1 billion investing in a Ponzi scheme run by Tom Petters, which claimed to finance receivables on electronic goods that were sold to large retailers; the goods never existed.

- Scott W. Rothstein: Ponzi scheme included a number of hedge funds as his victims; Rothstein lost over $1 billion collected from investors to finance a nonexistent program to finance insurance settlements in Florida.

BERNARD MADOFF AND PONZI SCHEMES

What Is a Ponzi Scheme?

A Ponzi scheme is a fraudulent investment operation that pays returns to its investors from their own money or the money paid by subsequent investors, rather than from profit earned by the individual or organization running the operation. The scheme is named after Charles Ponzi, who became notorious for using the technique in 1920.

To attract additional investors, the Ponzi scheme usually offers either higher returns than other investments or unusually consistent returns. Ponzi schemes are destined to collapse, although they have been known to run for years. (The Madoff scheme ran for nearly 20 years.) Perpetuation of the scheme requires that investors keep receiving high returns and that the fund be able to meet customer requests for redemptions. Since the scheme has little or no real earnings, the returns can only be provided by new investors and by the existing investors keeping their funds in the scheme. At some point, however, a Ponzi scheme is unable to meet the redemption requests of investors and the scheme collapses.

Ponzi schemes have a number of characteristics in common; they typically claim to provide returns that are high and consistent, but not so spectacular as to raise suspicion. They also have a plausible but relatively esoteric strategy for making money.

Recent Hedge Fund Ponzi Schemes

The past decade has had a number of Ponzi schemes that involved hedge funds either as investors or vehicles for the fraud. Examples include Bayou (involving equities), Petters (involving purported sales of electronic goods), and Rothstein (involving financing of legal settlements). However, the largest and most highly publicized is that run by Bernard Madoff.

Madoff's Ponzi Scheme

In December 2008, former NASDAQ chairman Bernard Madoff admitted that the wealth management arm of the Wall Street firm he founded in 1960, Bernard L. Madoff Investment Securities LLC (BLMIS), was an elaborate Ponzi scheme. On June 29, 2009, he was sentenced to 150 years in prison. Amazingly, the scheme may have begun in the 1970s. The estimated size of the fraud is $64.8 billion and included thousands of investors, including some of the most sophisticated investors in the world.

One of the reasons the Madoff scheme persisted was his stature in the financial industry. Unlike most Ponzi schemes, Madoff's company was a large and successful broker. Madoff Securities was one of the top market makers on Wall Street. Madoff himself had been the chairman of the board of directors and on the Board of Governors active in the National Association of Securities Dealers (NASD), a self-regulatory securities industry organization.

Purported Split-Strike Conversion Strategy

Madoff claimed to make money by purchasing S&P 100 stocks and then using a well-known option strategy known as a spread or collar to hedge the risk. Madoff claimed to purchase a put on the S&P 100 stock index to project his portfolio from market declines. The purchase of the put was funded via the sale of a call, which also limited the upside in case of market advances. He called the strategy a "split-strike conversion."

Red Flags

In extensive postmortems of the Madoff scheme, analysts point to a number of "red flags" that some claim should have led to the exposure of the Ponzi scheme, although it should be pointed out that the fraud was never "exposed"; rather, Madoff confessed to his sons who then turned him in to the authorities. These red flags include:

- Consistency of returns over many years with very few losing months
- Large volume of options activity to support the $15 billion in assets under management
- Use of a small accounting firm to audit results
- Lack of registration as an investment adviser until 2006
- Conversion of the strategy to U.S. Treasuries at the end of each quarter
- Madoff did not charge management fees, claiming to earn income from transaction fees

Green Flags

Thousands of investors placed billions of dollars with Madoff to manage because of green flags, including:

- Madoff's and Madoff Securities' legitimate and credible credentials, including SEC oversight as a broker/dealer.

- Madoff's returns were steady, but not spectacular by hedge fund industry standards.
- Madoff Securities was an SEC-registered broker dealer. SEC investigations of Madoff in 1999, 2000, 2004, 2005, and 2006 failed to turn up any evidence of a Ponzi scheme.

Madoff's Scheme Collapses

The credit crisis in 2008 led to large-scale redemption by investors in Madoff's scheme. Despite desperate efforts, Madoff was unable to raise new funds to meet these redemptions. Faced with the certainty of exposure, he allowed himself to be turned in.

INSIDER TRADING SCANDALS

The extent to which hedge funds engage in insider trading has received increased attention as a result of the conviction of a prominent hedge fund manager, Raj Rajaratnam, the founder of the Galleon Group, and dozens of others for trading on illegal stock tips. While insider trading cases are not limited to hedge funds, they are a natural target for investigation. Hedge funds command large sums of capital; many have contacts with well-placed Wall Street and corporate sources, and they operate hidden from public view. In addition, the hedge fund business is immensely lucrative and highly competitive, which provides an incentive for some to engage in this activity.

In early 2013, the SEC had filed insider trading charges against a hedge fund manager with close links to SAC Capital Advisors, one of the largest and most successful hedge funds.

What Constitutes Insider Trading?

The law on insider trading has developed over the years from judicial rulings and is not specifically found in a statute. The courts have established that it is illegal to trade on "material" information in breach of a duty to keep the information private. However, the definition of "material" is sometimes ambiguous. Information, including rumors and gossip, constantly flows among market participants; however, most is not "material." The advanced use of Twitter and services that dissect Twitter's content looking for investment information has accelerated the flow of information. One distinguishing feature of insider trading may be the intent of the participants.

No one knows how much cheating of this kind occurs. However, in a survey of 2,500 traders taken in 2007, more than half said they would take advantage of an illegal tip if they were assured they would not be caught. Insider trading is part of the debate on efficient markets we discussed elsewhere in this book since equal access to information by market participants is one of the key requirements if markets are to be efficient. The 1933 Securities Act, which established the SEC, was based on the tenet that a corporation issuing securities to the public has to provide full disclosure about its financial results and outlook. The traditional theory of insider trading applies to corporate insiders and other fiduciaries (even to executives' psychiatrists); it also covers traders who pay insiders for information or otherwise induce them to leak. Ivan Boesky, the arbitrageur who pleaded guilty to securities fraud in the 1980s, was the classic case.

Regulators have devoted considerable resources to uncovering insider trading. FINRA, an industry group, has developed a computer system for spotting insider trading. Every time there is market-moving news, such as a merger or an earnings report, computers at FINRA scan millions of buy-and-sell orders, looking for suspicious trades such as a big stock purchase in advance of a takeover. FINRA refers some 250 trades a year to the SEC for a closer look.

One consequence for hedge funds has been the growth of the compliance function and the increased emphasis on evaluating the source of content of trading information to make sure it does not constitute insider trading. Another consequence is that hedge funds have sharply cut their use of so-called expert networks. These networks hire people with knowledge of specific industries to talk to traders. Networks serve a valid research function, but the potential for experts to cross the line into illegal tipping is plain.

It is worth noting that insider trading is especially an issue for hedge funds that engage in short-term trading, where information of upcoming events may offer an edge. Hedge funds with a longer time horizon depend on analyzing information that is already public.

CONCLUSION

The preface set out a number of themes that provided a framework for this book. It is time to revisit and review these themes, taking into account the information contained in the book.

WHAT MAKES HEDGE FUNDS UNIQUE?

Hedge funds and other investment managers all trawl the same equities, fixed-income, and commodities markets. However, hedge funds have distinctive objectives that they pursue using distinctive tools and strategies. Hedge funds belong to the world of active investment management, in sharp contrast to the world of *passive management*, in which managers use capitalization-weighted index funds to mimic the performance of various markets such as the S&P 500 index instead of trying to beat the markets.

Other *active managers* include traditional, long-only active managers whose goal is to beat a passive market benchmark. Typically, however, these managers only attempt to beat their benchmarks by a relatively small amount. Furthermore, they are willing to follow their benchmark on the way down as long as their decline is less steep than their benchmark. Thus, if the benchmark is down 15% but the manager is only down 14%, the manager has achieved his or her objective and investors are delighted.

In contrast to traditional active managers, hedge funds belong to the world of *absolute return* investment management whose participants attempt to deliver a positive return in all market conditions. While this may have been the historical objective of hedge funds, the losses of the past several years have made this definition of absolute return untenable. A more relevant definition may be that they attempt to suffer smaller losses than traditional active managers during market declines. However, in this they also typically give up some upside during market rallies, giving their gain–loss profile the look of a call option on a benchmark.

In pursuit of their absolute return objective, hedge fund managers use a wide variety of investment strategies and techniques, including leverage, short selling, and derivatives.

THE ROLE OF SKILL IN HEDGE FUND PERFORMANCE

As discussed in this book, hedge fund managers are extremely well compensated for their efforts. This compensation is ostensibly earned because of their skill in providing investment returns that are not available elsewhere. However, this premise needs to be evaluated in light of the disappointing returns of hedge fund managers in recent years as well as the *efficient market* theory that precludes excess returns (i.e., returns above market returns) over a sustained period of time.

Efficient market theory states that increased investment returns can only be gained by taking on additional risk. A free lunch is impossible because the fierce competition between market participants means that any short-term advantage is quickly arbitraged out of existence. A related concept is that the past does not predict the future and that trends do not go on forever because money managers, by taking positions on both sides of a trend, cause a reversion to the mean.

Isolating the discrete role of skill in hedge fund performance is complicated by the multiple factors that contribute to hedge fund risk and returns. The issue is important because of the view in some quarters that the hedge fund industry has a near-monopoly on skilled managers. Of course this is an argument favored by hedge fund professionals in that it justifies the hedge fund fee structure.

DIRECTIONAL MARKET FACTORS

Perhaps the most important influence on hedge fund performance is directional market trends. Very few hedge funds are immune from the effects of a 40% decline in the stock market, no matter what their approach or strategy. However, hedge funds do vary in the extent to which they have market bias. For example, long-biased equity hedge funds and stock short sellers and hedge funds that invest in markets that are difficult to hedge—such as some emerging markets, distressed debt, or structured products—have a long bias that also makes them sensitive to market movements.

Some strategies are less sensitive to market direction—notably relative value managers that seek to be genuinely hedged at all times, with long and short positions offsetting each other's asset allocators. Risk arbitrage and distressed debt have modest levels of directional market risk since the forces that create weak equity markets also tend to create a headwind for these strategies.

Global macro hedge funds vary in their sensitivity to market direction because they can be long, or short, or neutral, depending on the circumstances. This means that they may at times be exposed to market direction; this exposure is not "chronic" in the same way as long-biased equity hedge funds.

Hedge funds are also influenced by factors that are *market related* but not *directional*. Some of these factors are *intramarket variables* that depend on relationships between two different parts of a market. Within the equity market, the growth–value distinction is especially important. If a hedge fund manager tends to be long value and short growth, then he will do well in some environments and will suffer terribly in others. Within the bond market, yield spreads are a critical factor. If a hedge fund manager tends to be long "spread product" (bonds that offer a yield premium over Treasuries) and short Treasuries, then the manager will thrive when spreads are narrowing and will suffer when they are expanding.

There are other important factors that are market related but not directional. The convertible hedger needs volatility. The momentum-oriented investor needs trends. The contrarian investor needs trendless, mean-reverting markets. The risk arbitrageur needs deal flow and decent deal spreads. The distressed debt investor needs a decent supply of opportunities and a congenial credit environment.

A WIDER DEFINITION OF SKILL

Skill is sometimes defined entirely as the ability to beat the market, or generate positive alpha. Some investors are more skilled than others. But skill is not merely brainpower. The investment world is filled with very smart people who produce mediocre results. There are other types of skills that hedge fund managers bring to bear that are crucial to their ability to generate positive returns. These include managerial and organizational skills, operational and risk management capabilities, flexibility and open-mindedness, and the like. These skills are increasingly important, especially, as seems likely, the growth of individual hedge funds continues at its present rate. The hedge fund manager of the future may be more akin to an investment bank manager.

CHANGING RATIONALE FOR HEDGE FUND INVESTING

One of the recurring themes in this book is the changes in the rationale for investing in hedge funds. In the early days of the industry, investors—largely high-net-worth individuals—were primarily interested in outsized returns and willing to accept large losses if hedge fund bets went awry.

As the industry matured, institutional investors replaced individuals as the largest group of investors, and absolute return became the primary rationale for investing in hedge funds. Hedge funds were seen as a form of catastrophe insurance, with the ability to produce positive returns in the face of fierce market turmoil.

However, in recent years, hedge funds have failed to live up to the expectations of absolute return by turning in losing or mediocre returns. This has led to a focus on the supposed diversification benefits of hedge funds in an overall investment portfolio. Some investors are thus willing to accept mediocre returns and large losses as long as hedge funds provide the benefit of diversification. If indeed hedge funds live up to this benefit, they will play an important role in investment portfolios. The increasing correlation between the performances of various markets makes any source of portfolio diversification highly desirable. However, recent hedge fund performance has also been correlated to traditional markets, especially during times of market turmoil, which means that the jury may be out about this "benefit" of hedge funds.

There is no doubt that some hedge fund strategies deliver diversification in traditional portfolios by virtue of their use of short positions and investment in virtually every market from stocks to pork bellies. However, some of these strategies—notably distressed debt, small-cap stocks, and some commodity markets— are constrained in the amount of capital that can be put to work without overwhelming the market. This becomes more problematic as institutions pour more and more money into hedge funds. In addition, there are limits to the ability of hedge funds to short many markets.

HEDGE FUND DEFENDERS AND DETRACTORS

Hedge funds generate strong feelings from their defenders and from their detractors. This book was designed to present a balanced portrait of the world of hedge funds, steering a course between the exaggerations on both sides.

Detractors claim that hedge funds are secretive, unregulated investment vehicles that make highly leveraged speculative bets in the global financial markets. If the performance is not good enough to generate attractive fees, then the hedge fund managers simply redistribute wealth from investors to themselves. Considered as a whole, hedge funds are momentum investors who add volatility and instability to the markets.

On the other side of the debate are those who will insist that hedge funds have the ability to deliver steady, consistent returns that have low correlation with traditional stock and bond markets. The key source of return is the skill of the manager. The hedge fund community is the "smart-money" community, the beneficiary of the massive brain drain that moves talented investors away from the huge investment bureaucracies into small and nimble investment organizations. But skill is not the sole source of return. Some hedge funds take advantage of market inefficiencies created by the behavior of the large investment organizations. On a systemic level, hedge funds are said to deliver liquidity to the marketplace and improve market efficiency by their ability to go short.

INVESTOR EXPECTATIONS AND THE FUTURE OF HEDGE FUNDS

The current economic and investment climate has had a profound effect on the expectations of investors, including their expectations of hedge fund performance. With interest rates near historical lows, anemic economic growth, a massive deleveraging of the financial system, and periodic systemic shocks, investors are scrambling to find strategies and vehicles that offer some semblance of stability, protection of investment principal, and at least some positive returns. Most investors would be satisfied with investment returns of 5% if these returns were relatively predictable and were accompanied by a low probability of large losses.

Investors have a large number of alternatives in pursuing these objectives. They can choose from a wide range of mutual funds, both index and actively managed, in most markets. They can also choose alternative investments, including real estate, commodities, hedge funds, and private equity firms. Then, they can construct portfolios of investment strategies and vehicles attempting to balance risk and return.

One thing is certain: hedge funds are now widely accepted as an integral part of investors' portfolios. Additionally, all signs point to continued growth of hedge funds and an increasing role in investors' portfolios. This means that investors need to become familiar with the pros and cons of hedge funds and their potential role in their investment portfolio. This is no easy task. Hedge funds are complex, varied, and, to many investors, baffling. However, the work needed to master hedge fund investments can yield significant rewards. This book is an attempt to assist in this task.

APPENDIX A

Model Due Diligence Questionnaire for
Hedge Fund Investors

A. Firm Overview

1. Firm Headquarters:
2. Placement Agent, if any:
3. Placement Agent Address:
4. Contact Name:
5. Contact Telephone Number:
6. Contact Fax:
7. Contact E-mail:

B. Firm Description

Please provide a brief description of the firm.

C. Investment Manager Entities and Organizational Structure

Please describe the relevant entities of the investment manager or adviser and their ownership structure. Have there been any material changes to the entities themselves (e.g., additions or deletions) or to the ownership structure of those entities in the past three years?

D. Personnel

1. Please briefly describe the background of the firm's key investment personnel.
2. For the firm's key investment personnel that have left the firm over the past three years, please explain any nonroutine reasons for the departures.
3. Please describe the firm's supervisory structures (e.g., management committees).

How many employees does the firm have supporting investment management businesses in total? How many by function? If the firm or its affiliates maintain multiple offices, how are these employees distributed geographically?

E.   Service Providers

Auditor

1. Who audits the investment vehicles managed by the firm?

2. Does the auditor have an affiliation or any business relationship with the firm or any of its affiliates outside of the audit relationship itself? Has the firm or any of its affiliates retained the auditor or any of its affiliates for other engagements, such as consulting services, financial statement preparation, or tax services? If so, please describe.

3. Has the current auditor audited the firm's investment vehicles in each of the last three years? If not, please describe the circumstances of any audit engagement changes made.

4. Has any investment vehicle managed by the firm ever received a qualified audit opinion? If so, please describe.

5. Has an auditor ever requested a material restatement of financial statements or performance results of any investment vehicle managed by the firm? If so, please describe.

6. Has the firm engaged any third-party marketing agent? If so, please describe the terms of this engagement.

7. Who serves as legal counsel for the firm?

8. Does the firm outsource any accounting or operational functions to third parties? If so, please describe. Does the firm periodically review the performance of any such service providers? How is this review conducted?

F.   Compliance System and Registrations with Regulatory Authorities

1. Please describe the firm's compliance regime. Does the firm have a designated Chief Compliance Officer (CCO)? If so, please briefly describe the background of the CCO, and explain whether the CCO has any responsibilities other than those relating to compliance matters.

2. Is the firm or any of its affiliates registered with any regulatory authorities? If so, please describe. If the firm has not registered with the U.S. Securities and Exchange Commission as an investment adviser, please explain the exemption

upon which the firm currently relies and if it intends to register in the next 12 months.

3. Does the firm maintain and periodically review written compliance policies and procedures, including a code of ethics? If not, please explain.

4. Does the firm have a written policy on the handling and safe guarding of any material, nonpublic information in its possession, including a process to educate employees? If not, how is material, nonpublic information protected, and how are these processes communicated to employees?

5. Does the firm have written policies regarding personal account trading by employees? If so, please describe. If not, is personal account trading monitored, and how are standards of conduct communicated to employees?

6. Does the firm maintain written procedures on the provision and receipt of gifts and entertainment? If not, how is such activity monitored, and how are standards of conduct communicated to employees?

7. Does the firm maintain written anti–money laundering (AML) procedures? Is there a designated AML compliance officer? If not, how are AML checks conducted?

8. Please describe any material soft dollar arrangements the firm currently maintains.

Please describe any material directed brokerage arrangements the firm currently maintains.

G. Legal Proceedings

1. In the past five years: (a) have there been any criminal or administrative proceedings or investigations against the firm, a principal or key employee of the firm, or any affiliate of the firm; or (b) have there been any civil proceedings against the firm, a principal or key employee of the firm, or any affiliate of the firm in each case that resulted in an adverse disposition? If so, please describe.

2. Is the firm currently aware of any pending criminal or administrative proceedings against the firm, a principal or key employee of the firm, or any affiliate of the firm?

Have any adverse dispositions materially affected any of the funds or accounts managed by the firm?

H.   Infrastructure and Controls

1. Please describe the firm's current trading, portfolio management, and post-trade reconciliation and accounting infrastructure, identifying any significant deployments of third-party software.

2. Please describe how trades are generally executed. What types of controls are typically used to help prevent unwanted executions from occurring?

3. Please describe the typical trade reconciliation process and frequency. What segregations of duty are generally employed in the process?

4. Please describe how cash or other asset transfers can be authorized, both for transfers within a vehicle managed by the firm, as well as to external parties. What types of controls are generally used to prevent unwanted transfers from occurring?

5. Please describe how the firm handles trading errors.

Does the firm or its affiliates retain errors and omissions insurance?

I.   Business Continuity

Does the firm maintain a written BC/DR plan? If not, how does the firm plan to maximize its ability to recover from business interruptions?

II. OVERVIEW OF ACTIVITIES OF THE INVESTMENT MANAGER

A.   Vehicles Managed

1. Please provide a description of the major investment vehicles managed by the investment manager.

2. What are the aggregate assets under management of the investment manager?

3. Does the firm manage separate accounts? If so, please describe.

4. Does the investment manager or any of its employees have an interest in any of the investment vehicles managed by the investment manager? If so, what is the amount of this interest in the aggregate?

B. Other Businesses

Does the investment manager engage materially in other businesses apart from asset management? If so, please describe.

C. Conflicts of Interest

1. Please describe those conflicts of interest that you consider material to the management of the investment vehicles. How do you address these conflicts?
2. Does the firm engage in cross-trades or principal cross-trades with or among the accounts and/or investment vehicles it manages? If so, what controls are generally in place to protect the participating investment vehicles or accounts?
3. Does the firm have any affiliates or subsidiaries that are broker/dealers or execution agents? If yes, do these broker–dealers or execution agents (a) execute on behalf of investment vehicles managed by the firm; and (b) charge commissions or markups on these executions or otherwise bill expenses to investment vehicles managed by the firm in instances in which the investment vehicle is not the sole owner of the execution agent or broker/dealer? If so, please describe these arrangements.

III. FUND INFORMATION

A. Fund Overview and Investment Approach

1. Please describe the fund's legal structure.
2. Please provide a brief description of the investment strategies generally deployed by the fund.
3. What types of financial instruments does the fund generally trade?
4. In which geographical markets does the fund generally trade?

5. Approximately how many positions does the fund generally hold? What is the typical maximum position size?

Please describe the portfolio turnover.

B.   **Fund Capital and Investor Base**

1. What is the capital base of the fund?
2. How many investors are currently invested in the fund?

If the fund maintains a master–feeder structure with both U.S. and non-U.S. "feeder" entities, what percentage of the capital base is invested in the U.S. fund? The non-U.S. feeder fund?

C.   **Fund Terms**

1. Are there multiple classes of interests or multiple "feeder" entities in the fund?
2. Please list, for each class of interest or feeder:
   a) Investment minimum
   b) Management fee
   c) Performance fee, including hurdle rates, high-water marks, and loss carryforwards, if any
   d) Redemption terms, including any fees payable, lockups, gating provisions, or other restrictions
3. Can the investment manager suspend redemptions, suspend the payment of redemption proceeds, pay redemption proceeds in kind, or otherwise elect to deviate from the redemption terms described in 2 above? If so, please describe.
4. Have gates been imposed in the past? If so, under what circumstances were the gates imposed? If gates have been imposed in the past, have those gates been lifted? If so, under what circumstances were the gates lifted?
5. Does the firm generally charge additional expenses to the fund, including operating expenses, audit fees, administrative fees, fund organizational expenses, legal fees, sales fees, salaries, rent, or other charges not detailed in 2 above? If so, please describe. What was the total amount of these expenses in each of the last three calendar years as a percentage of total fund assets under management, if applicable?

What is the firm's policy with regard to side letters? Do any investors in the fund experience fee or redemption terms that differ materially from those listed above? If so, please describe.

D. Performance History

Please provide a performance history for the fund.

E. Risk Management

1. Please describe the firm's risk management philosophy and discuss the approach used by the firm in the management of the fund's exposure to equity, interest rate, currency, and credit market risk (as applicable); financing and counterparty risk; and operational risk.
2. Does the firm rely on third parties to perform any portion of its risk management function?
3. What types of risk measures does the firm use in its risk management function?

F. Valuation

1. Please describe the process of valuation of the fund's positions, including valuation process for positions that do not have a market price. Please discuss in particular the frequency of valuation and whether any third-party services are employed in the valuation process (and, if so, how these third parties are monitored).
2. Has the fund had a material restatement of its financial statements or any prior results since inception? If so, please describe. Was the restatement the result of an audit by an external auditing firm?

G. Fund Service Providers

1. If the fund employs an administrator, please provide its name.
2. Please provide information concerning legal counsel used by the fund, if any.
3. Please name the main prime brokers used by the fund.

H.   Investor Communications

What types of investor communication does the fund currently provide, and with what frequency?

APPENDIX B

Overview of Major Hedge Fund Replication Products

Promoter	Product	Launch Date	Replication Target	Methodology
AlphaSwiss	AlphaSwiss Alternative Beta Fund	Dec-05	Composite	Rules based
Arrow Funds	Arrow Alternative Solutions Fund	Oct-07	Composite (hedged equity + fixed income arbitrage + managed futures)	Factor based + rules based
Barclays	Barclays Hedge Fund Replicator Fund	Sep-10	Long Barclays Alternatives Replicator	Factor based
BlueWhite Alternative Investments	BlueWhite Alternative Beta Fund	May-07	Portfolio of thousands of hedge funds	Factor based
Credit Suisse	Liquid Alternative Beta Index Event Driven Liquid Index Global Strategies Liquid Index Long/Short Liquid Index Managed Futures Liquid Index Merger Arbitrage Liquid Index	Jan-98	Dow Jones Credit Suisse Hedge Fund Index Event Driven Sector of Dow Jones Credit Suisse Hedge Fund Index Non-Long/Short or Event Driven Strategies within DJ CS HFI Long/Short Equity Sector of DJ CS HFI Managed Futures Liquid Index Merger Arbitrage Liquid Index	Rules based
Deutsche Bank	db Absolute Return Beta Index	May-07	HFRI Fund of Funds Composite Index	Rules based
Fulcrum Asset Management	Fulcrum Alternative Beta Plus	Jun-05	Composite	Rules based
Global X Funds	Global X Top Guru Holdings Index ETF	Jun-12	Top Guru Holdings Index	Rules based
Goldman Sachs	Goldman Sachs Absolute Return Tracker	Dec-06	Portfolio of thousands of hedge funds	Factor based

Guggenheim Investments	Guggenheim Multi-Hedge Strategies Fund	May-10	Composite Long/Short Equity Equity Market Neutral Fixed Income Merger Arbitrage Global Macro	Rules based
Ice Capital Fund Management Company	Ice Capital Alternative Beta	Mar-07	Composite	Factor based
IndexIQ	IQ Hedge Composite IQ Hedge Long Short IQ Hedge Market Neutral IQ Hedge Fixed Income Arbitrage IQ Hedge Global Macro IQ Hedge Event Driven IQ Hedge Multi Strategy IQ Hedge Emerging Market	Jul-07	Composite	Factor based + rules based
J.P. Morgan	J.P. Morgan Alternative Beta Index	Feb-07	HFRI Fund of Funds Composite Index	Factor based
J.P. Morgan	J.P. Morgan BMAST EUR Index J.P. Morgan BMAST USD Index	Apr-07	Swap Rates	Rules based

(continued)

Promoter	Product	Launch Date	Replication Target	Methodology
Merrill Lynch	Merrill Lynch FX Clone Merrill Lynch Factor Index Merrill Lynch Equity Volatility Arbitrage Index	Mar-07 Aug-06 Feb-07	Parker FX Index HFRI Fund Weighted Composite Index S&P 500 Volatility Arbitrage Strategy	Rules based Factor based Rules based
Morgan Stanley	Altera	Aug-07	MSCI Hedge Fund Indices	Factor based + rules based
Partners Group	Partners Group Alternative Beta Strategies	Oct-04	CTA, Equity Hedge, Equity Market Neutral, Fixed Income Arbitrage, Volatility Arbitrage, Event Driven, Global Macro, Emerging Markets, Long/Short, Carry FX, Carry Bonds, Insurance Linked	Factor based + rules based
ProShares	ProShares Hedge Replication ETF	Jul-11	HFRI Fund Weighted Composite Index	Factor based
Ramius Alternative Solutions	Ramius Dynamic Replication Fund	Jul-10	Ramius Custom Actively Managed Composite	Factor based
Stonebrook Capital Management	Stonebrook Alternative Beta Fund	Jun-07	HFRI Fund of Funds Composite Index	Factor based

APPENDIX C

Internet Resources for Hedge Fund News and Research

Absolute Return + Alpha	www.absolutereturn-alpha.com
All About Alpha	www.allaboutalpha.com
EurekaHedge	www.eurekahedge.com
eVestmentlHFN	www.hedgefund.net
Finalternatives	www.finalternatives.com
Hedge Fund Alert	www.hfalert.com
Hedge Fund Intelligence	www.hedgefundintelligence.com
Hedge Week	www.hedgeweek.com
Hedge World	www.hedgeworld.com
HedgeCo.net	www.hedgeco.net
HFM Week	www.hfmweek.com
InvestHedge	www.hedgefundintelligence.com/ investhedge
Institutional Investor Journals	www.iijournals.com
Opalesque	www.opalesque.com
Pensions and Investments Online	www.pionline.com
Seeking Alpha	www.seekingalpha.com
The Hedge Fund Law Report	www.hflawreport.com
The Journal of Alternative Investments	www.iijournals.com/jai
Zero Hedge	www.zerohedge.com

APPENDIX D

U.S. Securities and Exchange Commission

Chairman: Mary Schapiro

Contact Information:

http://www.sec.gov

Toll-Free Investor Information Service: +1-800-SEC-0330

Address:

SEC Headquarters

100 F Street, NE

Washington, DC 20549

The mission of the SEC is to protect investors; maintain fair, orderly, and efficient markets; and facilitate capital formation. Its responsibilities include interpreting federal securities law; issuing new rules and amending existing rules; overseeing the inspection of securities firms, brokers, investment advisers, and ratings agencies; overseeing private regulatory organizations in the securities, accounting, and auditing fields; and coordinating U.S. securities regulation with federal, state, and foreign authorities.

U.S. Commodity Futures Trading Commission

Chairman: Gary Gensler

Contact Information:

http://www.cftc.gov/index.htm

Telephone: +1-202-418-5000

Address:

Commodity Futures Trading Commission

Three Lafayette Centre

1155 21st Street, NW

Washington, DC 20581

The CFTC is an independent agency with the mandate to regulate commodity futures and option markets in the United States. The CFTC aims to assure the economic utility of the futures markets by encouraging their competitiveness and efficiency; protecting market participants against fraud, manipulation, and abusive trading practices; and by ensuring the financial integrity of the clearing process.

Financial Industry Regulatory Authority (U.S.)
Chairman: Richard G. Ketchum
Contact Information:
http://www.finra.org/
Telephone: +1-301-590-6500
Address:
FINRA
1735 K Street
Washington DC, 20006
FINRA is the largest independent regulator for all securities firms doing business in the United States. FINRA's mission is to protect America's investors by making sure the securities industry operates fairly and honestly.

Financial Services Authority (U.K.)
Chairman: Lord Adair Turner
Contact Information:
http://www.fsa.gov.uk
Telephone: +44-20-7066-1000
Address:
FSA
25 The North Colonnade, Canary Wharf, London E14 5HS
United Kingdom
The FSA has four statutory objectives: maintaining confidence in the U.K. financial system, contributing to the protection and enhancement of stability of the U.K. financial system, securing the appropriate degree of protection for consumers, and reducing the extent to which it is possible for a regulated business to be used for a purpose connected with financial crime.

Securities and Futures Commission (Hong Kong)
Chairman: Eddy Fong
Contact Information:
http://www.sfc.hk/sfc/html/EN/
Telephone: (852) 2840 9222
Address:
Securities and Futures Commission

8th Floor, Chater House
8 Connaught Road Central
Hong Kong

The SFC is an independent statutory body established by the Securities and Futures Commission Ordinance (SFCO). It is responsible for administering the laws governing the securities and futures markets in Hong Kong and facilitating and encouraging the development of these markets.

Cayman Islands Monetary Authority
Chairman: George McCarthy

Contact Information:
http://www.cimoney.com.ky/
Telephone: (345) 949-7089

Address:
Cayman Islands Monetary Authority
PO Box 10052
80e Shedden Road
Elizabethan Square
Grand Cayman KY1-1001
Cayman Islands

The Cayman Islands Monetary Authority is responsible for issuing and redeeming Cayman Islands currency; managing currency reserves; regulating and supervising financial services; monitoring compliance with money laundering regulations; issuing rules and statements of principle and guidance; providing assistance to overseas regulatory authorities; and providing advice to the Cayman Islands Government on monetary, regulatory, and cooperative matters.

Central Bank of Ireland
Governor of the Central Bank: Patrick Honohan

Contact Information:
http://www.centralbank.ie/Pages/home.aspx
Telephone: +353-1-224-6000

Address:
Central Bank of Ireland
PO Box 559

Dame Street
Dublin 2
Ireland

The Central Bank of Ireland is responsible for contributing to Eurosystem effectiveness and price stability; contributing to financial stability; ensuring proper and effective regulation of financial institutions and markets; ensuring that the best interests of consumers of financial services are protected; providing independent economic advice and high-quality financial statistics; and ensuring that payment and securities settlement systems are safe, effective, and efficient.

Bermuda Monetary Authority
Chairman: Alan Cossar

Contact Information:
http://www.bma.bm/
Telephone: +441-295-5278

Address:
Bermuda Monetary Authority
BMA House
43 Victoria Street
Hamilton
Bermuda

The Bermuda Monetary Authority is the integrated regulator of the financial services sector in Bermuda. The BMA supervises, regulates, and inspects financial institutions operating in or from within the jurisdiction. It also issues Bermuda's national currency; manages exchange control transactions; assists other authorities in Bermuda with the detection and prevention of financial crime; and advises the government and public bodies on banking and other financial and monetary matters.

Securities and Exchange Commission of Brazil
Chairperson: Maria Helena dos Santos Fernandes de Santana

Contact Information:
http://www.cvm.gov.br/ingl/indexing.asp
Telephone: +55-21-3554-8686

Address:
Rua Sete de Setembro, 111
2°, 3°, 5°, 6° (parte), 23°, 26° ao 34° Andares-Centro
CEP-20050-901
Rio de Janeiro
Brazil

The Securities and Exchange Commission of Brazil was established to assure the proper functioning of the exchange and over-the-counter markets, to protect all securities holders against fraudulent issues and illegal actions, to avoid or inhibit any kind of fraud or manipulation that may give rise to artificial price formation in the securities market, to assure public access to all relevant information about the securities traded and the companies that have issued them, to ensure that all market participants adopt fair trading practices, to stimulate the formation of savings and their investment in securities, and to promote the expansion and efficiency of the securities market and the capitalization of Brazilian publicly held companies.

Federal Financial Markets Service (Russia)
Head: Vladimir Milovidov

Contact Information:
http://www.fcsm.ru/ru/
Telephone: +495-935-87-90

Address:
Central Office of the Federal Financial Markets Service of Russia
119991, GSP-1, Moscow, Leninsky Prospect, 9
Russia

The Federal Financial Markets Service is responsible for regulation of securities, financial markets, and economic analysis.

Securities and Exchange Board of India
Chairman: Shri U.K. Sinha

Contact Information:
http://www.sebi.gov.in/sebiweb/
Telephone: +91-22-26449188

Address:
Plot No.C4-A, 'G' Block Bandra Kurla Complex

Bandra (East), Mumbai 400051
India
The Securities and Exchange Board of India was created to protect the interests of investors in securities and to promote the development of, and to regulate the securities market and for matters connected therewith or incidental thereto.

China Securities Regulatory Commission
Chairman: Guo Shuqing
Contact Information:
http://www.csrc.gov.cn/pub/newsite/
Fax: +86 010-66210205
Address:
China Securities Regulatory Commission
Focus Place 19, Jin Rong Street
West District, Beijing 100033
China
The CSRC is responsible for maintaining a fair and efficient market, protecting investors, and designing and implementing regulations for securities and futures markets.

Financial Services Agency (Japan)
Commissioner: Katsunori Mikuniya
Contact Information:
http://www.fsa.go.jp/en/index.html
Address:
Financial Services Agency
The Central Common Government Offices No. 7,
3-2-1 Kasumigaseki, Chiyoda-ku, Tokyo 100-8967
Japan
The FSA is responsible for ensuring the stability of Japan's financial system; protection of depositors, insurance policyholders, and securities investors; and smooth finance through such measures as planning and policymaking concerning the financial system, inspection and supervision of private sector financial institutions, and surveillance of securities transactions.

GLOSSARY

Accredited investor Wealthy individual or well-capitalized institutions covered under Regulation D of the Securities Act of 1933.

Administrator Third-party service provider offering certain back and front office administrative services to a hedge fund and/or hedge fund manager. Such services may include maintaining the principal corporate records; communicating with a hedge fund's investors and sending financial statements to its investors; providing registrar and transfer agent services in connection with the issuance, transfer, and redemption of interests in a hedge fund; processing subscription and redemptions; calculation of NAV; and providing other clerical services.

Alpha A numerical value indicating a manager's risk-adjusted excess rate of return relative to a benchmark. Measures a manager's "value-added" in selecting individual securities, independent of the effect of overall market movements.

Auditor A certified public accountant that examines a hedge fund's books according to a set of procedures and issues a report, typically annually.

AUM Asset under management.

Average portfolio turnover The percentage of the portfolio that is bought and sold each year.

Back-test An examination of the results generated by a model (e.g., a value-at-risk model) as compared with actual or realized results in order to assess the accuracy of the model.

Beta Beta is the measure of a fund's volatility relative to the market. (Almost all fund managers correlate themselves to the S&P 500.) A beta of greater than 1.0 indicates that the fund is more volatile than the market, and less than 1.0 is less volatile than the market. For example, if the market rises 1% and a fund has a beta greater than 2.5, the fund will rise, on average, 2.5%. For a fund with a beta of 0.4, if the market rises 1%, the fund will rise on average, 0.4%. The relationship is the same in a falling market. (Please note that funds can have a negative beta, meaning that on average they rise when the market falls and vice versa.)

Borrowing capacity The amount of money a hedge fund can borrow from a broker or dealer or other credit provider (e.g., in order to fund purchases of securities). For example, according to Regulation T of the Federal Reserve Board (12 C.F.R. 220.4), a borrower may borrow up to 50% of the value of a security, depending on the type of security.

Bottom–up investing An approach to investing that seeks to identify well-performing individual securities before considering the impact of economic trends.

Calmar ratio A return-to-risk ratio. Return (numerator) is defined as the compound annualized rate of return over the last 3 years. Risk (denominator) is defined as the maximum drawdown over the last 3 years.

Capital structure arbitrage Investment strategy that seeks to exploit pricing inefficiencies in a firm's capital structure.

Collateral An asset that is pledged as security, or whose title is transferred to a secured party, in order to secure payment or performance obligations.

Collateral event An event that triggers an increase in the amount of collateral related to a transaction or group of transactions under a collateral agreement or master agreement.

Commodity pool Commodity pools are investment funds that pool the money of numerous investors together to invest in the futures markets.

Commodity pool operator (CPO) The general partner (GP) of a commodity pool is typically registered as a CPO with the Commodities Futures Trading Commission (CFTC) and the National Futures Association (NFA).

Commodity trading adviser (CTA) Manager hired by CPOs to manage commodity pools.

Convertible arbitrage Investment strategy that seeks to exploit pricing inefficiencies between a convertible bond and the underlying stock. The manager will typically long the convertible bond and short the underlying stock.

Corporate debt Non-government-issued interest-bearing or discounted debt instrument that obligates the issuing corporation to pay the bondholder a specified sum of money, at specific intervals, and to repay the principal amount of the loan at maturity.

Correlation A standardized measure of the relative movement between two variables, such as the prices of two different securities.

Credit risk The risk that an issuer of a security (asset credit risk) or a counterparty (counterparty credit risk) will not meet its obligations when due.

Credit spread The difference between the yield (or percentage rate of return) of a Treasury security and a non-Treasury debt security (e.g., a corporate bond), which are identical in most respects (particularly the term of the obligation) except with credit rating.

Current leverage The amount of leverage currently used by the fund as a percentage of the fund.

Current net exposure The exposure level of the fund to the market at the present time. It is calculated by subtracting the short percentage from the long percentage.

Derivative A financial instrument in which the value depends on, or is derived from, the value of an underlying asset, index, rate, or instrument.

Direct investor Investor who invests in a hedge fund as principal and not for the benefit of any third party.

Distressed securities investing Investment strategy focusing on troubled or restructuring companies at deep discounts through stocks, fixed income, bank debt, or trade claims.

Diversification Minimization of nonsystematic portfolio risk by investing assets in several securities and investment categories with low correlation between each other.

Downside deviation Similar to the loss standard deviation except the downside deviation considers only returns that fall below a defined minimum acceptable return (MAR) rather than the arithmetic mean.

Drawdown The percentage loss from a fund's highest value to its lowest, over a particular time frame. A fund's "maximum drawdown" is often looked at as a measure of potential risk, particularly in the analysis of CTA managers.

Equalization amounts Distribution to limited partnership interests according to high water provisions, to properly account for performance-based fees, which may differ among investors, depending on the investor's entry points into a fund.

Equity market neutral investing Equity investing on both the long and short side, with equal dollar amounts. Will attempt to neutralize market risk, and isolate a manager's alpha, to achieve absolute returns.

Event-driven investing Investment strategy seeking to identify and exploit pricing inefficiencies that have been caused by some sort of corporate event, such as a merger, spinoff, distressed situation, or recapitalization.

Fair value Generally refers to the price at which a single unit of an instrument would trade between disinterested parties in an arm's-length transaction.

Fixed-income arbitrage Investment strategy that seeks to exploit pricing inefficiencies in fixed-income securities and their derivative instruments. Typical investment will involve long a fixed-income security or related instrument that is perceived to be undervalued, and short a similar, related fixed-income security or related instrument.

Form ADV The SEC's uniform application for investment adviser registration. Contains basic information about a registered investment adviser, including AUM and contact information.

Fund of funds Investment partnership that invests in a series of other hedge funds. Portfolio will typically diversify across a variety of investment managers, investment strategies, and subcategories.

Fundamental investment analysis Analysis of the balance sheet and income statements of companies in order to forecast their future stock price movements.

Gate Refers to a restriction on withdrawals or redemptions from a hedge fund whereby the hedge fund limits redemptions to a pro rata portion of requested redemptions up to a predetermined percentage of capital for a specific redemption period.

General partner Managing partner of a limited partnership, who is responsible for the operation of the limited partnership. The general partner's liability is unlimited.

Global macro investing Investment strategy that seeks to profit by making leveraged bets on anticipated price movements of global stock markets, interest rates, foreign exchange rates, and physical commodities.

Growth stocks Equity of a corporation that has displayed faster-than-average earnings gains over the past few years and is expected to continue to show high rates of earnings growth. Growth stocks will typically have a higher price-to-earnings ratio because of their higher expected earnings growth.

Haircuts The difference between the market value of an asset posted as collateral and the value attributed to the asset by a secured party in determining whether the collateral requirements related to the asset have been met. A haircut is intended to protect a party that receives collateral from fluctuations in the value of such collateral.

Hedge fund A pooled investment vehicle that generally meets the following criteria: (1) it is not marketed to the general public (i.e., it is privately offered); (2) it is limited to high-net-worth individuals and institutions; (3) it is not registered as an investment company under relevant laws (e.g., U.S. Investment Company Act of 1940); (4) its assets are managed by a professional investment management firm that shares in the gains of the investment vehicle based on the investment performance of the vehicle; and (5) it has periodic but restricted or limited investor redemption rights.

High-water mark The assurance that a fund only takes fees on profits unique to an individual investment. For example, a $1,000,000 investment is made in year 1 and the fund declines by 50%, leaving $500,000 in the fund. In year 2, the fund returns 100%, bringing the investment value back to $1,000,000. If a fund has a high-water mark, it will not take incentive fees on the return in year 2 since the investment has never grown. The fund will only take incentive fees if the investment grows above the initial level of $1,000,000.

Hurdle rate The return above which a hedge fund manager begins taking incentive fees. For example, if a fund has a hurdle rate of 10%, and the fund returns 25% for the year, the fund will only take incentive fees on the 15% return above the hurdle rate.

Incentive fee The fee on new profits earned by the fund for the period, typically 20%. For example, if the initial investment was $1,000,000 and the fund returned 25% during the period (creating profits of $250,000) and the fund has an incentive fee of 20%, then the fund receives 20% of the $250,000 in profits, or $50,000.

Jensen ratio The Jensen ratio, developed by Michael Jensen, quantifies the extent to which an investment has added value relative to a benchmark. The Jensen alpha is equal to the investment's average return in excess of the risk free rate minus the beta times the benchmark's average return in excess of the risk free rate.

Legal risk The risk of loss arising from uncertainty in laws, regulations, or legal actions that may affect transactions between parties. Legal risk may include issues related to the enforceability of netting agreements, the perfection of collateral, the capacity of parties, and the legality of contracts, among others.

Leverage A factor that influences the rapidity with which changes in market risk, credit risk, or liquidity risk change the value of a portfolio.

Liquidity There are two separate but related types of liquidity. Funding liquidity is the ability of a hedge fund to hold its market positions and meet the cash and/or collateral demands of counterparties, other credit providers, and investors. Asset liquidity refers to the ability to liquidate an asset quickly, and in large volume, without substantially affecting the asset's price. An asset that cannot be liquidated in a short period without substantially affecting the asset's price is considered an illiquid instrument.

Liquidity risk The inability to sell an asset quickly and/or in large volume at a reasonable price, or the risk that a party will not have or cannot obtain sufficient funds to meet its obligations.

Lockup Time period that the initial investment cannot be redeemed from the fund.

Management fee The fees taken by the manager on the entire asset level of the investment, typically 2%.

Margin A certain amount of assets that must be deposited in a margin account in order to secure a portion of a party's obligations under a contract. For example, to buy or sell an exchange-traded futures contract, a party must post a specified amount that is determined by the exchange, referred to as an "initial margin." In addition, a party will be required to post additional margin if the futures contracts change in value. Margin is also required in connection with the purchase and sale of securities when the full purchase price is not paid upfront or the securities sold are not owned by the seller.

Margin accounts The account in which margin is held for securities or exchange-traded futures or options. Positions that are subject to margin requirements are generally valued, or "marked to market" daily.

Market factors Refers collectively to interest rates, foreign exchange rates, equity prices, commodity prices, and indices constructed from these rates and prices, as well as their volatility and correlation.

Market risk Narrowly defined, it is the risk of a decline in value of a hedge fund's portfolio resulting from changes in market factors. Since asset liquidity risk and the credit risk of an asset's issuer may also affect the value of instruments in a portfolio, hedge funds frequently manage all of these risks jointly as market risk.

Master agreement An agreement, such as the 1992 ISDA Master Agreement form published by the International Swaps and Derivatives Association Inc., that sets forth the overarching terms and conditions governing all OTC transactions between two parties that are subject to such master agreement. A master agreement typically includes payment netting and closeout netting provisions (see netting).

Master–feeder fund A typical structure for a hedge fund. It involves a master trading vehicle that is domiciled offshore. The master fund has two investors: another offshore fund, and a U.S.

(usually Delaware-domiciled) limited partnership. These two funds are the feeder funds. Investors invest in the feeder funds, which in turn invest all the money in the master fund, which is traded by the manager.

Maximum drawdown The worst period of "peak-to-valley" performance for the fund, regardless of whether or not the drawdown consisted of consecutive months of negative performance.

Minimum investment The minimum initial investment for the fund.

Net asset value The fair value of a hedge fund's assets minus the fair value of its liabilities. Under U.S. GAAP, NAV computations should include accrued interest, dividends, and other receivables of the hedge fund, as well as accrued expenses and other payables. NAV would generally not include special adjustments that may be made to valuations for risk-monitoring purposes, such as adjustments for illiquidity concerns. NAV is the basis for determining the prices applicable to investor subscription and redemptions, and is typically provider by a third-party administrator.

Netting Involves aggregating payment amount, collateral, or close-out valuation exposures on multiple transactions between the same two counterparties and reducing them down to a single net exposure amount by offsetting the positive exposures with the negative. Netting provisions are typically included in master agreements and collateral agreements between a hedge fund and its counterparty.

Nondirectional Investment strategy with absolute return objectives, irrespective of market movements.

Offering documents Refers to documents such as an offering memorandum, limited partnership or limited liability company agreement, subscription agreement, or similar contracts governing the relationship between a hedge fund and its investors.

Omega ratio The omega ratio is a measure of the risk of an investment asset, portfolio, or strategy involving partitioning returns into loss and gain above and below a given threshold. The omega ratio is therefore the ratio of the probability of having a gain by the probability of having a loss.

Operational risk The risk of loss due to system breakdowns, employee fraud or misconduct, errors in models, or natural or manmade catastrophes, among other risks. It may also include the risk of loss due to the incomplete or incorrect documentation of trades. Operational risk may also be defined by what it does not include: market risk, credit risk, and liquidity risk.

Over-the-counter transaction (OTC) A transaction between parties that is not executed on an organized exchange but instead privately negotiated on a bilateral basis between the parties.

Pairs trading Nondirectional relative value investment strategy that seeks to identify two companies with similar characteristics whose equity securities are currently trading at a price relationship that is out of their historical trading range.

Portfolio turnover The number of times an average portfolio security is replaced during an accounting period, usually a year.

Prime broker A brokerage firm providing multiple services to a hedge fund that are beyond the scope of those offered by a traditional broker, such as clearing and settlement of securities transactions, financing, recordkeeping, custodial services, and research capabilities.

Redemption The redemption of shares or other interests in, or withdrawals of funds from, a hedge fund by an investor.

Redemption fee Fee charged upon a voluntary redemption from an investment vehicle.

Redemption notice period Required notification period of an intended redemption request. Notification is usually required in writing.

Relative value Nondirectional market neutral investment strategy that seeks to exploit pricing discrepancies between a pair of related securities. The strategy will entail buying the undervalued security and short selling the overvalued security.

Risk arbitrage Relative value investment strategy that seeks to exploit pricing discrepancies in the equity securities of two companies involved in a merger-related transaction. The strategy will entail the purchase of a security of the company being acquired, along with a simultaneous sale in the acquiring company.

Scenario analysis Similar to a stress test, the practice of subjecting a model (e.g., a value-at-risk model) to adjusted inputs in order to assess the impact of a specified scenario of market events on a hedge fund's portfolio.

Settlement risk The risk that a counterparty will fail to perform its obligations under a contract on the settlement date; a form of credit risk.

Sharpe ratio A measure that is widely used by investors to evaluate the performance of a portfolio or to compare the performance of different portfolios on a "risk-adjusted" basis. The numerator of the Sharpe ratio is a measure of a portfolio's return during a given period, generally the return earned on the portfolio in excess of the risk-free rate of return over one year. The denominator of the ratio is a measure of the risk incurred in achieving the return, usually measured as the standard deviation of the portfolio's daily return. The higher the Sharpe ratio, the better the portfolio's return in risk-adjusted terms.

Short sale Generally means borrowing a security (or commodity futures contract) from a broker and selling it, with the understanding that it must later be bought back (hopefully at a lower price) and returned to the broker. Short selling is a technique used by investors who try to profit from the falling price of a stock.

Side letter Generally refers to an agreement with an investor that varies the terms of a hedge fund's governing documents with respect to that investor.

Side pocket Generally refers to an investment in an illiquid or nonmarketable instrument that is accounted for separately from the other assets of the hedge fund.

Sortino ratio The Sortino ratio is similar to the Sharpe ratio, except that instead of using standard deviation as the denominator, it uses downside deviation. The Sortino ratio was developed to differentiate between "good" and "bad" volatility in the Sharpe ratio. If a fund is volatile to the upside (which is generally a good thing), its Sharpe ratio would still be low.

Special situations investing Investment strategy that seeks to profit from pricing discrepancies resulting from corporate "event" transactions such as mergers and acquisitions, spinoffs, bankruptcies, or recapitalizations.

Spread The excess of the price or yield on a particular security or instrument relative to a benchmark. For example, the "spread over Treasury" is the difference between the yield for a certain fixed-income instrument and the yield for a comparable U.S. Treasury security.

Standard deviation Technically, a statistical measure of the dispersion of a set of numbers around a central point. Standard deviation measures the volatility, or uncertainty, of investment returns, and is therefore commonly used to measure the risk of a portfolio. The higher the standard deviation of a portfolio, the higher the uncertainty of the portfolio's return.

Statistical arbitrage Market neutral relative value investment strategy that involves the utilization of a quantitatively based investment method that identifies securities or groups of securities that are currently trading at prices out of their historical range.

Sterling ratio This is a return-to-risk ratio. Return (numerator) is defined as the compound annualized rate of return over the last three years. Risk (denominator) is defined as the average yearly maximum drawdown over the last three years less an arbitrary 10%.

Stress test A general term for the practice of subjecting a model (e.g., a value-at-risk model) to inputs that are adjusted to represent extreme or unusual changes in market factors. The sources of stress may be actual historical changes in market factors or hypothetical changes.

Systemic risk The risk that the failure of a significant market participant in a payment or settlement system to meet its obligations when due will cause other participants or financial institutions to be unable to meet their obligations. Such a failure could potentially cause significant market liquidity or credit problems and threaten the stability of financial markets.

Third-party service provider A firm that provides certain administrative, technical, financial, or other services to a hedge fund manager that chooses to outsource parts of its operations.

Transportable alpha The alpha of one active strategy can be combined with another asset class. For example, an equity market neutral strategy's value-added can be "transported" to a fixed-income asset class by simply buying a fixed-income futures contract. The total return comes from both sources.

Treynor ratio The Treynor ratio, developed by Jack Treynor, is similar to the Sharpe ratio, except that it uses beta as the volatility measurement. Return (numerator) is defined as the incremental average return of an investment over the risk-free rate. Risk (denominator) is defined as the beta of the investment returns relative to a benchmark.

Turnarounds Favorable reversal in the fortunes of a company, a market, or the economy at large. Turnaround specialists seek to exploit market pricing inefficiencies in securities of companies that might be on the verge of a turnaround situation.

Typical leverage The amount of leverage typically used by the fund as a percentage of the fund. For example, if the fund has $1,000,000 and borrowing another $2,000,000, to bring the total dollars invested to $3,000,000, then the leverage used is 200%.

Typical net exposure The exposure level of the fund to the market that the fund attempts to maintain over time. It is calculated by subtracting the short percentage from the long percentage. For example, if a fund is 100% long and 25% short, then the net exposure is 75%.

Valuation The process of determining the value of positions in a hedge fund portfolio. Valuation serves two distinct purposes: it provides the base input for both the risk-monitoring process and the calculation of a hedge fund's NAV, which serves as the basis for pricing investor subscriptions and redemptions.

Value at risk (VAR) An integrated measure of the market risk of a portfolio of assets and/or liabilities. At the most general level, VAR is a measure of the potential change in value of a specified portfolio over a specified time interval or holding period, resulting from potential changes in market factors (e.g., prices and volatilities). The VAR measure is based on the distribution of potential changes in the value of the portfolio and is expressed in terms of a confidence level. A hedge fund manager's risk management team may choose to use VAR to estimate the maximum expected amount a hedge fund could lose over a specified time horizon at a specified probability level.

Volatility A measure of risk based on the standard deviation of an asset's return. The greater the degree of an asset's volatility, the greater the risk of the asset.

Worst historical drawdown The largest decrease in the value of a hedge fund measured as the difference between the highest and lowest value since its inception or during a given period of time (e.g., last five years).

BIBLIOGRAPHY

Anson, Mark. *Handbook of Alternative Assets*. 2nd ed. Hoboken, NJ: John Wiley & Sons, 2006.

Asness, Clifford, Robert Krail, and John Liew. "Do Hedge Funds Hedge?" *Journal of Portfolio Management* 28, no. 1 (2001): 6–19.

Fama, Eugene. *Foundations of Finance*. New York: Basic Books, 1976.

Fung, William, and David Hsieh. "A Primer on Hedge Funds." *Journal of Empirical Finance* 6, no. 3 (September 1999): 309–331.

Fung, William, and David Hsieh. "Hedge Fund Benchmarks: A Risk-Based Approach." *Financial Analysts Journal* (September/October 2004): 65–80.

Fung, William, and David Hsieh. "Hedge Funds: An Industry in Its Adolescence." *Federal Reserve Bank of Atlanta Economic Review*, May 2006.

Horwitz, Richard. *Hedge Fund Risk Fundamentals*. New York: Bloomberg Press. 2004.

Ibbotson, Roger G., Peng Chen, and Kevin X. Zhu. "The ABCs of Hedge Funds: Alphas, Betas, & Costs" (March 30, 2010). Available at SSRN: http://ssrn.com/abstract=1581559, accessed November 14, 2012.

Lack, Simon. *The Hedge Fund Mirage: The Illusion of Big Money and Why It's Too Good to Be True*. Hoboken, NJ: Wiley. 2012.

Lhabitant, Francois-Serge. *Handbook of Hedge Funds*. Chichester, England: John Wiley & Sons, 2006.

Lo, Andrew W., and A. Craig MacKinlay. *A Non-Random Walk Down Wall Street*. Princeton, NJ: Princeton University Press. 2001.

Longo, John M., ed. *Hedge Fund Alpha: A Framework for Generating and Understanding Investment Performance*. Singapore: World Scientific Publishing Company. 2009.

Lowenstein, Roger. *When Genius Failed: The Rise and Fall of Long-Term Capital Management*. New York: Random House. 2000.

Mallaby, Sebastian. *More Money Than God: Hedge Funds and the Making of the New Elite*. New York: Penguin Press. 2010.

Nicholas, Joseph G. *Hedge Fund of Funds Investing: An Investor's Guide*. New York: Bloomberg Press. 2004.

Nicholas, Joseph G. *Investing in Hedge Funds.* 2nd ed. New York: Bloomberg Press. 2005.

Patterson, Scott. *The Quants: How a New Breed of Math Shizzes Conquered Wall Street and Nearly Destroyed It.* New York. Crown Business. 2010.

PerTrac, Impact of Fund Size and Age on Hedge Fund Performance, September 2011.

PerTrac, Investment Statistics: A Reference Guide, September 2012.

Rittereiser, Cathleen, and Lawrence Kochard. *Top Hedge Fund Investors: Stories, Strategies, and Advice.* Hoboken, NJ: Wiley Publishing, 2010.

Scaramucci, Anthony. *The Little Book of Hedge Funds.* New York: John Wiley & Sons. 2012.

Schwager, Jack D. *Hedge Fund Market Wizards.* New Jersey. John Wiley & Sons. 2012.

Shiller, Robert J. *Irrational Exuberance,* 2nd ed. Princeton, NJ: Princeton University Press. 2005.

Soros, George. *The Alchemy of Finance.* Hoboken, NJ: John Wiley & Sons, 1994.

Thomas, Lee R., III. "Active Management." *Journal of Portfolio Management* 26, no. 2 (Winter 2000): 25–32.

"The Value of the Hedge Fund Industry to Investors, Markets, and the Broader Economy." KPMG and AIMA, 2012.

Zask, Ezra, ed. *Global Investment Risk Management.* New York: McGraw-Hill, 1999.

INDEX

CPSIA information can be obtained
at www.ICGtesting.com
Printed in the USA
BVOW06s1228151116

467905BV00009B/42/P